Mass Politics

THE POLITICS OF
POPULAR CULTURE

Mass Politics

THE POLITICS OF
POPULAR CULTURE

Edited by
Daniel M. Shea
LAFAYETTE COLLEGE

St. Martin's/WORTH

Mass Politics:
The Politics of Popular Culture

Executive Editor: James R. Headley
Project Director: Scott E. Hitchcock
Editorial Assistant: Brian Nobile
Design Director: Jennie R. Nichols
Production Editor: Douglas Bell
Production Manager: Barbara Anne Seixas
Project Coordination: Publisher's Studio
Cover Design: Paul Lacey
Cover Photo: MacDuff Everton/Corbis
Cover Printer: Phoenix Color Corporation
Composition: Stratford Publishing Services
Printing and Binding: R. R. Donnelley & Sons Company

ISBN: 0-312-17101-3 (paperback)   ISBN: 0-312-21949-0 (hardcover)

For information (College):   For information (Scholarly/Reference):

Worth Publishers   **St. Martin's Press, Inc.**
33 Irving Place   175 Fifth Avenue
New York, NY 10003   New York, NY 10010

www.worthpublishers.com   **www.stmartins.com**

Acknowledgments

Acknowledgments and copyrights are continued at the back of the book on page 161, which constitutes an extension of the copyright page.

It is a violation of the law to reproduce the following selections by any means whatsoever without the written permission of the copyright holder.

Bonnie J. Dow. "*Murphy Brown:* Postfeminism Personified" from *Prime-Time Feminism.* Copyright © 1996 University of Pennsylvania Press. Reprinted by permission of the publisher. Portions of this essay appeared in "Femininity and Feminism in *Murphy Brown,*" *Southern Communication Journal,* 57 (Winter 1992): 143-155. Reprinted by permission of the Southern Speech Communication Association.

About the Editor

Daniel M. Shea (Ph.D., State University of New York at Albany, 1993) is assistant professor in the Department of Government and Law, Lafayette College. Before receiving his doctorate, Shea was a campaign operative for the New York State Democratic Assembly Campaign Committee. His research interests include campaign management, political parties, Congress and state legislatures, and most recently the politics of the media. He has written or edited seven books, including *Transforming Democracy* (State University of New York Press, 1995), *Campaign Craft* (Praeger Books, 1996), and along with John K. White, *Political Parties in the Information Age* (St. Martins's/Worth, forthcoming). His articles have appeared in many leading journals, including the *American Review of Politics, Campaigns and Elections,* and *Southeastern Political Review.* Dr. Shea lives in Easton, Pennsylvania, with his wife, Christine Gatto-Shea, and two-year-old daughter, Abigail.

To my nifty siblings,
Mike, Brian, Pat, Dennis, Matt, and of course Mary Kate

Contents

Preface

The manuscript for this book was finished the same week two boys saw fit to don camouflage outfits, pull the fire alarm at their school, and while hiding in the bushes shoot their junior high classmates and teachers with high-powered hunting rifles as they fled the building. The horror of Jonesboro, Arkansas, was followed, almost two weeks later, with a similar incident in Edinboro, Pennsylvania, and shortly thereafter in Springfield, Oregon. During the spring of 1998, the nation was paralyzed with grief and disbelief. How could this have happened? Where was society headed?

Unfortunately, incidences like these have become all too familiar. Sociologists, psychologists, community leaders, and parents have frantically searched for an explanation. What forces would lead children to commit such unfathomable acts of savagery? Many suspect the answer is obvious—and indeed all around us. The degree of murder, violence, and gore that American children are exposed to is staggering. Unlike in other nations, where the real thing can be seen out the window or down the street, most American kids get their dose of brutality from television, video games, compact discs, movies, and even sports stadiums. How could a couple of junior high students blow away their classmates with high-powered guns? Perhaps the answer, or at least part of the puzzle, can be found by spending a night in front of the tube or at the movies.

Many would strongly disagree with such "simplistic" pronouncements. They might argue that entertainment merely echoes changes in society and that blaming television or video games is akin to burying one's head in the sand, ignoring more pressing societal ills—like the declining attention and responsibility of parents. "Parents can always shut off the television or monitor their children's Internet activities," they might say. Popular culture can be a catalyst for progressive social change as well, they would point out. Moreover, theorizing a connection between modes of entertainment and adverse social trends is an old story—mostly a "generational thing." After all, pundits of popular culture have lamented everything from baseball at the turn of the century to rock 'n' roll in the 1950s. Just as we have survived the menace of Ty Cobb and Chuck Berry, we will get through Ice-T and Rambo.

The chorus of scholars, community leaders, and parents decrying the evils of popular culture in the 1990s, however, is getting louder. Condemnations of how Americans, especially children, spend their free time has become a growth industry of late. If nothing else, the scope of "information age" entertainment in the lives of ordinary Americans is cause for serious reflection. No form of leisure has ever approached the dominant position television now holds in the everyday lives of citizens. Coupled with changes in the socialization process (i.e., the weakening of family as the primary socialization agent), popular "entertainment" may well be a powder keg of trouble.

But how does this relate to politics—the focus of this book? Simply put, it makes sense that if we are willing to accept the possibility that popular culture can bring about profound changes in society, we might also better appreciate its potential to shape politics. This idea, of course, is also nothing new; many have contemplated the role entertainment can play in the course of politics. Surprisingly, this line of inquiry is better understood by scholars of communications than by students of government. It is entirely likely that one could receive an advanced degree in political science from any number of prestigious schools, and never confront the "politics of fun and games." What is more, while most of us who teach government might spend a perfunctory hour or two on political culture, rarely do we explore the effects of popular culture on politics. What makes this even more perplexing is that students might really connect to the topic and, in fact, teach *us* a good bit about the process. Academics are all too often insulated from trends in popular culture. Who better to help bring us up to speed than those in the trenches?

This book, then, is not about the link between popular culture and social trends per se, but rather an attempt to draw attention to the "political connection." It is about the role of popular culture in shaping American politics as we move toward a new millennium.

To some extent, this book heads out on thinner ice than sociological works. Suggesting a link between leisure activities and social trends is hazy enough, and indeed difficult to pin down. It would seem even more tenuous to argue the political process is altered by the tube and silver screen, the content of magazines and books, or music lyrics. A number of theoretical possibilities of how this might occur are discussed in the Introduction, but it is only honest to admit many readers will find it a "hard sell." The core supposition woven into the pages that follow, nevertheless, is that the way we spend our free time can mold our expectations, world view, and attitudes toward others. Powerful ideas and themes can be found in sports, music, literature, and virtually every form of leisure activity. Some of these ideas are implied, while others are clear. They build upon and reconfigure prior information and, in the end, shape each person's identity and our political culture. And political culture surely constrains public policy.

One of the most frequent comments from students who confront arguments about the implicit political themes found in popular culture is, "relax, it's just fun and games" or "what's the big deal?" On one level they may be right, but I don't think so. Politics, very serious politics, does not take place only in legislatures, court houses, smoke-filled rooms, and on the campaign trail. As is said of many endeavors, the devil is in the details. This book is about flushing out some of those details and raising possibilities. The real trick for students of government is to understand what they cannot easily put their fingers on.

Not surprisingly, the idea for this book came from my students. I had the fortunate insight to assign Michael Parenti's book, *Make-Believe Media,* to students in one of my Politics of the Media classes. He offers a thoughtful, comprehensive look at the political themes found in film and television. Students attacked the pages of his book and came to class anxious to debate its contents. Not all agreed with his basic premise that the media presents a consistent pro-capitalist, status quo message, but few scholarly books, at least the ones that I have assigned to students, spur as much debate. Those were wonderful, dynamic class sessions.

Thinking about how Parenti's book produced such lively discussion—though it was limited to movies and television and was getting a tad out-dated—I broached the possibility of similar work with my steadfast career consultant, Dennis M. Shea. Having recently retired after teaching government at the State University of New York at Oneonta for thirty-six years, Dad has a keen ability to draw out nuances about politics and explore possibilities. Why not expand the analysis to other forms of entertainment, like sports, music, the Internet, and talk radio, and update it to better fit what has been going on in the 1990s? After a few cold beers and a bag of pretzels, a book proposal had been written, at least in my head, and the search was on for a publisher.

It seemed logical to approach Parenti's publisher, St. Martin's Press. Thankfully, editors Beth Gillett and James Headley agreed the topic is important and were willing to take a chance. Beth has since moved on to another publishing group, but James has proven to be an integral part of the project. His keen insight helped sort out the appropriate mix of chapters and fine-tune the Introduction. James is clearly a rising star in the publishing field and it has been a pleasure working with him. Also at St. Martin's, Sandy Schecter helped with the arduous chore of securing copyrights for many of the chapters. The staff at Publisher's Studio was very helpful with production—including probably breaking the all-time manuscript-to-bound-book speed record.

A heartfelt thanks goes out to the authors of the chapters. Several of the pieces were pulled from previously written material, but many are original works. These authors confronted not only the labyrinth of frequent, vague instructions concerning themes and level of analysis, but also stark page limits. Readers will surely agree that the strength of the book lies in these carefully constructed chapters.

I am especially grateful for the constructive comments that were provided by those scholars who reviewed this manuscript: David Clark, Florida State University; Daniel Franklin, Georgia State University; William Kelly, Auburn University; Carol Liebler, Syracuse University; Anthony Nownes, University of Tennessee; Rex Peebles, Austin Community College; John Pitney, Jr., Claremont McKenna College; and Scott Waalkes, Calvin College.

A number of students helped with this project. At the University of Akron, Connie Krouss, Adam Smith, and Megan Pavlik aided my efforts in compiling lists of potential articles. Here at Lafayette College, Kathryn

Lundwall helped write the review questions at the end of the chapters and Wendy Erdly lent a hand with the final manuscript preparation.

Also at Lafayette College, Dr. James Lennertz, of the government and law department, was kind enough to read a first draft of the Introduction and provide many thoughtful suggestions. This book was finished during my first year at Lafayette, and it was reassuring to get such earnest assistance from such an accomplished teacher and scholar. Ruth Panovec, the departmental secretary, had the difficult job of retyping several of the chapters. A special thanks goes out to her for completing a tedious chore in such a cheerful, expedient manner.

Finally, I am indebted to my wife, Christine Gatto-Shea. She helped edit several pieces of the book and, perhaps more than anyone else, was an unfailing source of support during a busy, turbulent year. With Chrissy in my corner, every project will be a success.

Daniel M. Shea

Mass Politics

THE POLITICS OF
POPULAR CULTURE

Introduction: Popular Culture—The Trojan Horse of American Politics?

DANIEL M. SHEA

Pondering the state of civil society has become a growth industry in recent years. Questions of who we are and where we are going resonate through the halls of academia, in coffee shops and in restaurants, and at kitchen tables across the country. Much of this introspection is probably caused by our march toward a new millennium. If we do not contemplate "big" questions every one hundred years or so, when should we? It is likely that this reflection is also due to the rapid pace of technological "developments." The breadth of such change is staggering and a great deal of our world appears caught in its torrent.

This soul-searching has spread in many directions, but a growing target has been American popular culture. Although a multifaceted term, *popular culture* implies the numerous forms, meanings, and practices that members of society find appealing—especially as they relate to leisure. Put differently, popular culture is "those shifting sets of social and cultural relations, meanings, and texts which in varying ways emerge as contemporary forms of pleasure, leisure, style, and identity . . ."[1] But Americans have always taken to fads in their dress and entertainment, so why all the attention to popular culture in the 1990s? The current preoccupation with modes of entertainment is not because we have more leisure time—in fact the opposite is true—but rather because things seem so radically different. For example, today Americans spend 70 percent of their nonworking, waking hours watching television. This comes out to roughly 7.4 hours per household *each day.*[2] By the time today's teenagers reach the age of seventy, they will have watched *seven years* of television.[3] These figures are astounding, especially when one considers that television was not a household feature until the late 1950s. No other leisure activity has ever approached the dominant place television now holds in the day-to-day lives of ordinary people. And television is only part of the story; much the same can be said about video games, movies (rentals as well), music, and sporting activities. Whereas a decade ago only few scholars and business leaders had access to the World Wide Web, today tens of millions of American households are "wired," with their inhabitants spending countless hours "surfing."

Another possibility for the recent flurry of inquiries into popular culture might be its emerging homogeneity around the globe. Simply put, American popular culture is spreading and for the first time in history we are approaching a "global popular culture." No one should be surprised that

Dolly Parton's are among the most sought-after records in the rural areas of Zimbabwe, that MTV is hugely popular with teenagers in Hungary, or that Kirk Douglas should be greeted on the streets of Moscow by a fan "with tears running down his face, giving the impression that he had found a long-lost brother."[4]

There is also growing recognition, particularly in academic circles, that trends in popular culture may not be just "fun and games." Many now recognize that modes of entertainment are linked to changes in civil society. As noted by one commentator, "There are, no doubt, complex causes for illegitimacy and violence in today's society, but it seems impossible to deny that one cause is the messages popular culture insistently presses on us."[5] The same cause-and-effect argument is increasingly heard in reference to attitudes toward minority groups, women, law enforcement officials, political institutions, politicians, and much else. Others argue it is not simply the messages transmitted through popular culture, but how we now spend our time that matters. Michael Medved, a well-known political-social commentator, notes: "When consumed in the American pattern of several hours each day, TV inevitably promotes impatience, self pity, and superficiality."[6] Still others argue that while popular culture may not directly shape civil society, at the very least it affords a barometer of public attitudes.

This book probes the fit between politics and popular culture. As will be seen here and in the chapters to follow, the relationship is murky and quite contentious. Suggesting popular culture is a significant piece of the political process is much easier said than proven. This is not to say we should be discouraged from the task, only mindful of its complexity. Social scientific inquiry is often arduous and it may be helpful to draw a distinction between applied research and basic research. The former refers to investigation designed to solve a particular problem, while the latter suggests inquiry to enhance one's understanding of a political phenomenon—to better explain political life. Basic research leads to the development of theories to explain political events and helps sustain the democratic process, where a premium is put on an informed citizenry. This book adopts that approach and should be considered basic research into the convergence of politics and entertainment.

THE INTRICATE LINK OF POPULAR CULTURE AND POLITICS

Few would doubt that entertainment is somehow related to politics, but how and in what ways? Does taking in a movie or listening to a CD rank with the state of the economy, religious trends, school activities, or changes in political institutions? Which is a better indicator of the state of the American polity, the fact that we spend countless hours in front of the tube or that more children are now born out of wedlock than at any point in our nation's history? Are the two related? Where do current events, such as wars, assassinations, natural disasters, or acts of terrorism, fit into the mix? The number of pieces to the puzzle is staggering and trying to sort out the import of popular culture is a daunting task.

Moreover, assuming a link between entertainment and politics, a second obstacle is causation. Does popular culture modify the political process, or do political changes in values and attitudes affect modes of entertainment? In other words, should popular culture be considered an independent or dependent variable? Did Americans, for instance, rethink racial stereotypes when Jackie Robinson stepped into Ebbits's Field wearing a Brooklyn Dodgers uniform in 1947, or did the act—an African American being allowed to play major-league baseball—suggest changes in public attitudes?

This section is intended to set some theoretical guideposts for answering these questions and evaluating the remaining chapters of the book.

Popular Culture as a Catalyst

If we were to contemplate how movies, television, sports, music, and other aspects of entertainment might affect society, and in the end politics, one strategy would be to search for the "smoking gun." That is, we might infer a direct causal relationship between a stimulus (a movie, song, television program, etc.) and behavior. There is a good deal of research to support this assertion. For example, the *Christian Science Monitor* reported that more than three thousand studies over the last thirty years offer evidence that violent movies and television programs have a measurable effect on children. Several studies find that after viewing violent cartoons, children are more aggressive during playtime.[7] William J. Bennett, one of the most respected social-political commentators of our day, has written extensively about the connection between popular culture and behavior. Among other things, he suggests the rate of teenage suicide in the United States (now the second leading cause of death among adolescents and eleven times higher than in any other nation) skyrocketed at precisely the same period that television viewing hours mushroomed and the content of television programs became more violent.[8]

We can be more specific: After *The Deer Hunter* was released in 1979, at least twenty-five viewers reenacted the movie's Russian roulette scene and blew their own heads off.[9] Controversy surrounded the 1993 release of *The Program* because the movie depicted college football players testing their masculinity by allowing a car to run over them. Several real-life kids tried the stunt, with serious consequences. Some parents have argued in court that the lyrics of heavy metal music pushed their children to commit suicide. And certainly product market specialists believe there is a direct link between popular culture and behavior; why else pay chests of money to have a celebrity drink *their* beer or smoke *their* brand of cigarette on screen?

The stimulus/action argument is the theme of *Natural Born Killers,* a 1994 film written and directed by Oliver Stone. It is a satirical depiction of two youths, Mickey and Mallory (Woody Harrelson and Juliette Lewis), who, after viewing a never-ending stream of violence on television and at the movies, head out on a killing spree of their own. Because Americans are fixated on celebrity, particularly when violence is involved, the two become stars. "Mass murder is wrong," says a teenager in the movie to the television cameras, "but if I were a mass-murderer, I'd be Mickey and Mallory!"

Stone's cutting satire aside, this approach makes good sense because there are often serious ramifications to what might, at first glance, seem only to be "entertainment." Yet the rationale also has limitations. The vast majority of us do not club someone after watching a violent TV show, badger a police officer as a result of listening to rap music, or send a check to an animal rights organization after taking our kids to see *Bambi*. To many, the stimulus-action argument is a hard sell because even though there may be a link between entertainment and unwanted consequences, most people realize it is just a movie, song, game, or advertisement. Few are anxious to let a Buick run over them because they saw it in a movie.

Perhaps the real impact of popular culture, then, may not be the direct action it triggers but its power to shape attitudes and perceptions over the long run. The way we spend our free time can mold our expectations, views of the world, and attitudes toward others. Powerful messages and themes are often found in sports, music, literature, and virtually every form of entertainment. Sometimes these ideas are implied, at other times, quite clear. We are bombarded with them when we pick up the remote, plug in a CD, or spend a day at the ballpark. These messages have a collective effect, building upon and reconfiguring prior information, and in the end shaping each person's political identity and our political culture.

Political culture implies the fundamental values and beliefs that form a rough consensus in society, and within which political behavior and government policies are bound. It is the umbrella under which political activities take place and where public questions are resolved. The exact dimensions of any nation's political culture are not easy to discern. Political culture springs from numerous sources, including documents held in high esteem, the thoughts and deeds of past leaders, important legal decisions, the ideological underpinnings of the political system, and the "creation myth" (the circumstances under which the nation was formed). It is also reasonable to assume that any nation's political culture is partially a product of its entertainment culture. (The inverse—that pop culture is shaped by political culture—is also likely and will be discussed later.)

There are many possibilities where popular culture may have played a role in reshaping American political culture. The abolitionist movement was simmering in the North during the early part of the nineteenth century, but it was not until the publication of *Uncle Tom's Cabin*, written by Harriet Beecher Stowe in 1852, that antislavery sentiment became mainstream. Several decades later, *The Birth of a Nation* (1915), possibly the most racist film ever made, was shown to schoolchildren in the South as a "history lesson." The film was widely criticized for its positive portrayal of the Ku Klux Klan and had a negative impact on race relations throughout the United

States. Folk music probably played a hand in changing political attitudes in the 1960s, especially among the young, as rap music has during the last decade.

Evidence of the cumulative impact of popular culture might also be found in the recent debate over health care reform. There has been much speculation as to why President Clinton's health care program (first advanced in 1994) never got off the ground. On the one hand, the plan flopped because it was devised without much public input, was exceedingly costly, and called for a new bureaucracy. Many members of Clinton's own party were lukewarm to its provisions. But it is also fair to say that any *government-sponsored* health care system would face an uphill battle in America because our political culture places a premium on individualism and minimal governmental intrusion. This idea is a legacy of our nation's formative years, where freedom from a domineering monarchy was paramount, and where a make-it-on-your-own ethos grew out of the realities of living in a vast, unsettled land. The celebration of rugged individualism during westward expansion in the mid-1800s surely had a lasting influence as well. Lone heroes and "making it on your own" are recurring themes in American entertainment, immortalized in hundreds of books, movies, songs, and television programs. Why is baseball the "great American pastime"? Perhaps because it pits individuals against each other—the pitcher faces the batter. Cowboy films, a purely American invention, are often little else than stories of rugged individualism. It would seem entirely reasonable to speculate that popular culture played a hand in the Clinton health care debacle.

It is, of course, not just an individualism ethos that has been echoed in American popular culture, but myriad themes and messages—many less auspicious. The steady, cumulative impact of popular culture can be seen in many directions: It was not one "cowboy-and-Indian" western that shaped stereotypes of Native Americans, but hundreds of movies, dime novels, television programs, and advertisements that nearly always portrayed them as dim-witted savages. We have probably not come to think of most rural people as toothless, barefoot simpletons just by watching *Deliverance* (1979), but by viewing endless reruns of *The Beverly Hillbillies* and *Green Acres,* and by listening to scores of country songs where Bubba pulls out a .45 and shoots a jukebox because "it played a sad song, and made 'em cry." It is not only countless magazine covers depicting half-naked, emaciated women that has perpetuated the notion that women are worth more when they are thin and sexy, but endless hours of situation comedies, movies, and MTV rock videos that hardly ever feature normal looking women. Once these and other stereotypes are established, reinforcement comes easily.

What makes cumulative indoctrination especially powerful is that often the message is veiled. In some instances the political theme is clear because it is the central point. For example, Upton Sinclair's goal in writing *The Jungle* (1906) was to change public policy. Commenting on the purpose of the book, Sinclair himself said that he had "aimed at the public's heart . . ."[10]

But the overtly political examples are far outweighed by subtle ones. Most film directors or television producers probably aim only to be entertaining—and, of course, to make a profit. Political messages may be incidental, but they are no less serious. In fact, it is when people think they are just being entertained that political messages have their greatest impact. As one critic of political entertainment noted, "Beliefs are less likely to be preached than assumed. Woven into the story line and into the characterizations, they are perceived as entertainment rather than as political judgements about the world."[11] Explicitly political movies, books, or songs can be scrutinized, challenged, debated. Subtle themes are often overlooked because they are assumed to be "just fun."

It should be noted that entertainment is only one piece of the political culture puzzle. Trends in religion, education, technology, the economy, and other areas are equally important, and popular culture is also a *product* of attitudes and beliefs. Likewise, not every piece of pop culture has political connotations. The heart of this line of reasoning, however, is that entertainment can be linked to individual values, beliefs, and priorities. Once these attitudes become widely shared, government action in accordance has legitimacy. The surest path to changing public policy is to first transform the attitudes, fears, and prejudices of the public.

Popular Culture as a Barometer

Not all would endow popular culture with such power in shaping attitudes, reconfiguring political culture, and redirecting public policy. Many would argue that modes of entertainment *reflect* values and beliefs. In other words, art is simply imitating life and by analyzing popular culture we get a bearing on society. We might consider, for instance, the relevance of Ellen DeGeneres coming out as an openly gay character in her situation comedy in the spring of 1997. It is possible that viewer attitudes toward homosexuals were changed by the program—leading to a more tolerant society. But it is at least equally likely that the program reflected changing American values and beliefs about gay men and women. One media critic wrote: "Does Ellen Morgan's coming out in what is still our massest medium legitimize homosexuality, or does the sponsorship of a bottom-line business like ABC merely reflect its acceptance by a significant portion of the population?"[12] The answer is debatable, but all agree such a program would have never aired a few decades ago because homosexuality was not considered an admissible public lifestyle by a vast majority of Americans. Simply put, this line of reasoning suggests popular culture reflects changes in society and by examining these trends we gain knowledge about who we are.

An Interactive Process

Still another possibility, perhaps the most likely, is that there is an interaction between art and reality, where social conditions push writers and producers to focus on certain themes and their handiwork influences what happens in the real world. Sometimes the balance is even and other times it is not. Let us consider one of the hottest topics these days—violence in entertainment and crime in America.

Few would dispute that we live in a rough world. In the past, a rebellious high school student may have wished to smuggle a switchblade into class; today, metal detectors and security guards try to keep out handguns and assault rifles. Drive-by shootings, car jackings, assaults, and general lawlessness are so common in some cities that they hardly make news. The *New York Times* recently noted a decline of civility and rise of assaults even in local politics—such as at city and town council meetings.[13] It is little wonder, then, that violence would be echoed in movies, television, music, and sports. Should be we shocked that in one movie alone, *Face-Off,* we are privy to over two hundred killings? Is it any wonder that Mike Tyson would bite off Evander Holyfield's ear during a boxing match, that Roberto Alomar would spit in the face of a baseball umpire, or that Latrell Sprewell, a professional basketball player, would choke and threaten to kill his coach? How shocking is it that rapper Ice-T would release a song called "Cop Killer," where the character is "bout to dust some cop off"? Entertainment has become more violent because society has become more violent.

But what role does violent entertainment play in real-life lawlessness and violence? Perhaps people are thrashing each other at city council meetings because they are besieged with similar conduct on television, at the movies, and in music. As noted earlier, there is much scholarly research to suggest a connection. "Young males" writes one commentator, "witness so many gory depictions of killings that they are bound to become desensitized to it. We now have teenagers, and even subteenagers who shoot if they feel they have been 'dissed.'"[14]

We might also consider *perceptions* of crime. Even though crime rates are much higher than several decades ago, during the past few years they have actually declined. In some cities, such as New York, the drop is upwards of 30 percent from just a few years ago.[15] Yet most Americans believe crime is on the rise and are demanding public officials do something about it. There are rival explanations for this paradox but one must surely be that the barrage of violence on television, at the movies, and in song lyrics has jumped far ahead of reality. Does it matter that the average child watches up to eight thousand made-for-TV murders and ten thousand acts of violence by the end of grade school?[16] Does this reflect "reality"? George Gerbner has conducted extensive research on how safe Americans feel. His findings suggest that while there is a very low correlation between anxiety and the actual crime rate, a "sense of danger" is highly connected to levels of television viewing.[17]

Is There a "Correct" Perspective?

So which perspective is right? Does popular culture spur changes in attitudes and beliefs, thus modifying our political culture and in the end public policy, or does popular culture simply reflect changes in society? Maybe the interactive model ties things up in a neat package? Figure 1 highlights the three theoretical possibilities. Unfortunately, there is no clear answer and, to a large extent, the "right" approach depends upon one's outlook about human nature. How flexible are core values and beliefs? How susceptible

Possibility 1
Popular Culture as a Catalyst for Change

Popular Culture   shapes   Individual Attitudes and Beliefs

EXAMPLE: Jackie Robinson's debut with the Brooklyn Dodgers pushes many Americans to rethink racial stereotypes.

Possibility 2
Popular Culture as a Barometer of Public Attitudes and Beliefs

Individual Attitudes and Beliefs   shape   Popular Culture

EXAMPLE: Ellen Morgan is able to come out as an openly gay character in the sitcom *Ellen* because of growing tolerance toward homosexual men and women.

Possibility 3
Popular Culture as an Interactive Process

Individual Attitudes and Beliefs   shape   Popular Culture

while at the same time

Popular Culture   shapes   Individual Attitudes and Beliefs

EXAMPLE: Much rap music depicts acts of violence as a reflection of the crime and brutality in society, especially in inner cities. Rap fans become more violent as a result of repeatedly hearing these themes.

Figure 1 / The Nexus between Popular Culture and Individual Attitudes and Beliefs: Some Theoretical Possibilities are we to external stimuli? One sure thing is that few commentators straddle the fence when it comes to which model they believe is most appropriate. Each of the chapters to follow is grounded in one of these assumptions, sometimes explicitly but usually implicitly. A chore for readers, then, is to identify each author's "angle" and evaluate its strengths juxtaposed with their own perspective.

A FEW ADDITIONAL TOPICS TO CONSIDER

To this point, we have discussed the complexity of sorting out cause and effect, which would certainly be enough to spur discussion for some time. But there are additional topics that further confound our inquiry into the politics of popular culture, three of which are briefly outlined below.

Changes in Political Socialization

The process by which Americans acquire information about their world, termed *political socialization,* has changed over the last decade. This idea refers to the transition of customs and belief of a political system through the conscious and unconscious instilling of values.[18] It is the process by which political culture spreads from generation to generation. The primary socialization "agent" is generally believed to be the family, with schools as a distant second. Yet it is only honest to admit that the media and other forms of entertainment have emerged as the new socialization powerhouse. Whereas a few decades ago most homes did not have a television, today it is estimated that kids spend upwards of twenty-five hours per week watching TV. If we add to this time spent at the movies, listening to music, reading magazines, attending sporting events, playing video games, etc., the potential role of popular culture in conveying values is staggering. In addition, the very nature of "family life" has changed, with the number of single-parent households tripling since the mid-1960s (from about 10 to 30 percent) and the rate of births to unmarried teenagers jumping by almost 200 percent.[19] Of those families with two parents at home, most have two wage earners. All this suggests children spend more time "home alone" than ever before. What impact might changes in the socialization process have on the link between culture and politics? Although we might optimistically speculate that the family remains the primary socialization agent, popular culture is storming the gates.

A Free Market of Ideas

We might also consider the extent to which popular culture reflects the free market of ideas. Saying that popular culture promotes themes about politics is, by itself, not particularly troublesome. We might wish to be more astute about the messages espoused, but it is probably no big deal so long as diverse themes are being expressed. Many civil libertarians, for example, believe that the brawn of the First Amendment is that it allows *any* speech, no matter how loathsome, from which citizens can make informed judgments. The "marketplace of ideas" is a key element of democracy, they argue. Unfortunately, most agree that our choices in popular culture are limited.

In a lively, informative book on the political themes found in television and film, Michael Parenti argues that Hollywood regularly propagates some ideas and carefully avoids others. Themes stressed include racism, sexism, violence, vigilantism, authoritarian violence, and the virtues of capitalism and imperialism.[20] His book does an excellent job explaining the conformity of ideas found in film and on television.

Fortunately, other entertainment mediums like music, literature, and to an extent sports, reflect progressive ideas a bit more often. One could hardly discount the importance of folk and rock 'n' roll music in the 1960s as expressions of countercultural ideas, and the significance of hip-hop in giving African Americans a way to speak out against the problems of inner cities. Literature has always been at the forefront of important social movements, including those to the rights of women, Native Americans, persons with disabilities, and the poor. Radio has recently emerged as an outlet for Christian/conservative themes. And while sports has often perpetuated disparaging stereotypes, it has also exemplified our nation's reformative, healing powers.

So, does popular culture reflect a free market of ideas? Probably not. The "heavyweights"—television and film—continue to perpetuate violent, sexist, racist, and pro-capitalist themes. Maybe the good news is that "the times they are a-changin'," to use one of Bob Dylan's more celebrated lyrics from the 1960s, as more independent filmmakers are undertaking offbeat projects and the number of cable channels grows, allowing for more diversity on television and in theaters.

The Demands of Consumers

Finally, to what extent does American entertainment reflect consumer demand? How can we disparage television and film for promoting degrading, stereotypical themes if they are responding to market forces? Artistic considerations aside, conceivably *Rambo*'s "celebration of Reaganite cinema," as Parenti puts it, was exactly what viewers wanted; after all, it was a box-office smash (as was Reagan). Are not tales of lone heroes inspiring, and shows about the rich kids—perhaps those living in Melrose, California—more entertaining than programs about common folks? Maybe criticism of the content of popular culture is elitist—coming from a small group of academics holed up in "ivory towers." If we do not want to hear the violent, sexist messages espoused in rap music, we will buy other records or listen to other radio stations. If we disagree with the content of a situation comedy, we can pick up the remote and change channels (heaven knows we have options!). Or we will spend our eight dollars on one film, rather than another.

Others suggest we are not actually given real choices, but rather pseudo-choices.[21] We are afforded variety, but only within a small range of options.

For instance, seldom do we actually have the choice of seeing television programs that challenge the status quo or present unconventional ideas. Ellen's coming out notwithstanding, where can we turn to watch shows portraying gay life? For that matter, which networks air programs on the virtues of Christian fundamentalism? Americans can choose from an array of professional sports to watch on television or at a stadium, but only a fraction are played by women. The same is true of the types of music, books, and magazines available in the commercial marketplace. An analogy would be having the option of picking from a menu at McDonald's—there are choices, but they're all fast food. And remember, couched as entertainment, the themes espoused in popular culture are often not noticeable. If we are not fully aware of the subtle messages, choosing a politically acceptable option is never considered.

THE CHAPTERS THAT FOLLOW

The fit between popular culture and politics is a new area of scholarly interest and there is a growing body of research. The remaining fourteen chapters represent a fraction of this literature. They are organized into four of the most pressing topics in American politics: gender equality, race relations, the politics of social class, and the decline of civil society. The goal in selecting these chapters was to draw attention to novel viewpoints, suggesting unique ways of thinking about what otherwise might be seen as just entertainment.

Gender concerns are certainly nothing new in American politics. Women have been struggling to achieve economic, social, and political equality for hundreds of years. There are, to be sure, signs of improvement and few would dispute that we are heading in the right direction. More women now graduate from college, for example, than do men and the number of women entering traditionally male professions, like medicine, law, and politics is mushrooming. But should the fight for women's equality come to an end? Has the war been won? This book begins with a chapter by Bonnie Dow, who offers a novel spin on the hit television sitcom *Murphy Brown*. Rather than assuming the show celebrates the virtues of feminism and the potential of women in today's fast-paced world, as most would, Dow argues the real theme of Murphy Brown is quite the opposite. Murphy is successful precisely because she is not "feminine." Next is a lively, controversial piece by Mariah Burton Nelson. Her research is on the role of sports in the women's rights movement and this chapter is an excerpt from her book *The Stronger Women Get, the More Men Love Football* (1995). Women are advancing in all areas of society, she argues, which is perhaps why many men cling to the final refuge of male providence—violent sports. If nothing else, the chapter is sure to arouse discussion. The final chapter of the section, by Susan J. Douglas, sets its sights on the Spice Girls. This new, all-women group can hardly be ignored—they sold more than ten million albums in five months in

1997 and their list of hits is growing. The group proclaims to be "girl power for the nineties," but with their "Wonderbras, bare thighs, pouty lips, and top-of-the-head ponytails" the message afforded young girls might suggest otherwise. Douglas discusses the controversy, suggesting the good probably outweighs the bad.

Similar to the women's rights movement, the struggle for racial equality has taken center stage in American politics for more than two hundred years. Some gains have been made, but the dream of a color-blind society envisioned by the Reverend Martin Luther King, Jr. and many others has not become a reality. Race relations remain America's nagging embarrassment. But how does entertainment reflect and perhaps intensify racial problems? The lead chapter in the section, penned by Michael Lapchick, looks at race in collegiate athletics. "College sports," he writes, "has been portrayed as a beacon for democracy and opportunity." As one might guess, Lapchick's findings suggest otherwise. Next is Neil Englehart's essay on messages imbued in sports mascots, namely the use of Native American images and symbols. Shifting to music, David Hershey-Webb draws our attention to the racial undertones inherent in criticisms in rap music. Finally, Marilyn Kern-Foxworth presents a powerful argument, buttressed by scores of illustrations, of how racial and ethnic stereotypes are used to sell products.

Part III examines the politics of economic class. One of the hottest topics these days is how the shift from a production-based economy to service-sector economy will affect class politics in America. Who will be the losers in the global interdependent, high-tech economy of the twenty-first century? Michael Parenti, one of the most outspoken critics of America's economic system, begins the section by arguing that television and film have inundated us with status quo, antilabor messages. Some might take exception with this argument and a few of his examples, but Parenti never fails to be thought-provoking. This is followed by Nick Gillespie's brisk, unorthodox critique of Howard Stern's morning radio program. Stern has been the target of much criticism, but Gillespie believes the shock jock is "in the tradition of such folks as Mark Twain and Lenny Bruce." He suggests Stern is "particularly brilliant at deconstructing the pat, cliched, narrative that actors, politicians, and other public figures spin to their own advantage." Some might disagree. Finally, Stephen Smith and Jamie Rogers offer a unique look at country music. Disparaged for decades as simpleminded and perhaps even racist, these scholars believe country music echoes a consistent libertarian/populist message.

The final section addresses changes in political community more generally. Not long ago, renowned sociologist Robert Putnam published an article with the clever title, "Bowling Alone." America, he argues, is losing its social capital—that is, the connection between citizens in the public sphere. We are abandoning communal activities for television sets and computer screens. "The new 'virtual reality' helmets that we will soon don to be entertained in total isolation are merely the latest extension of this trend."[22] Others have sounded a similar alarm. The final four chapters of the book confront the broad topic of how popular culture affects families, communities, and society.

The section is kicked off by Robert Bork, one of America's leading conservative intellectuals. He presents a powerful critique of popular culture, finding things to be so bad that censorship is a viable solution. This idea would certainly not be shared by Oliver Stone, the author of the next chapter. Distinguished for writing, directing, and producing cutting-edge films, Stone was assailed following the release of *JFK* (1992) and *Nixon* (1995) for his "fast-and-loose" play with historical facts. The chapter answers this criticism and offers a statement on the role of art, more generally, in politics and society. Michael Medved shifts the blame for much of society's recent woes away from the content of television to the simple act of watching the tube for endless hours each day. The final chapter of the book takes a similar tract, but is also rather unique. It is written by Mary Pipher, whose most celebrated work, *Reviving Ophelia* (1994), is about the crisis facing adolescent girls brought about through popular culture. This chapter comes from her subsequent book, also a best-seller, *The Shelter of Each Other* (1996). Pipher expounds on the "profound crisis, of decency, of civility, of character" in which she feels today's society is mired—and the damaging effect it has on families. The prime culprits are, of course, television, advertising, and the "new tools" available in the Information Age. At first glance this chapter might seem only to be about families, but if we broaden our view of "family" to include community, it suggests a great deal about contemporary politics.

A FEW PARTING THOUGHTS

The reader will note contradictions between chapters. For instance, Pipher will disparage daytime television for radicalizing and ruining culture, while Parenti suggests popular culture is not radical enough. Bork attacks sex and vulgarity, while Gillespie defends Howard Stern. Stone sees Hollywood as a liberating force, while Medved views film and television watching as symptoms of cultural decay. Moreover, this book is not easily pigeonholed as "conservative" or "liberal," as there are chapters by lead scholars from both sides of the ideological fence. Uniting Mariah Burton Nelson and Robert Bork in the same volume would certainly guarantee a diversity of viewpoints. This might create a bit of frustration. On the other hand, it merely reflects the state of contemporary research on the topic, as well as the wide disagreement the topic provokes. These contradictions also reflect how notions regarding human nature and fundamental political values shape commentary and analysis. In politics, as in much of life, truisms or easy answers rarely emerge. All we might do is be open to unique ideas, anxious to appraise the validity of arguments, and willing to broaden the view of the world. Readers are encouraged to enter into the debate, not necessarily to agree with an author's premise, but to expand their core of knowledge. To help with sorting through conflicting arguments, I provide review questions at the end of each chapter.

One of the most widespread misnomers about politics is that it takes place only in legislatures, courthouses, smoke-filled rooms, and on the campaign trail. This is certainly not true and the core objective of this book is to recast the reader's conception of the political process. By understanding the diversity of political cues, activities, and messages, we are better able to uncover the underpinnings of politics. This will help us become more informed and, at the very least, more discerning consumers of entertainment.

Notes

1. David Rowe, *Popular Cultures: Rock Music, Sport, and the Politics of Pleasure* (Thousand Oaks, Calif.: Sage, 1995), p. 8.

2. Ibid., p. 102.

3. Ibid.

4. These three claims are from the following sources, respectively: Jonathan Zilbert, "Yes, It's True: Zimbabweans Love Dolly Parton," *Journal of Popular Culture* 29 (Summer 1995); Beverly James, "The Reception of American Popular Culture by Hungarians," *Journal of Popular Culture* 29 (Fall 1995): pp. 97–108; John K. White, *The New Politics of Old Values,* 2nd ed. (Hanover, Mass.: University Press of New England, February 1990), p. 108.

5. Robert H. Bork, *Slouching towards Gamorrah: Modern Liberalism and American Decline* (New York: ReganBooks, 1996), p. 143.

6. Michael Medved, "TV Vice? Sex and Violence Aren't the Problem," *American Enterprise,* September/October 1997, p. 54.

7. Keith Henderson, "Activists Say Need Is Less Violence on TV, Not More Warnings About It," *Christian Science Monitor,* July 6, 1993, p. 7.

8. William J. Bennett, *The Index of Leading Cultural Indicators: Facts and Figures on the State of American Society* (New York: Simon and Schuster, 1994).

9. Michael Parenti, *Make-Believe Media: The Politics of Entertainment* (New York: St. Martin's Press, 1992), p. 7, citing Tim Lahaye, *The Hidden Censors* (Old Tappan, N.J.: Revell, 1984).

10. Quoted in Greg Mitchell, *Campaign of the Century* (New York: Grove/Atlantic, Inc., September 1991), p. xv.

11. Parenti, *Make-Believe Media,* p. 3.

12. Bruce Handy, "Roll Over, Ward Cleaver," *Time,* April 14, 1997, p. 80.

13. Dirk Johnson, "Civility in Politics Going, Going, Gone," *New York Times,* December 10, 1997, sec. A, p. 20.

14. Bork, *Slouching towards Gamorrah,* p. 143.

15. See, for example, David Firestone, "Experts Call Giuliani's Term One of Modest Achievements," *New York Times,* October 27, 1997, p. A1. The article notes that while Giuliani may have failed in his term as mayor of New York City in some regards, crime rates have dropped dramatically in the last four years—upwards of 40 percent.

16. Bennett, *The Index of Leading Cultural Indicators,* p. 104.

17. As cited in W. Lance Bennett, *News: The Politics of Illusion,* 3rd ed. (New York: Longman, 1998), p. 5.

18. Jay M. Shafritz, *The Dorsey Dictionary of American Government and Politics* (Chicago: Dorsey Press, 1988), p. 419.

19. Bennett, *The Index of Leading Cultural Indicators,* pp. 50–73.

20. Parenti, *Make-Believe Media,* p. 2.

21. Ibid., pp. 207–213.

22. Robert D. Putnam, "Bowling Alone: America's Declining Social Capital," *Journal of Democracy* 6 (January 5, 1995).

1 / *Murphy Brown* and Postfeminist Politics

BONNIE J. DOW

Since its debut in 1988, *Murphy Brown* has been viewed as a "political" situation comedy, in at least two senses. First, it has been discussed in the popular press as a television show influenced by or representative of a political movement—feminism. Second, it is a show that *talks about* politics—story lines center on political events or issues (often thinly veiled representations of "real" events), political figures such as Bob Dole or Newt Gingrich or John F. Kennedy, Jr. have made guest appearances, and characters on the sitcom consistently allude to current events and make reference to public figures. Because feminism is generally perceived as a liberal political movement, and because the show's lead character, Murphy Brown, is depicted as a politically liberal journalist with a radical past, viewers and commentators have tended to assume that a liberal bias emanates from the sitcom. Generally, however, such assessments miss the mark; that is, claims about *Murphy Brown*'s politics are usually based on superficial characteristics of the sitcom (its topicality, the personality of its lead character, the use of political humor) rather than on examination of the deeper political implications of its treatment of issues or characters.

For example, *Murphy Brown*'s status as a feminist icon is based largely on the show's reworking of a television staple associated with 1970s feminism—the single, working-woman sitcom. *The Mary Tyler Moore Show* is generally credited as the first situation comedy to clearly illustrate the influence of the feminist movement that emerged in the late 1960s, and the numerous comparisons between *Mary Tyler Moore* and *Murphy Brown* position the latter sitcom as the heir to television's feminist tradition. For example, in *Newsweek*'s 1989 cover story on the new "womanpower" in television, entitled "Networking Women" and featuring Candice Bergen, the star of *Murphy Brown,* on the cover, *Murphy Brown* is heralded as an exemplar of the triumph of feminism on the small screen. The authors of the article note that "the critics . . . haven't lavished so much attention on an unmarried woman since Mary Richards walked into that other TV newsroom in Minneapolis."[1] In the same article, Linda Bloodworth-Thomason, producer of *Designing Women,* also spoke of *Mary Tyler Moore* as the baseline for representations of working women: "When Mary Richards threw that hat in the air for the last time, it stayed up. The contemporary TV

Note: *Murphy Brown* was one of America's top-rated situation comedies during the late 1980s and early 1990s. In spring of 1998, after the show's tenth season, it was canceled. It is currently in syndication—Ed.

15

woman is making it on her own."[2] Indeed, while Mary Richards was a rather tentative depiction of the implications of women's liberation, there is no doubt that Murphy Brown has made it. She is no struggling producer-cum-secretary in local news. Rather, she is a powerful network coanchor of a prime-time news magazine. Murphy presumably proves that "TV women have come a long, *long* way since Mrs. Cleaver whipped up her last breakfast for the Beav."[3]

This point is made again and again in media treatment of *Murphy Brown*.[4] Not only was a CBS special focusing on the twentieth anniversary of *Mary Tyler Moore* broadcast on a Monday evening (February 18, 1991) with *Murphy Brown* as its lead-in show, but the special was advertised as "An Evening with Murphy and Mary." *Primetime Live,* the ABC news magazine show, introduced a July 25, 1991 feature on *Murphy Brown* by placing the show on a continuum of "liberated woman" sitcoms that included *That Girl* and *Mary Tyler Moore*. If Mary Richards was the feminist television icon of the 1970s, then Murphy is the postfeminist icon for the 1990s. The show's producers have claimed that they "intend Murphy to be for the '90s what Mary Richards was for the '70s."[5] Media critic Jane Feuer has perhaps put it most explicitly by claiming that "the two shows [*Mary Tyler Moore* and *Murphy Brown*] really represent a continuation of the same cultural theme—the earlier show riding the crest of the feminist movement, the later one detailing its ebb in the 'postfeminist' era."[6]

But what is "postfeminism"? *Postfeminism* is a term used to refer to attitudes toward women's liberation that began to emerge in media coverage in the late 1980s. In various journalistic efforts to assess the progress of women and their attitudes toward changes in their lives, two basic themes recurred. The first, signified by the term "postfeminism," was that the feminist movement was over, having accomplished its major goals (accomplishments in this category usually include women's increasing access to education, their entrance into male-dominated professions, and the increasing number of women combining family and career).[7] The second theme emerged in press accounts focusing on women's dissatisfaction with the aftermath of these feminist advances—their difficulties combining family and work (including the "second shift" experienced by many women who were expected to work outside the home and yet still fulfill all housework and child care responsibilities within it[8]), the "infertility epidemic" among career women, the guilt and anxiety of working mothers over the problem of "toxic" day care,[9] and the supposed "marriage crunch" experienced by women who had deferred marriage in their twenties, only to find that their chances of ever securing a mate had drastically declined.[10] The implication of this second theme was that, regardless of their progress in the public sphere, success in the private sphere of romance, marriage, and motherhood was still the key priority in women's lives.

Many of the claims about postfeminist problems were inaccurate or exaggerated, and these stories too seldom made the point that many of these conflicts were created by the reluctance of business, government, and spouses to adjust to the reality of women's lives as workers and mothers.[11] Regardless, however, the rash of postfeminist trend stories in 1980s media created the impression that women's liberation was the source of the problems in women's lives, rather than the solution to them.

In this chapter, I argue that a key part of *Murphy Brown*'s political function is its representation of postfeminist themes, both in its validation of women's progress embodied in the power of the lead character and in its exploration of the costs of that progress. Although media treatment of the sitcom emphasizes the progressive portrait of a professional woman, it also contains subtler themes about the lessons of liberation. The *Newsweek* article already mentioned, for example, claims that "beneath their self-assured veneers," television's new, powerful women "carry stretch marks on their psyches. They've been roughed up by life and are coming to terms with their limits."[12] Candice Bergen adds to this theme in a 1989 *Playboy* interview in which she notes that "Murphy is at the top of her profession but . . . she is, in a very realistic way, paying the price for it."[13]

POSTFEMINIST WOMANHOOD

The regulars on *Murphy Brown* consist primarily of Murphy's colleagues at "FYI," the weekly prime-time news magazine show of which she is a coanchor. The other "FYI" anchor is Jim Dial, an older, experienced television newsman known for his rigid, uptight nature and his stiff, laconic style. Miles Silverberg was, throughout most of the show's tenure, the executive producer of "FYI" and Murphy's boss. He is less experienced and younger than Murphy, a situation that she finds consistently irritating in early seasons of the sitcom. Two other regulars are Frank Fontana and Corky Sherwood, reporters for the program. Frank is an experienced investigative reporter and Murphy's closest friend in the group.

In contrast, Corky has little journalistic experience. She is an ex-Miss America who was hired at "FYI" for her beauty queen status. Corky is young, pretty, and perky, a softer character than Murphy, and she provides a traditionally feminine foil for Murphy's feminist character. Murphy's relation to Corky is competitive rather than cooperative. Corky's role on "FYI" is to produce "soft" news features (e.g., "Twelve Angry Women in Hairdresser Horror Stories," "Dinner with the Van Patten Family") that appeal to female viewers. Although the two women become friends over time, Murphy does not see Corky as her professional equal, and a strong theme in their relationship is Murphy's disdain for Corky's journalistic ability. Two other regulars on the show are not connected to "FYI." They are Murphy's ever-present house painter, Eldin Bernecky, who appears in most of the scenes set in Murphy's home, and Phil, the owner of a bar frequented by the "FYI" staff.[14]

This review of characters shows kinship between *Murphy Brown* and *Mary Tyler Moore*. Like Mary Richards, Murphy is "a woman in a man's world." However, Murphy is a media "star," a knowledgeable, driven, investigative reporter who has won numerous awards. Unlike *Mary Tyler Moore*, in which the narrative problem was "can she make it on her own?", *Murphy Brown* has moved beyond such a question. She has indeed made it on her own, in the process becoming what Phyllis Japp calls "a male persona in a female body."[15]

Murphy Brown signifies Murphy's masculinized persona in numerous ways. Her name is not traditionally feminine; generally, "Murphy" would be more likely to refer to a man than a woman. Moreover, although Candice Bergen is a strikingly beautiful woman, her style, as Murphy Brown, is not traditionally feminine. Murphy's clothing is severely tailored, and she tends to wear high collars and boxy suits with straight lines. The contrast of Murphy's look and manner with that of the ultrafeminine Corky give Murphy's "difference" additional weight. Reinforcing the idea that she and Corky are two extremes on a spectrum, Murphy's tendency toward black, brown, and strong colors are a clear contrast to Corky's frequent pastels, soft scarves, and bows. While Murphy often wears flats, Corky always wears high heels. Murphy's subdued makeup and hair also are striking in comparison to Corky's teased, bleached hair and bright lips. Corky's appearance is part of her general femininity, while Murphy's style reflects the goal of gaining credibility in a male world.

Murphy's physical presence also is noteworthy in defining her character. Her stride is aggressive, her gestures are strong, her manner of speaking is forceful, and she commands primary attention in any scene in which she is involved. Murphy's physical aura is reinforced by her aggressive communication style. She is supremely confident about her own opinions, and she expresses them easily, often with little regard for others' feelings. For example, in "The Strike"[16] (1989), Murphy is disgusted by the way the men around her are handling a management-union dispute. She accuses them of being blinded by male pride, and comments, "just pull down your pants, I'll get a ruler, and we'll settle this once and for all." This line, in fact, illustrates the double edge to Murphy's character. It can be taken, simultaneously, as a salient feminist comment on a masculine obsession with power at the expense of reasonable problem solving and as further evidence of Murphy's insensitivity and her taste for harsh sarcasm.

A clear message of *Murphy Brown* is that the personality traits alluded to above, such as aggression, competitiveness, and lack of interpersonal sensitivity, are key to Murphy's professional success in a patriarchal world. For example, in "The Unshrinkable Murphy Brown" (1989) Murphy is so relentless while interviewing a subject that he has a heart attack and dies on the air. Guilt-stricken, Murphy vows to be a nicer person, and in subsequent scenes she is uncharacteristically polite and considerate to her colleagues. They are shocked and dismayed at the change in her behavior, concerned that it is affecting the quality of her work.

This episode is instructive, because it implies that Murphy's display of traditionally "nice," feminine qualities is not only shocking, but incompatible with her success as a journalist. In order to be successful she must be tough and competitive, and she must reject behaviors that contradict such a persona. While other reporters on "FYI" are also capable and successful, notably Jim Dial and Frank Fontana, they do not behave as ruthlessly as Murphy. To compete in a male culture, Murphy becomes an extreme version of it—a caricature of the consequences of liberal feminism. Alison Jaggar has noted that a typical liberal feminist argument is that "women are capable of participating in male culture and of living up to male values."[17] In *Murphy Brown*, consistent with postfeminism, this success has its costs. A theme in early seasons is Murphy's recovery from alcoholism, a disease that she attributes to her driven lifestyle. She has little success with romantic relationships and does not bond easily with other women.

The earlier seasons of *Murphy Brown* are the most direct about exploiting aspects of Murphy's stereotypical liberal feminist character. A classic example occurs in "The Morning Show" (1989), in which the major plotline concerns Murphy's week-long stint as the substitute coanchor of "Today America," a program much like *Good Morning America*. Murphy ridicules the "soft news" orientation of the program, and she is unhappy to discover that Corky is to be her cohost. Corky is excited by the assignment and spends significant time preparing. Murphy, in contrast, does not see the job as challenging and does no preparation.

The contrasts between Murphy and Corky as coanchors are the context within which Corky's traditional femininity is validated, while Murphy's aggressive competitiveness only creates difficulties. In the first morning show, they interview the male author of a popular children's book. While Corky praises the inventiveness and popularity of the book, Murphy asserts that the setting of the book, the "Land of the Woogies," emulates a male-dominated society, and that the story represents the larger culture's "struggle for sexual equality in the workplace." The author protests that his characters are not gendered, but Murphy is relentless, claiming that the "Fifis," another group in the book, are female and represent "an oppressed minority of sorts." At this point, Corky steps in, soothes the author, and ends the interview.

The contrast between Murphy's feminism and Corky's femininity are clear in this scene. Murphy personifies the intensity and humorlessness of the stereotypical feminist ideologue, refusing to enact the supportive, gracious role required in such a situation. While her argument that the children's book is sexist indeed may be correct (and some viewers may see it as a salient point to make), the laugh track encourages the audience to view her claim as absurd and her behavior as inappropriate for the situation. Corky, in contrast, is at home in the soft news format that reflects traditionally female interests.

While Corky is praised for her performance, Murphy is described by colleagues as "acerbic, humorless, inflexible, and unprepared." The next day, Murphy panics when she hears that she must participate in a segment with a bake-off champion, and moans, "The last time I tried to bake brownies, I had to call in an industrial cleaning service." During the segment, Corky startles Murphy by separating an egg with one hand. Corky's baking expertise is manifest—and Murphy is challenged. She becomes obsessed with learning to separate eggs and annoys the bake-off champion. Murphy ruins the segment as she and the bake-off champion do verbal (and nearly physical) battle and have to be pried apart by Corky. Murphy's dearth of culinary skills, and her inability to acquiesce graciously to Corky's superiority in this arena further demonstrate her lack of stereotypical feminine qualities.

By the end of this episode, Murphy is humbled, and she must admit that Corky did the better job. Murphy is humiliated because she is not traditionally feminine enough, in terms of social facilitation or cooking skills, to fulfill the assigned role. Despite the fact that her particular traits have led to success in "hard news," when she fails at soft news she is punished. Again, Murphy is the victim of conflicting expectations. Corky, whose more traditionally female skills are appropriate for the situation, shines on the morning show, although she has failed in the past at hard news assignments. This episode adds strength to a theme that dominates early seasons of the program: a woman cannot both be professionally successful and retain traditional qualities of femininity. Murphy is rich and famous but not a "real" woman in personality or personal relationships. Corky, in contrast, is more traditionally feminine in appearance and behavior but is professionally competent only in the feminine province of lower-status, soft news situations. In *Murphy Brown,* neither major female character can be totally complete, and the "weaknesses" of each are highlighted through contrast with the other.

The sharp contrast between Murphy and Corky that feeds the dichotomy in *Murphy Brown* between professional and personal competence eases in later seasons of the sitcom, largely as a result of the development of Corky's character through her marriage, divorce, and increasing professional ambition. Corky's ultimately unsuccessful first marriage extends the program's message about the incompatibility of personal and professional success to encompass Corky's life as well. Although Corky still handles only soft news features, she becomes more competent, successful, and ambitious. Despite Corky's development, the disturbing element of competition that fuels Murphy and Corky's relationship is never lost. Corky frequently uses her new skills at Murphy's expense, which feeds the competition between them and functions to discipline Murphy for her excesses. A 1991 episode, in which Corky is given a network special of her own, is illustrative.

In that episode, Corky decides to frame the special as a tea-party, in which she will interview people such as Mrs. Fields (of Mrs. Fields' cookies fame) and Mary Ann Mobley and Gary Collins (best known as hosts of the Miss America pageant). Corky also wants Murphy to be a guest, a request Murphy disdains ("What self-respecting journalist would let himself[18] be interviewed at a tea-party?"), until Miles manages to talk her into it by appealing to her ego. On the day the special is to be broadcast live, a newspaper columnist ridicules the special so thoroughly that Corky is completely demoralized, convinced that she can never be as good as the other members of FYI, that she will never be able to "ask the tough questions." Uncharacteristically, Murphy offers Corky encouragement and convinces her to go ahead with the special. Corky promises that she will "try to live up to your [Murphy's] standards."

During the special, instead of asking Murphy questions about her professional experiences, Corky turns the conversation to Murphy's troubled personal life with questions such as "Earlier in your career, you were, in your own words, a 'major booze hound.' I was just wondering, could America trust your accuracy and judgment in reporting information?" Corky's relentless probing eventually leads to various highly personal revelations from Murphy, such as "Maybe I deliberately sabotage my personal relationships because I fear losing some professional edge." After the special, Murphy is completely humiliated, convinced that her reputation has been destroyed. When she confronts Corky, threatening to "kill" her, Corky's reply is that she was modeling herself after Murphy: "I did what I thought you would have done in the same situation. . . . I'm right, aren't I, Murphy?"

Murphy is hoisted on her own petard in this episode. She has disdained Corky's abilities for years while asserting her own superiority as a journalist, only to be the unwitting victim when Corky finally is able "to ask the tough questions" (it is doubly interesting, of course, that Murphy's dysfunctional personal life is the focus). Murphy suffers this kind of deflation regularly in the show, frequently at Corky's hands. In true sitcom style, Murphy never really learns her lesson (to do so would eliminate the "sit"), and she keeps returning for yet more comeuppances. Moreover, Murphy's comment to Corky about sabotaging personal relationships reflects a theme that surfaces in various plot-lines focusing on Murphy's private life. Unmarried, childless, and without a satisfying romantic relationship, Murphy's character embodies what media constructions of postfeminism suggest are the negative consequences of female independence. For example, *Time* magazine's 1989 cover story asking "Is there a future for feminism?" maintains that many career women resent feminists for not foreseeing the sacrifices women would have to make, noting that "the bitterest complaints come from the growing ranks of women who have reached 40 and find themselves childless, having put their careers first."[19] The emphasis on Murphy's barren personal life enacts this postfeminist scenario; several episodes comment on the effect of Murphy's life choices on her personal relations, offering the message that her professional ambition precludes lasting personal relationships.

For example, in a 1988 episode, Murphy's ex-husband, a political activist to whom she was married for five days twenty years earlier, appears on "FYI." They reignite their attraction and decide to marry again. However, Murphy cannot find time for a wedding and they give up on the idea. Her excuses range from "I gotta fly to Moscow to interview Gorbachev" to "I can't plan that far in advance—I've got to be ready to hop a plane at a moment's notice." Murphy's devotion to her work seems extreme in this circumstance, with the result that she sacrifices her own personal happiness. In the 1990–91 season, Murphy began a relationship with Jerry Gold, an abrasive talk show host. In their first try at a relationship, Murphy eventually called it off, saying, "I'm good at a lot of things, but this isn't one of them. I start saying things I don't normally say, I start doing things I don't normally do. . . . Oh, God, I'm wearing an apron. See what I mean?" This remark comes after a failed dinner party that Murphy concocted to introduce Jerry to her colleagues. It is telling that Murphy equates her failure at the relationship with her unsuitability for a domestic role, reinforcing the dichotomy between the private and public spheres.

THE POLITICS OF SINGLE MOTHERHOOD

At the conclusion of the 1991 season, *Murphy Brown*'s producers presented the possibility of a drastic alteration in the narrative premise of the sitcom when Murphy discovered that she was pregnant. As I will discuss, Murphy's decision to become a single mother ultimately had little effect on the dynamics of the sitcom. However, the series of events surrounding Murphy's pregnancy and birth, both inside and outside the text of the show, deserves discussion for its illustration of the intersections of postfeminism, politics, and media intertextuality.

Press reaction to Murphy's pregnancy was mixed. Rather than viewing it as shocking, some writers[20] interpreted it as part of a trend on series television, which was experiencing a spate of baby-related storylines in shows such as *Designing Women, Cheers, Moonlighting,* and *The Days and Nights of Molly Dodd.* Murphy's pregnancy did spark some moral outrage, from editorial columnists who accused television producers of irresponsibly weakening "the rule against illegitimacy [that] helps to prevent women and children from being abandoned by men,"[21] to viewers who protested that the show was sending the wrong message about the joys of single motherhood.[22] Even Candice Bergen herself made a point of asserting that "I myself, as a parent, believe that the ideal is that you have a two-parent family. I'm the last person to think fathers are obsolete."[23]

Yet, given the possibilities, the handling of Murphy's pregnancy within the narrative of the sitcom was remarkably conservative. In the concluding episode to the 1990–91 season both of Murphy's former loves reenter her life at the same time. Jerry Gold returns from California to resume a relationship with Murphy at the same time that Murphy's ex-husband, Jake Lowenstein, reappears. Murphy juggles the two men briefly, unable to decide between them. In the episode's final scene, Murphy is shocked by the result of a home pregnancy test, creating the cliffhanger question: Who is the father?

The show takes care, in later episodes, to downplay implications of sexual irresponsibility. When Frank chastises Murphy for having unprotected sex with two men, Murphy reminds him that it was a fluke, that she has sex about as often as Democrats occupy the White House. Moreover, the father turns out to be Jake, who makes the choice not to be involved in the pregnancy or the child's life, citing his commitment to political activism around the world. Finally, although Murphy considers abortion, she ultimately rejects it. By this point, it has been established the Murphy is not promiscuous, that the child has an aura of legitimacy derived from the fact that Murphy was once married to the father, that the father is deserting her through his own choice,[24] and that Murphy will not abort the pregnancy simply to avoid the inconvenience of single motherhood. Beyond the fact that Murphy engaged in unprotected extramarital sex in the first place, the portrayal of her journey to single motherhood is relatively timid.

Indeed, Murphy's surrender to women's supposed biological imperative, is, in my view, the ultimate postfeminist moment in *Murphy Brown,* giving credence to the claims about biological clocks, about the emptiness experienced by childless career women, and women's "natural" destiny to mother. Various characters in the program, including Murphy herself, reiterate that Murphy is unsuited for motherhood. After she has decided to keep the baby, Phil comments that her decision was "pretty gutsy for a woman with no maternal instinct whatsoever," to which Murphy replies, "Not everyone is born with maternal instincts, Phil. I can get some. I'm sure there's a class." At another point, Corky comments that she is sure Murphy will "make a wonderful mother, once she gets a little practice and maybe some estrogen supplements."

Given her personality and lifestyle, Murphy's decision to bear the child hardly seems rational. It makes sense only as a reflection of the sexist adage that all women have a deep and irrepressible desire (duty?) to reproduce that is merely waiting to be triggered. Indeed, this essentialist interpretation of Murphy's motivation is given support in the "birth" episode from the end of the 1992 season—an episode viewed by some thirty-eight million people. In the final scene, Murphy cradles her new infant in her arms, singing to him words from one of her favorite songs, "Natural Woman," by Aretha Franklin. The lines that Murphy sings, including "I didn't know what was wrong with me, 'til you helped me name it," and "You make me feel like a natural woman," take on a powerful meaning in this context. Having given birth, Murphy is miraculously transformed, albeit briefly, from an "unnatural" (professional) to a "natural" (maternal) woman.[25]

Apparently, then-Vice President Dan Quayle did not view this episode before making his remarks about the poverty of family values represented by *Murphy Brown.* If he had, he might have noticed how closely it dovetailed with his wife's (and presumably his own) view, expressed at the Republican National Convention a few months later, that, contrary to feminist claims, "women do not wish to be liberated from their essential natures." However, given that the treatment of Murphy's pregnancy and birth is hardly radical, the most interesting aspects of the Quayle-Murphy media phenomenon to me is the way in which a popular sitcom, and the underlying values of the entertainment industry, became the dominant focus in reaction to a speech that was predominantly an attack on poor women. Focusing on the theme of family values, as though its implications were gender, race, and class neutral, both mainstream media and the text of *Murphy Brown* itself (through its intertextual appropriation and interpretation of Quayle's statement) created a debate that left untouched what Bell Hooks usefully calls "white supremacist capitalist patriarchy."[26]

Quayle's famous comment about *Murphy Brown* occurred in a May 19, 1992 speech to the Commonwealth Club of California, an elite political group dominated by white men.[27] Attempting to make sense of the recent Los Angeles riots, Quayle argued that "the lawless social anarchy which we saw is directly related to the breakdown of family structure, personal responsibility, and social order in too many areas of our society." He went on to note that, while baby boomers such as himself participated in the "war against traditional values" waged in the 1960s and 1970s, now that the boomers are "middle-aged and middle-class . . . the responsibility of having families has helped many recover traditional values."

Quayle maintains that the poor, unfortunately, have never managed to regain those traditional values. The result is that "the intergenerational poverty that troubles us so much today is predominantly a poverty of values. . . . The anarchy and lack of structure in our inner cities are testament to how quickly civilization falls apart when the family foundation cracks." The vice president then asserts the necessity of male role models for inner-city children, touts marriage as "the best antipoverty program of all," and calls for a return to the moral stigmatization of illegitimacy. At this point he mentions *Murphy Brown,* claiming that "it doesn't help matters when prime-time TV has Murphy Brown—a character who supposedly epitomizes today's intelligent, highly paid, professional woman—mocking the importance of fathers by bearing a child alone and calling it just another 'lifestyle choice.'" Moments later, Quayle extends his censure to the "cultural leaders in Hollywood, network TV, the national newspapers" who "routinely jeer" at moral values.

Quayle's remarks made the front pages of national newspapers—notably the *New York Times* and *USA Today*—and became the lead story on ABC's *World News Tonight,* the most popular national television newscast in America. In its May 20 edition, *USA Today* ran a photograph of Murphy Brown holding her baby next to the headline: "Quayle: Murphy No Role Model." The following day, the *New York Times* ran the same photograph of Murphy Brown on its front page, juxtaposed with photos of Quayle and White House spokesperson Marlin Fitzwater and the headline "Appeal of 'Murphy Brown' Now Clear at White House." The *Times* article made clear the extent to which Quayle's brief comment about Murphy Brown was influencing reaction to his speech, noting that in his tour of Los Angeles, "Mr. Quayle was greeted at every stop and in six local television interviews with questions about the 'Murphy Brown' program."[28] Press coverage of President Bush's trade talks with Canadian Prime Minister Brian Mulroney also was dominated by questions about the *Murphy Brown* issue.[29]

Generally, reports on Quayle's remarks were dominated by analysis of the White House campaign strategy to emphasize family values, by the comical contradictions in Quayle's and Fitzwater's follow-up remarks, and by reactions from the show's producers. Fitzwater, for instance, noted that Murphy's decision to bear the child "[exhibits] pro-life values which we think are good,"[30] an opinion that Quayle later countered, claiming that *Murphy Brown* "does not represent pro-life policies."[31] Quayle's disagreement with Fitzwater was no doubt prompted by the widely reported response of Diane English to the vice president's attack: "'If the vice president thinks it's disgraceful for an unmarried woman to bear a child, and if he believes that a woman cannot adequately raise a child without a father, then he'd better make sure abortion remains safe and legal.'"[32]

English's comment was one of the few that made it into coverage of the incident that indicated even a slight sense of the substance and the politics of Quayle's speech. Nonetheless, even English overlooked Quayle's classism. Quayle did not suggest that *women in general* could not raise children adequately without fathers; rather, he suggested that *poor women,* in particular, were "bearing babies irresponsibly." Murphy Brown's contribution to the crisis was that she was failing to provide a worthy role model for poor women, apparently a key issue in the "trickle-down theory of values" which holds that prime-time television is a major influence on inner-city mothers.[33] A point that was never raised in the debate over Hollywood's poverty of values was that, in fact, the overwhelming majority of families on television have always been headed by two parents, a factor that has apparently made little difference in checking the "anarchy and lack of structure in our inner cities."

Quayle's claims in his speech that poverty is traceable to a lack of moral fiber, that single, poor women are inadequate mothers, that poor mothering is responsible for inner-city problems, and that marriage will save the inner city from decline are the most interesting and disturbing in his speech to the Commonwealth Club. That these claims were largely overlooked is fairly easy to explain. First, the mass media loves to inflate its own importance and found it far more interesting to highlight its own minor role in Quayle's speech than to examine the implications of the vice president's remarks for welfare and urban policy. Second, it is a media convention to focus on an individual—even a fictional one—rather than to grapple with the structural problems (e.g., lack of economic opportunity, racism, sexism) that contribute to inner-city poverty.

Media emphasis on the "Murphy Brown angle" transformed a vicious attack on poor, presumably black (given the emphasis on the inner cities and the L.A. riots) women into a debate about Hollywood liberalism, middle-class morality, and the constitution of the nuclear family.[34] *Murphy Brown* itself, in its famous and much hyped response to Quayle in the premiere episode of the 1992 fall season, frames the debate in this fashion. This episode's pivotal moment is a scene in which Murphy and Frank see Quayle's remarks on the evening news. After hearing Quayle's brief remarks about her "lifestyle choice," Murphy explodes:

Glamorize single motherhood? What planet is he on? Look at me, Frank, am I glamorous? . . . And what was that crack about just another lifestyle choice? I agonized over that decision. I didn't know if I could raise a kid myself. I worried about what it would do to him, I worried about what it would do to me. I didn't just wake up one morning and say "Oh, gee, I can't get in for a facial, I might as well have a baby!"

Murphy's debunking of Quayle's characterization of her motives is humorous, but it takes Quayle's comments largely at face value and ignores their context, as did media accounts. As the controversy escalates, Murphy decides that she must make a response to the vice president on "FYI." Although media accounts positioned this episode as an oppositional response to the vice president, the substance of Murphy's argument on "FYI" is consistent with the framing of the debate as a referendum on the proper definition of a family:

These are difficult times for our country, and in searching for the causes of our social ills, we could choose to blame the media, or the Congress, or an administration that's been in power for twelve years, or we could blame it on me. . . . I doubt that my status as a single mother has contributed all that much to the breakdown of Western civilization. . . . The vice president says he felt it was important to open a dialogue about family values, and on that point we agree. Unfortunately, it seems that for him, the only acceptable definition of family is a mother, a father, and children, and in a country where millions of children grow up in nontraditional families, that definition seems painfully unfair. Perhaps it's time for the vice president to expand his definition and recognize that, whether by choice or circumstance, families come in all shapes and sizes, and ultimately what really defines a family is commitment, caring, and love.

By the time that this episode aired in September of 1992, both the White House and the producers of *Murphy Brown* were enjoying the fruits of the publicity the incident had created. Candice Bergen, only partly tongue-in-cheek, thanked Quayle in her acceptance speech after she won the Emmy for best actress in a comedy series. Quayle obtained yet more attention when he arranged to watch the episode with a group of single mothers. The producers of the show benefitted from the ratings boost and the rise in advertising prices that the incident gave the sitcom,[35] and the Bush administration gained publicity for its "family values" campaign agenda. The only losers were the poor women of the inner cities, who became invisible in a debate that began with an assertion of their moral failings.[36]

POSTFEMINIST POLITICS IN *MURPHY BROWN*

Despite all of the controversy, Murphy's child, Avery, makes little difference in the patterns of Murphy's character or in the narrative of the show. Avery is not featured in every episode, and Murphy's personality remains largely unchanged. Initially, the child functions as a comic device to provide plotlines for Murphy's antics. Within a couple of seasons, he disappears almost entirely from the sitcom's narrative. In fact, at least one article, originally published in the *Los Angeles Times,* featured complaints from a number of women and child-care experts that Murphy was unrealistically well-adjusted to working motherhood and that she was not "guilty, anguished, or exhausted" enough. The consensus among those interviewed in this article was that *Murphy Brown,* having defended Murphy's right to be a single mother, has "failed to prove Dan Quayle wrong" by neglecting to portray Murphy as a classically "good" mother and refusing to focus on "what [her] child's life was like."[37]

Putting aside the obvious arguments that could be made about the possibilities for realism in television, I find a number of fascinating postfeminist contradictions at work in critiques of Murphy's motherhood. The postfeminist working mothers who dominated television in the 1980s (in shows such as *The Cosby Show, Family Ties,* and *Growing Pains*) never inspired such a reaction, even though they were hardly realistic in that their highly paid professional jobs never seemed to interfere with their constant availability for family matters. However, these women were characters in sitcoms about *family,* not work. *Murphy Brown,* in turn, has always been a sitcom about *work,* not family. Yet, the possibility that, after initial adjustment, Murphy's professional life might continue largely unaffected by her maternity is interpreted by critics of the show as irresponsibility on the part of the show's producers (as if Dan Quayle was really concerned about the maternal fitness of white, wealthy, career women in the first place). For some reason, Murphy's motherhood should dominate her life. Such a move would have brought the program even closer to the "unstated but ever-present suggestion of postfeminist television . . . that women should combine work with family, and that normal women prioritize the latter."[38] To its credit, in one of its rare refusals of postfeminist ideology, *Murphy Brown* does not provide this satisfaction. After a brief flirtation with essentialist womanhood in the "Natural Woman" scene, the sitcom seems to take the position that Murphy's dedication to her job, and her personality as a strong-willed, belligerent woman, will not be drastically altered by motherhood.

This interpretation of Murphy's motherhood has a number of ideological edges, as does Murphy's character generally. The show gives in to the postfeminist notion that a woman's life is incomplete without reproduction, but does not, in turn, use Murphy's motherhood to further essentialist ideas about the effect of maternity on women's thinking and/or behavior. Nor does it argue that careerism and motherhood are incompatible. Likewise, Murphy's difficulties with the tasks of motherhood and her lack of "maternal instincts" can be interpreted as subtle debunking of essential constructions of motherhood or as further demonstration of how Murphy's stereotypical feminist lifestyle has "defeminized" her and made her (humorously) unsuitable to be a mother.

More than any other popular television show, *Murphy Brown* represents and comments on various strands of postfeminist thought in the late 1980s and early 1990s: the personal costs of professional success, the conflicts between work and motherhood, and the emphasis on the "choices" women make. Despite the clear coding of its main character as a liberal feminist success story, the show still leaves room for ambivalence. For profeminist viewers, Murphy is a rare and satisfying portrait of a powerful woman. From this perspective, even Murphy's frequent comeuppances, from which she always bounces back to endure yet more of them, can be viewed as evidence of the continuing discomfort of Americans with powerful women and of the need for continued feminist struggle. For an audience uncomfortable with the confrontation that feminism presents for many cherished assumptions, however, Murphy's function as a comedic character, whose extreme personality traits are often the source of humor, provides the relief necessary to keep her character appealing. The fact that Murphy "suffers" for her success makes it easier to accept her rejection of traditional womanhood. Ultimately, *Murphy Brown*'s potential to satisfy viewers from both camps (if only partially) tells us something about why it is so popular.

Even with its potential doubleness, the program stops far short of offering any substantive challenge to postfeminism. *Murphy Brown* appears to eschew any acknowledgment of women's collective problems or of the need for collective action to solve them. To me, the fact that so much of the humor generated by Murphy's character derives from her failure to meet conventional expectations for womanhood indicates that we are far from living in post-patriarchy. However, as *Murphy Brown* tells it, Murphy sabotages herself and pays the price for it. Even those critics of the program who claim that Murphy integrates motherhood and work too easily are not motivated by a desire to dramatize the need for structural change to benefit working mothers. Rather, they are concerned that Murphy is failing to fulfill adequately her responsibility as a postfeminist role model. The onus is not on a workplace, or government, or cultural mindset that has failed to adapt to the realities of women's lives—it is on the woman, the character (or those who write her).

Indeed, it is difficult to view someone as privileged and powerful as Murphy as a victim because she is the kind of woman who has benefitted the most from the liberal feminist advances of the past two decades: she is white, wealthy, and well educated. For me, this is the ultimate problem of uncritically accepting Murphy as a representation of what feminism hath wrought: in doing so, all we are gaining is the possibility for a kind of rugged individualism on the part of exceptional women whose lives are cushioned by privileges of education, race, and class. In doing so, we are encouraged to overlook the profound inequalities that burden women who are not like Murphy Brown (a category that, in fact, includes most women). The Quayle incident reveals, at once, just how easily Murphy Brown has been accorded status as the icon of liberated womanhood and how different her circumstances are from the poor, black women who have benefitted little from liberal feminism and who were Quayle's primary target.

Murphy Brown is a popular sitcom because it taps into the postfeminist anxieties of both those who think feminism went too far and those who think it did not go far enough. In the end, however, I view the program as a sitcom which, beyond the "lifestyle feminism" popularized more than twenty years ago by *Mary Tyler Moore,* has no genuine feminist politics of its own, no sense that women's problems can be understood "not as symptoms of individual failure but as symptoms of oppression by a system of male dominance."[39] That *Murphy Brown* can be so widely interpreted as a vision of feminist success is a testament to how firmly postfeminist attitudes and expectations have taken hold of popular consciousness.

REVIEW QUESTIONS

1. Should *Murphy Brown* be viewed as a valuable commentary on the status of women in our society—one that is valuable for exposing the difficulty many women face in the public realm while also trying to find satisfaction at the personal level? Or does *Murphy Brown* fall short of feminism's goals of demanding that the workplace be changed to accommodate the needs of working women? Put a bit differently, should those of us concerned with issues of gender equality applaud this sitcom?

2. Despite the fact that only about 25 percent of American households are composed of a married couple and their children, and less than 10 percent of American households account for the traditional version in which the father is the sole family breadwinner (Susan Lehrer, "Family and Women's Lives," in *Women: Images and Realities: A Multicultural Anthology,* eds. Amy Kesselman, Lily D. McNair, and Nancy Schniedewind [Mountain View, Calif.: Mayfield Publishing Company, 1995], pp. 184–88) some, like Dan Quayle, strive to maintain the notion that the nuclear family predominates. Do shows like *Murphy Brown* dismantle such claims? If so, is that a good or bad thing?

3. Murphy Brown is a woman who assumes masculine characteristics and assimilates into the patriarchal working world. What does *Murphy Brown* say about the structure of the workplace and how success is defined? Does the creation of a character who has battled alcohol abuse and who has had several failed romantic relationships help to reveal the problems that working women face? According to Dow, what price does Murphy Brown pay?

4. Does Murphy Brown's decision to have a baby serve to reinforce the idea that women have a "natural" inclination toward parenthood, that women are somehow incomplete if they are childless?

5. In your opinion, does *Murphy Brown* contribute to the notion that women's liberation is the source of the problem in women's lives rather than the solution?

Notes

1. Harry F. Waters, and Janet Huck, "Networking Women," *Newsweek,* March 13, 1989, pp. 48–55.

2. Ibid., p. 50.

3. Ibid., p. 48.

4. For other examples of press coverage that make this claim, see Robert S. Alley, and Irby B. Brown, *Love Is All Around: The Making of The Mary Tyler Moore Show* (New York: Delta, 1989); Joanna Elm, "What TV's Real Newswomen Think of Murphy Brown." *TV Guide,* December 23, 1989, pp. 4–7; Joy Horowitz, "On TV, Ms. Macho and Mr. Wimp," *New York Times,* April 19, 1989, pp. 1H, 36H; John J. O'Connor, "One Day at a Time," *New York Times,* December 16, 1975, p. 79; Jane O'Reilly, "At Last! Women Worth Watching." *TV Guide,* May 27, 1989, pp. 18–21; Bill Wisehart, "Murphy and Mary: Similar but So Unlike," *Star Tribune* (Minneapolis), December 24, 1989, pp. 39.

5. Joy Horowitz, "On TV, Ms. Macho and Mr. Wimp," p. 1H.

6. Jane Feuer, "Genre Study and Television," in "Audience-Oriented Criticism and Television," *Channels of Discourse, Reassembled: Television and Contemporary Criticism,* 2nd ed., ed. Robert Allen (Chapel Hill: University of North Carolina Press, 1992), pp. 101–137.

7. See Bonnie J. Dow, *Prime-Time Feminism: Television, Media Culture, and the Women's Movement Since 1970* (Philadelphia: University of Pennsylvania Press, 1996), pp. 87–92.

8. See Arlie Hochschild, *The Second Shift* (New York: Avon, 1989); Barbara Kantrowitz, "A Mother's Choice," *Newsweek,* March 31, 1986, pp. 46–51; Claudia Wallis, "Onward, Women!" *Time,* December 4, 1989, pp. 80–89.

9. See Susan Faludi, *Backlash: The Undeclared War against American Women* (New York: Crown, 1991), pp. 27–32, 42–45.

10. Eloise Salholz, "Too Late for Prince Charming?" *Newsweek,* June 2, 1986, pp. 54–61.

11. See Susan Faludi, *Backlash;* and Bonnie J. Dow, *Prime-Time Feminism.*

12. Harry F. Waters, and Janet Huck, "Networking Women," pp. 50–51.

13. "Candice Bergen," *Playboy,* December 1989, p. 62.

14. This cast of characters is consistent for the first seven years of *Murphy Brown,* the period of time I am concerned with in this analysis.

15. Phyllis Japp, 1991. "Gender and Work in the 1980s: Television's Working Women as Displaced Persons," *Women's Studies in Communication* 14 (1991): p. 71.

16. The names that identify episodes used in this analysis are from Robert S. Alley, and Irby B. Brown, *Murphy Brown: Anatomy of a Sitcom* (New York: Delta, 1990).

17. Alison Jaggar, *Feminist Politics and Human Nature* (Totowa, N.J.: Rowman and Allanheld, 1983), p. 250.

18. Remarkably, Murphy does indeed refer to herself with a masculine pronoun in this comment.

19. Claudia Wallis, "Onward, Women!" *Time,* December 4, 1989, p. 82.

20. See, for example, Mona Charen, "Sitcoms Treat Unwed Motherhood as Laughing Matter," *Cincinnati Post,* October 3, 1991, p. 15A; and Caryn James, "A Baby Boom on TV as Biological Clock Ticks Cruelly Away," *New York Times,* October 16, 1991, pp. B1, B7.

21. Mona Charen, "Sitcoms Treat Unwed Motherhood as Laughing Matter," p. 15A.

22. See "Murphy Is Not Reality," *USA Today,* May 20, 1992, p. 10A; and "Mixed Messages," *USA Today,* May 20, 1992, p. 10A.

23. Joe Rhodes, "When Baby Makes Two," *TV Guide,* September 19, 1992, p. 8.

24. After Jake leaves, Murphy and Jerry Gold make a brief attempt to live together, but they cannot get along. Murphy decides that their relationship makes her feel too dependent and "needy." Murphy's most consistent companion throughout her pregnancy is Eldin, her house-painter, who is motivated, he claims, by the realization that whereas Murphy would be a rotten mother, he would be an excellent one. Indeed, Murphy eventually hires Eldin to be the child's nanny. While Eldin's skill at child-rearing could be viewed as a feminist statement (i.e., men can be caretakers as well as women), it can also be viewed as underscoring Murphy's maternal incompetence (i.e., an itinerant housepainter can be as good a mother as she can).

25. The troubling implication of this scene was not lost on some viewers. In response to a *USA Today* editorial about *Murphy Brown*'s glorification of single motherhood, at least two viewers wrote letters expressing their dissatisfaction with the sitcom's message. One wrote, "Television writers, take a hint: Not every woman has to be fulfilled through the joys of

motherhood" ("Aghast at Writers," *USA Today,* May 20, 1992, p. 10A.), while another had a more expansive analysis:

> Why can't she "feel like a natural woman" without a child? Why does the entertainment industry insist on showing childless women as less than whole? . . . Is having a child supposed to "tame" Murphy and make her softer and more feminine? The entertainment industry's message seems to be that liberation has made women unhappy and unfulfilled. What's wrong with exalting an intelligent female character who is happy with her life and her choices?" ("A 'Natural Woman'?" *USA Today,* May 20, 1992, p. 10A.)

26. Bell Hooks, *Outlaw Culture: Resisting Representations* (New York: Routledge, 1994).

27. All quotations from the Quayle speech that I use here are from "Excerpts from the Vice President's Speech on Cities and Poverty," *New York Times,* May 20, 1992, p. A11.

28. Michael Wines, "Appeal of 'Murphy Brown' Now Clear at White House," *New York Times,* May 21, 1992, p. A12.

29. Ibid, pp. A1, A12.

30. Ibid, p. A1.

31. "Quayle vs. Brown," *Cincinnati Post,* May 21, 1992, pp. A1.

32. Andrew Rosenthal, "Quayle Says Riots Arose from Burst of Social Anarchy," *New York Times,* May 20, 1992, pp. A11.

33. Katha Pollitt, *Reasonable Creatures: Essays on Women and Feminism* (New York: Knopf, 1994), p. 32.

34. For example, the *Chicago Tribune,* alongside an analysis of the response to the *Murphy Brown* flap from politicians and members of the television community, ran a story entitled "Single Mom: Quayle Stance Is 'Ludicrous,'" which featured a single, white, female business executive describing the joys of single motherhood. The woman concludes that "she knows 'other single women who have children and who are strong and financially able—and they deserve to have a child if they want to'" (Carol Kleiman, "Single Mom: Quayle Stance is 'Ludicrous,'" *Chicago Tribune,* May 21, 1992, p. 2). By featuring a white, economically privileged woman, even this seemingly oppositional story fails to challenge the politics of race and class raised in Quayle's speech and, in fact, implicitly participates in the distinction between deserving and undeserving mothers that Quayle creates.

35. See Stuart Elliott, "Contretemps Lifts Ad Rate for 'Murphy,'" *New York Times,* September 17, 1992, p. C8; and "Murphy to Dan: Read My Ratings," *Time,* October 5, 1992, p. 25.

36. Katha Pollitt, one of the few journalists to point out the race, class, and gender politics that infused Quayle's speech, offered an incisive analysis of the Quayle/*Murphy Brown* incident that has greatly influenced my thinking about the issues involved. See Katha Pollitt, *Reasonable Creatures,* pp. 31–41.

37. Lynn Smith, "Critics Say Selfish 'Murphy Brown' Is Failing as a Career Mother Who Wants It All," *Saint Paul Pioneer Press,* January 24, 1993, p. E6.

38. Andrea Press, *Women Watching Television: Class, Gender, and Generation in the American Television Experience* (Philadelphia: University of Pennsylvania Press, 1991), p. 146.

39. Alison Jaggar, *Feminist Politics and Human Nature,* pp. 85–86.

2 / The Stronger Women Get, the More Men Love Football

MARIAH BURTON NELSON

WE DON'T LIKE FOOTBALL, DO WE?

If you grew up female in America, you heard this: Sports are unfeminine. And this: Girls who play sports are tomboys or lesbians. You got this message: Real women don't spend their free time sliding feet-first into home plate or smacking their fists into soft leather gloves.

So you didn't play or you did play and either way you didn't quite fit. You didn't fit in your body—didn't learn to live there, breathe there, feel dynamic and capable. Or maybe you fell madly, passionately in love with sports but didn't quite fit in society, never saw yourself—basketball player, cyclist, golfer—reflected in movies, billboards, magazines.

Or you took a middle ground, shying away at first but then later sprinting toward aerobics and weight lifting and in-line skating, relishing your increasing endurance and grace and strength. Even then, though, you sensed that something was wrong: all the ads and articles seemed to focus on weight loss and beauty. While those may have inspired you to get fit in the first place, there are more important things, you now know, than how you looked. No one seemed to be talking about pride, pleasure, power, possibility.

If you grew up male in America, you heard this: Boys who *don't* play sports are sissies or faggots. And this: Don't throw like a girl. You got this message: Sports are a male initiation rite, as fundamental and natural as shaving and deep voices—a prerequisite, somehow, to becoming an American man. So you played football or soccer or baseball and felt competent, strong, and bonded with your male buddies. Or you didn't play and risked ridicule.

Whether we were inspired by Babe Ruth or Babe Didrikson or neither, and whether we played kickball with our brothers or sisters or both, all of us, female and male, learned to associate sports prowess and sports privilege with masculinity. Even if the best athlete in the neighborhood was a girl, we learned from newspapers, television, and from our own parents' prejudices that batting, catching, throwing, and jumping are not neutral, human activities, but somehow more naturally a male domain. Insidiously, our culture's reverence for men's professional sports and its silence about women's athletic accomplishments shaped, defined, and limited how we felt about ourselves as women and men.

You may remember. There was a time not too long ago when women in bright tights did not run along highways, bike paths, forest trails. Now they do. "Horses make a landscape look more beautiful," the Sioux medicine man Lame Deer (and, later, Alice Walker) said. You may harbor a similar feeling about this endless stream of rainbow runners: Women make a landscape look more beautiful.

You may have noticed that boys are no longer the only ones shooting baskets in public parks. One girl often joins the boys now, her hair dark with sweat, her body alert as a squirrel's. Maybe they don't pass her the ball. Maybe she grabs it anyway, squeezes mightily through the barricade of bodies, leaps skyward, feet flying.

Or she teams with other girls. Gyms fill these days with the rowdy sounds of women hard at play: basketballs seized by calloused hands, sneakers squealing like shocked mice. The players' high, urgent voices resonate, too—"Here!" "Go!"—and right then nothing exists for them except the ball, the shifting constellation of women, the chance to be fluid, smooth, alive.

What does this mean? What does it mean that everywhere, women are running, shooting baskets, getting sweaty and exhausted and euphoric? What changes when a woman becomes an athlete?

Everything.

On playing fields and in gyms across America, women are engaged in a contest with higher stakes than trophies or ribbons or even prize money. Through women's play, and through their huddles behind the scenes, they are deciding who American women will be. Not just what games they will play, but what role they will play in this still-young nation. Not only what their bodies will look like, but what their bodies can do.

"Who's your team?" a man asks a boy he has just met in a doctor's office.

"The Atlanta Braves," the boy replies.

"Good choice," says the man. Actually, almost any men's pro or college team would suffice. The important thing is to "have" a team, love a team, follow a team. To identify with successful manly athletes is to feel successful and manly oneself, to feel a part of the dominant male culture. Millions of men affirm their manliness and manly ties by betting on sports, discussing sports, arguing over sports, agonizing over decisions such as, Should I root for Baltimore, where I grew up, or Cleveland, where I live now? These men argue over whether Pete Rose should be admitted into the Hall of Fame. They can become irritable for an entire day if "their" team loses.

To women, this can sound silly, but many men take manly sports seriously. The games become symbolic struggles, passion plays reenacted daily to define, affirm, and celebrate manliness. The games offer men a chance to admire huge bodies, "aggressive play" and "very physical teams," to gossip over who did what and in what year, to compete over statistics: "When did the Boston Red Sox win their last World Series?" "Who scored the most points in a single NBA game?" When discussing sports, men reminisce about their own high school sports "careers." They imagine that they themselves somehow "just missed" becoming famous athletes.

Few men take no interest in the World Series, the Super Bowl, the Final Four, or the latest boxing match. Of those who do abstain from the daily sports dialogue, some have failed at youth sports and retain an antagonism for the arena that injured their egos or their bodies. "I was big, slow, and clumsy," recalls Brent LaFever, a facilities manager from Winston-Salem, North Carolina. "Now I hate watching sports. They're so barbaric. When people come to visit, my wife and I don't let them turn on the television. Often they leave."

Other men develop an antipathy for sports because they did play and didn't like what they saw of the manly sport culture: the cutthroat competition, the cruel coaches, the required "toughness." Numerous men were humiliated by coaches who insisted on "making a man out of them" but ignored the sensitive boys that they were.

Regardless of his reasons, the grown man who pays no attention to male sporting dramas must be, it seems to me, among the most secure and confident of all men, because he relinquishes a daily opportunity to identify with the culture's primary male heroes and in the process risks censure or at least estrangement from other men. Yet even a man who steers clear of the daily barrage of sports events, sports pages, sports television, and sports talk radio shows will often devise ways to fake it. In response to overtures such as, "How 'bout those Redskins!" he may utter an ambiguous, noncommittal exclamation, such as, "They've got quite a quarterback!" Rare is the man who not only opts out of the manly sports system but also criticizes it— who, in response to "How 'bout those Redskins!" will say, "I hate football. It's racist, sexist, and far too violent for me."

STRONGER WOMEN

Laughing, Patrick Thevenard would scoop his wife, Gail Savage, off the floor and carry her around the house like a squirming child. This was early in the marriage, and Patrick, an ecologist from Hyattsville, Maryland, thought it was funny, a joke. Gail, a history professor, didn't like it. Feeling helpless and angry, she would ask to be put down. He would refuse.

Later, Gail became a dedicated runner. Patrick argued that she was running too much, or in the wrong way, or at the wrong times. They would quarrel, and he would yell. Patrick didn't literally lift her off the ground then, but to Gail the sensation was similar: Patrick's criticisms felt like physical restraints, as if he were trying to prevent her from going where she wanted to go.

Patrick says Gail used running as a "weapon" against him, a way "to escape out of our relationship—to literally put physical distance between us."

Gail says running became "the focus of a power struggle over who would control me."

The way Gail gained strength, and keeps gaining strength, is through sports. Women can become strong in other ways, without being athletes, but athletic strength holds particular meaning in this culture. It's tangible, visible, measurable. It has a history of symbolic importance. Joe Louis, Jackie Robinson, Jesse Owens, Billie Jean King: their athletic feats have represented to many Americans key victories over racism and sexism, key "wins" in a game that has historically been dominated by white men.

Sports have particular salience for men, who share childhood memories of having their masculinity confirmed or questioned because of their athletic ability or inability. Along with money or sex, sports in this culture define men for men. They embody a language men understand.

Women also understand sports—their power, their allure—but often from a spectator's perspective. When a woman steps out of the bleachers or slips off her cheerleader's costume and becomes an athlete herself, she implicitly challenges the association between masculinity and sports. She refutes the traditional feminine role (primarily for white women) of passivity, frailty, and subservience. If a woman can play a sport—especially if she can play it better than many men—then that sport can no longer be used as a yardstick of masculinity. The more women play a variety of sports, the more the entire notion of masculine and feminine roles—or any roles at all assigned by gender—becomes as ludicrous as the notion of roles assigned by race.

Female athletes provide obvious, confrontational evidence—"in your face" evidence, some might say—of women's physical prowess, tangible examples of just what women can achieve.

For a woman, especially for a married woman with a controlling husband, running is a feminist act. The athlete's feminism begins with the fact that her sports participation is, in Gail's words, "a declaration of independence." The runner runs on her own two feet, on her own time, in her own way, without male assistance. If a man wants to join her club, trot along next to her, watch her race, and leave a light on for her when she arrives home late, fine. If not, if she encounters male interference, she may not tolerate it. She may prioritize, instead, her own athletic joy. Running raises the possibility that the woman with the aggrieved husband will become the woman with no husband—that, in the process of running, women will run away from men.

Running also raises the possibility that mothers will leave fathers at home to wash dishes and put kids to bed. According to a 1993 Women's Sports Foundation survey of almost 1,600 working women, the more hours women devote to housework, the fewer they devote to sports or fitness. Twenty-nine percent of working women report that their husbands do no housework at all. Married women with children are the most likely to report a decrease in sports or fitness participation in the past five years.[1]

So if a woman runs in the morning while her husband dresses the children, feeds them, and gets them off to school, she tips the balance of power not only within the marriage but within the family. The runner who has no children, no husband, and no boyfriend—who instead carves out a life for

herself with other athletes and other women—is likewise committing feminist acts. Her running represents a world in which women are neither running toward nor alongside nor away from men; where men and their ideas
about what's too strenuous for women, what's acceptable for women, and
what's attractive in women become irrelevant.

Female athletes don't necessarily see it this way. They don't necessarily
call themselves feminists. They cycle or swim or surf because it's fun and
challenging, because it feels good, because they like the way it makes them
look, because it allows them to eat more without gaining weight, because it
gives them energy and confidence and time spent with friends, female or
male. Many are ignorant about the women's rights movement. I've heard
college students confuse feminism with feminine hygiene.

Female athletes have a long tradition of dissociating themselves from
feminism. Their desire to be accepted or to acquire or keep a boyfriend or a
job has often equaled their passion for sports. Thus, athletes have taken
great pains—and it can hurt—to send reassuring signals to those who would
oppose their play: "Don't worry, we're not feminists. We're not dykes, we're
not aggressive, we're not muscular, we're not a threat to you. We just want
to play ball." It has been a survival strategy.

It's time to tell the truth. We are feminists.[2] Some of us are dykes. Some
of us are aggressive, some of us are muscular. All of us, collectively, are a
threat—not to men exactly, but to male privilege and to masculinity as
defined through manly sports. By reserving time each day for basketball
dribbling, or for runs or rides or rows, women are changing themselves and
society. Feminism is rarely an individual's motivating force but always the
result: a woman's athletic training, regardless of the factors that lead to her
involvement, implicitly challenges patriarchal constraints on her behavior.
Sport for women changes the woman's experience of herself and others'
experience of her. It alters the balance of power between the sexes. It is dar-
ing. It is life changing. It is happening every day.

Feminism is about freedom: women's individual and collective liberty to
make their own decisions. For women, sports embody freedom: unrestricted
physical expression, travel across great distances, liberated movement.
Sports give meaning to the phrase "free time." Women find it, use it, and
insist on retaining it. Their time for sports becomes a time when they free
themselves of all the other people and projects they usually tend to. They
become the person, the project, who needs care. They take care of themselves. For a group of people who have historically been defined by their
ability to nurture others, the commitment to nurture themselves is radical.

Sports give a woman the confidence to try new things, including things
previously defined as dangerous or unfeminine. "Boys grow up trying lots of
new physical activities," notes University of Virginia sports psychologist
Linda Bunker. "They develop an overall sense of their ability to handle
unknown situations. Ask a male tennis player if he wants to play racquetball; he'll say 'sure,' even if he's never seen a racquetball court. But ask a

nonathletic woman to play racquetball, and she'll say, 'Gee, I don't know if I can do it.'"

Several writers have used sports as metaphor, depicting women emancipated by the process of building muscle and endurance. In Fannie Flagg's film, *Fried Green Tomatoes,* a meek and depressed Evelyn Couch (played by Kathy Bates) takes aerobics classes, meets with a women's support group, and develops a deep friendship with an old woman. Soon she has acquired a new persona, Tawanda, who skips up steps, knocks down walls, and asserts herself with her husband. "I'm trying to save our marriage," she tells him. "What's the point of my trying if you're gonna sit on your butt drinking beer and watching baseball, basketball, football, hockey, bowling, golf, and challenge of the gladiators?"

In *Daughters of Copperwoman,* Anne Cameron creates a fictional world (based on the lives of the native people of Vancouver Island) in which prepubescent girls practice sprinting in the sand, running backwards, and swimming while tied to a log "until we were so tired we ached, but our muscles got strong and our bodies grew straight." Finally, after a girl's first menses, she is paddled by canoe out to sea, where she disrobes, dives overboard, and swims back to the village. As she approaches the shore, the villagers "sing a victory song about how a girl went for a swim and a woman came home."[3]

In Alice Adams' short story, "A Public Pool,"[4] a shy, anxious, unemployed woman who feels too tall and too fat and who lives with her depressed mother is slowly and subtly transformed by the process of swimming laps. At first she feels embarrassed to appear, even in the locker room, in her bathing suit. Swimming twenty-six laps, a half-mile, seems a struggle. She feels flattered by attention from a blond, bearded swimmer not because he is kind or interesting—in fact he cuts rudely through the water with a "violent crawl"—but because he is male.

By the end of the story she becomes "aware of a long strong body (mine) pulling through the water, of marvelous muscles, a strong back, and long, long legs." She applies for a job she'll probably get and looks forward to moving out of her mother's house. When she happens upon "Blond Beard" outside a cafe, she realizes that he is a gum-chewing, spiffily dressed jerk. The story ends with his inviting her to join him for coffee, and her declining. "I leave him standing there, I swim away."

Nancy Murray, an equestrian and public health doctoral student from Houston, Texas, quit riding the day she got married because she thought her husband wanted her to. She also quit graduate school and stopped talking to her friends in the evenings. "I was not a sane person," she recalls. She became ill with severe thyroid disease that mysteriously cleared up when she started riding again, after eleven years. "It amazed the doctors," she says. Now she competes at fourth level, just below international level, in dressage.

"When I started riding again, I found my power," says Murray. That power transferred outside the ring. She is no longer able, she says, to play the subservient role her graduate school professors expect. Pursuing her dreams takes a toll, though. Murray says her husband now "supports my riding conceptually, but it's hard for him to have my attentions elsewhere." Like many of her married friends, Murray arrives at weekend competitions "blasted" with exhaustion, she says, "because it took so much energy just to leave—to leave our husbands, to get them to take care of the kids."

Traveling around the south to equestrian events, Murray drives a truck with horse-trailer attached. When she pulls off the road, she enjoys men's reactions. "My horse stands 17 hands high and weighs 1,500 pounds. I put a chain around his nose and hold a whip in my hand. He behaves. Men see me coming, controlling this huge beast, and they say, uh-oh." She laughs. She's in control. She's an athlete. She's free.

Feminism is about bodies: birth control, sexual harassment, child sexual abuse, pornography, rape, date rape, battering, breast cancer, breast enlargement, dieting, liposuction, abortion, anorexia, bulimia, sexuality.

Sports.

"The repossession by women of our bodies," wrote the poet and author Adrienne Rich in *Of Women Born,* "will bring far more essential change to human society than the seizing of the means of production by workers."

As athletes, we repossess our bodies. Told that we're weak, we develop our strengths. Told that certain sports are wrong for women, we decide what feels right. Told that our bodies are too dark, big, old, flabby, or wrinkly to be attractive to men, we look at naked women in locker rooms and discover for ourselves the beauty of actual women's bodies in all their colors, shapes, and sizes. Told that certain sports make women look "like men," we notice the truth: working out doesn't make us look like men, it makes us look happy. It makes us smile. More important, it makes us healthy and powerful. It makes us feel good.

According to the Women's Sports Foundation's 1993 survey, 71 percent of women who exercise said they work out primarily for the physical benefits.[5] The National Center for Health Statistics reports that physical fitness is linked to a general sense of well-being, a positive mood, and lower levels of anxiety and depression, especially among women. The athlete is more likely than her nonathletic sisters to have a good body image, studies have consistently shown. Female athletes also report that sports reduce stress and enhance self-esteem. And University of Maine psychology professor Richard Ryckman has found that girls in the '70s derived their self-esteem primarily from their physical attractiveness, whereas for girls in the early '90s, physical competence is as essential to self-esteem as beauty.

According to the Women's Sports Foundation, female high school athletes are more likely than nonathletes to do well in high school and college, to feel popular, to be involved in extracurricular activities, to stay involved in sport as adults, and to aspire to community leadership. Female high school athletes are 92 percent less likely to get involved with drugs, 80 percent less likely to get pregnant, and three times more likely than their nonathletic peers to graduate from high school.[6]

As little as two hours of weekly exercise can lower a teenage girl's life-long risk of breast cancer. Exercise reduces an older woman's chances of developing osteoporosis. Pregnant athletes report a lower incidence of back pain, easier labor and delivery, fewer stress-related complaints, and less postpartum depression than women who don't exercise.[7] And the effects of exercise seem to persist throughout a lifetime. Women who were athletic as children report greater confidence, self-esteem, and pride in their physical and social selves than those who were sedentary as children.[8] If, as a society, we were interested in the health and welfare of women, we would encourage and enable them to play sports.

In a country where male politicians and judges make key decisions about our bodies and all of us are vulnerable to random attacks of male violence, the simple act of women taking control of their own bodies—including their health, their pleasure, and their power—is radical. In a society in which real female bodies (as opposed to media images of female bodies) are unappreciated at best, the act of enjoying one's own female body is radical. It contradicts all feminine training to move, to extend our arms, to claim public space as our own, to use our bodies aggressively and instrumentally, and to make rough contact with other bodies.

When playing sports our bodies are ours to do with as we please. If in that process our bodies look unfeminine—if they become bruised or bloody or simply unattractive—that seems irrelevant. Our bodies are ours. We own them. While running to catch a ball, we remember that.

BOYS WILL BE BOYS AND GIRLS WILL NOT

Two scientists recently made this forecast: The fastest woman may eventually outrun the fastest man. Their prediction appeared only as a letter to the editor in *Nature* magazine,[9] yet it generated a stampede of interest from the media. *Time,* the *Chicago Tribune, USA Today,* the *New York Times,* the *Washington Post,* and *Sports Illustrated* printed stories. All quoted experts who ridiculed the conjecture as "ludicrous," "sheer ignorance," "a good laugh," "absurd," "asinine," "completely fallacious," and/or "laughable." In one Associated Press report, the word ridiculous was used five times. *Science News* ran the headline "Women on the verge of an athletic showdown." *Runner's World* entitled its article "Battle of the Sexes." Unlike questionable projections that are dismissed without fanfare, this one seems to have struck a nerve.

The researchers, Brian Whipp and Susan Ward of the University of California, Los Angeles, calculated runners' average speeds during record-breaking races over the past seventy years, then compared the rates of increase. Noting that women's average speeds are increasing at a faster rate than are men's, they projected that in the future, the best women may catch up to and even surpass the best men at various distances. For example: By 1998, the best woman and man would, if they continue to improve at current rates, complete the 26.2 mile marathon in two hours, two minutes. In subsequent years, the woman would sprint ahead.

Indisputably, neither women nor men will continue to improve at their current rates forever. Otherwise, humans would one day run the marathon in a matter of minutes. But the very idea that women might someday beat men elicited passionate responses. *Runner's World* writers Amby Burfoot and Marty Post, as if verbally to stop women in their tracks, pointed out that in the past five years, women have made few improvements in world-record times. This is a sure sign, they said, that women "have already stopped" improving.[10]

When I appear on radio and television shows to discuss women's sports or my first book, *Are We Winning Yet? How Women Are Changing Sports and Sports Are Changing Women*, I encounter a similar fury. Although some male callers tell stories about female martial artists or mountain climbers who taught them about female strength, at least half of the male callers act as if my views were heretical. What seems to make them angriest is my observation that men are not better athletes than women are. In no sport are all men better than all women, I point out, and in many sports, women routinely defeat men. Although single-sex competitions are often appropriate, and men do have physical advantages in some sports, women should see themselves as men's peers, I suggest, rather than exclusively competing against women.

These men don't want to hear any of that. In voices I can only describe as high-pitched and hysterical, they say, "Yeah, but you're never going to see a woman play pro football!"

It is a taunt and, I think, a genuine fear. I'm not talking about football. I've never met a woman who aspires to play pro football. I'm talking about auto racing, horse racing, dog sled racing, equestrian events, rifle shooting, and marathon swimming, where women and men compete together at the elite levels. I'm talking about tennis, golf, racquetball, bowling, skiing, and other recreational sports, where a wife and husband or a female and male pair of friends are likely to find themselves evenly matched. In sports, as in the rest of life, women do compete with men on a daily basis, and often win.

So it intrigues me that in response to my discussion of women's athletic excellence, men change the subject to football. They try to assert football as the sine qua non of athleticism. Because "women could never play football," they imply, men are physically, naturally, biologically superior. Most men can't play pro football themselves—but they can take vicarious comfort in the display of male physical competence and aggression. They take comfort in professional baseball ("Women could never play pro baseball") and in professional basketball ("Women could never play pro basketball") and in boxing ("Women could never box") and in footraces ("Women could never win the marathon").

Most men are not 320-pound linebackers. But, identified with these hulks, some men take great pleasure in the linebackers' exploits (a revealing term). Football, baseball, basketball, boxing, and hockey are important to men in part *because* they seem to be all-male pursuits, because they seem to be activities that *only men can do.* When women demonstrate excellence in sports like running, tennis, and golf, men take great pains to describe that excellence as less important, less worthy, less of an achievement than male excellence.

Psychiatrist Arnold R. Beisser explains the phenomenon this way: "It is small wonder that the American male has a strong affinity for sports. He has learned that this is one area where there is no doubt about sexual differences and where his biology is not obsolete. Athletics help assure his difference from women in a world where his functions have come to resemble theirs."[11]

THE LAST BASTION OF
MALE DOMINATION

Sport has been called the last bastion of male domination. Unfortunately, there are others—Congress, for instance. But sport constitutes the only large cultural institution where men and women are (sometimes) justifiably segregated according to gender. It is one of the few remaining endeavors where male muscle matters.

Women have always been strong. We have carried water, harvested crops, birthed and raised children. Women do two-thirds of the world's work, according to New Zealand economist Marilyn Waring. But as women in the late twentieth century gain increasing economic, political, and athletic strength, many men cling to manly sports as a symbol of "natural" male dominance. The stronger women get, the more enthusiastically male fans, players, coaches, and owners seem to be embracing a particular form of masculinity: toughness, aggression, denial of emotion, and a persistent denigration of all that's considered female. Attitudes learned on the playing fields, or by watching sports on television, leach into the soil of everyday life, where many men view women and treat women with disdain. They call baseball the national pastime—which, in a diverse society, "unites us all." But baseball, football, and other manly sports do not unite Americans. They unite American men in a celebration of male victory. By pointing to men's greater size and strength and by imbuing those qualities with meaning (dominance, conquest), many men justify to themselves a two-tiered gender system with men on top. As University of Iowa sports sociologist Susan Birrell has noted, "It's a short leap from seeing men as physically superior to seeing men as superior, period."[12]

Sports are an escape, men often say. One wonders what they are escaping from. Men who *must* watch "The Game" seem to me to be escaping from women's demands for freedom, equality, and simple attention—as well as from housework, child care, and other family responsibilities.

Many sports are more than a refuge from the reality of women's liberation. By creating a world where masculinity is equated with violence, where male bonding is based on the illusion of male supremacy, and where all of the visible women are cheerleaders, manly sports set the stage for violence against women. When we begin to understand how male coaches and play-ers speak and think about women and masculinity, it ceases to be surprising that college football and basketball players gang-rape women in numbers equaled only by fraternity brothers.[13] Or that male basketball and football players are reported to police for sexual assault 38 percent more often than their male college peers.[14] Or that football and basketball players are more likely to engage in sexually aggressive behaviors (including everything from whistling and unwanted touching to attempted rape) than their peers, including those who play other sports.[15]

"It's just a game," former commissioner Fay Vincent used to say about baseball. But baseball and other manly sports are more than games. They constitute a culture—the dominant culture in America today. Manly sports comprise a world where men are in charge and women are irrelevant at best. Where assaults that would be illegal off the field become an accepted, even celebrated part of "play" and replay. Where big men wearing tight pants embrace each other, openly loving men and male power. Where "girls" flash their underwear.

Feminists have tried to reduce sexual violence in all its forms: child sexual abuse, sexual harassment at work, battering and rape by husbands and "lovers," rape by strangers, and the glorification of rape through pornogra-phy. Women have tried to empower women through jobs, education, health care, politics, and therapy. For the most part, women haven't paid attention to sports. Women tend to ignore the sports section of the newspaper and to avoid living rooms and bars and college dormitories where men gather ritu-ally, as if to worship the televised game.

Women—and fair-minded men—need to pay attention. We live in a country in which the manly sports culture is so pervasive we may fail to rec-ognize the symbolic messages we all receive about men, women, love, sex, and power. We need to take sports seriously—not the scores or the statistics, but the process. Not to focus on who wins, but on who's losing. Who loses when a community spends millions of dollars in tax revenue to construct a new stadium and only men get to play in it, and only men get to work there? Who loses when football and baseball so dominate the public discourse that they eclipse all mention of female volleyball players, gymnasts, basketball players, swimmers? Who loses when coaches teach boys that the worst pos-sible insult is to be called "pussy" or "cunt?" Who loses when rape jokes comprise an accepted part of the game?

Sport is a women's issue because on playing fields, male athletes learn to talk about and think about women and women's bodies with contempt. It's a women's issue because male athletes have disproportionately high rates of sexual assaults on women—including female athletes. It's a women's issue because the media itself cheers for men's sports and rarely covers women's, thereby reinforcing the notion that men are naturally more athletic. It's a women's issue because of the veiled threat, this homage paid to bulky, brutal bodies. And it's a women's issue because female sports participation empowers women, thereby inexorably changing everything.

REVIEW QUESTIONS

1. Does the author suggest sports can have a powerful impact on attitudes and opinions about society and politics, or does it simply reflect changes already underway? Perhaps she suggests an interactive process?

2. Clearly, Burton Nelson believes that participation in sports is a political activity. She mentions several ways in which women athletes are changing themselves and society. Would you agree? In what ways might the presence of women in athletics change the status quo?

3. Burton Nelson argues that women can achieve a sort of independence by engaging in athletic activities, such as running. But are individual-centered activities enough, or should women demand greater access to team sports, many of which have traditionally been just for men? Put a bit differently, should women demand "a league of their own?"

4. Recently, two women's basketball leagues have been created: the WNBA and the ABL. What effects do you think these leagues might have on spectators, young women in particular? Do you think such changes are working to reshape our political culture?

5. Women are often excluded from sports and different occupations on the presumption that they are not strong enough. Do you think that there are differences between men and women that justify the exclusion of women from certain sports? In other words, is sports an institution where men and women are justifiably segregated?

Notes

1. Don Sabo and Marjorie Snyder, "Miller Lite Report on Sports and Fitness in the Lives of Working Women" (in cooperation with the Women's Sports Federation and *Working Woman*, March 8, 1993).

2. Susan Greendorfer, professor of Kinesiology at the University of Illinois, Urbana-Champaign, asserts that women's sports are inherently a political act. Susan Greendorfer, "Making Connections: Women's Sport Participation as a Political Act" (paper presented at the National Girls and Women in Sports Symposium, Slippery Rock State University, Slippery Rock, Pa., February 13, 1993).

3. Anne Cameron, *Daughters of Copperwoman* (Vancouver, British Columbia: Press Gang Publishers, 1981), pp. 101–102.

4. Alice Adams, "A Public Pool," *Mother Jones* (November 1984): p. 38.

5. Sabo and Snyder, "Miller Lite Report on Sports and Fitness."

6. Women's Sports Foundation, Eisenhower Park, East Meadow, N.Y. 11554 (1992).

7. Ibid.

8. L. Jaffee and J. Lutter, "A Change in Attitudes? A Report of Melpomene's Third Membership Survey," *Melpomene Journal* 10, no. 2 (1991): pp. 11–16; and L. Jaffee and R. Mantzer, "Girls' Perspectives: Physical Activity and Self-Esteem," *Melpomene Journal* 11, no. 3 (1992): pp. 14–23.

9. Brian Whipp and Susan Ward, letter to the editor, *Nature,* (January 2, 1992).

10. Amby Burfoot and Marty Post, "Battle of the Sexes," *Runner's World* (April 1992), p. 40.

11. Stephanie Twin, *Out of the Bleachers: Writings on Women and Sport* (Old Westbury, N.Y.: The Feminist Press, 1979), p. xxxvi.

12. Susan Birrell, "The Woman Athlete: Fact or Fiction?" (paper presented at the National Girls and Women in Sport Symposium, Slippery Rock State University, Slippery Rock, Pa., February 6–9, 1992).

13. Lester Munson, "Against Their Will," *National Sports Daily* (August 17, 1990), p. 30.

14. Rich Hoffman, "Rape and the College Athlete: Part One," *Philadelphia Daily News* (March 17, 1986), p. 104.

15. Mary P. Koss and John A. Gaines, "The Prediction of Sexual Aggression by Alcohol Use, Athletic Participation, and Fraternity Affiliation," *Journal of Interpersonal Violence* 8 (March 1993): pp. 94–108.

3 / Girls 'n' Spice: All Things Nice?

SUSAN J. DOUGLAS

It's 8:12 A.M. The feminist mom, who looks like she just got shot out of a wind turbine and has a cheap Chardonnay hangover, is making pancakes for four 8-year-old girls having a sleep-over party. Let's just say that she's not in the most festive mood. Then, blasting from the other room, she hears the now-familiar faux-rap riff, "I'll tell ya what I want, what I really really want. . . ." She peeks around the corner to see the four girls singing and dancing with abandon, sucking in "girl power" with every pore. Should she be happy that they're listening to bustier feminism instead of watching Barbie commercials on Saturday morning TV? Or should she run in, rip the CD out of the player and insist that they listen to Mary-Chapin Carpenter or Ani DiFranco instead?

Welcome to the Spice Girls debate, which has been raging in the British and American press since the beginning of 1997. With their Wonderbras, bare thighs, pouty lips, and top-of-the-head ponytails favored by Pebbles on *The Flintstones*, the Spice Girls advocate "girl power" and demand, in their colossal, intercontinental hit "Wannabe," that boys treat them with respect or take a hike. Their boldfaced liner notes claim that "The Future Is Female" and suggest that they and their fans are "Freedom Fighters." "We're freshening up feminism for the '90s," they told the *Guardian*. "Feminism has become a dirty word," they said. "Girl Power is just a '90s way of saying it." New Age feminism means "you have a brain, a voice, and an opinion."

In addition to their chart-topping CD, they have a magazine, a book (*Girl Power*), fan clubs everywhere, a new ad for Pepsi with the kind of production values previously reserved for Michael Jackson, and plans for a movie that would be a girls' version of *A Hard Day's Night*. They each have a nickname: red-headed Geri is "Ginger Spice"; Melanie C., who does backflips onstage, is "Sporty Spice"; Emma, the one with the Chatty Cathy ponytails, is "Baby Spice"; Victoria, allegedly upper class, is "Posh Spice"; and Melanie, the only woman of color, is, you guessed it, "Scary Spice." They are twenty-one to twenty-four years old. Their biggest fans are girls between the ages of eight and fourteen.

Are they a group of no-talent, flash-in-the-pan bimbos whose success comes primarily from a highly calculated and cynical marketing strategy that has fused bubble-gum music with a pseudo-feminist message? Or are they a refreshing fusion of politics and music that debunks antiquated stereotypes about feminism and helps empower young girls as they enter the treacherous process of discovering their sexuality?

Not since the Beatles has a British band conquered the worldwide pop charts with such speed or thoroughness. "Wannabe," their first single, hit No. 2 in *Billboard*'s Top 10 about fourteen minutes after its U.S. debut in January, and then hit No. 1. The song has topped the charts in thirty-five countries across four continents, and in Britain three subsequent singles also went to No. 1. In a five-month period, they sold ten million albums, grossing an estimated $165 million for Virgin records.

More than that, they insinuated themselves into British politics during the spring elections, and were courted by politicians on both sides. They were in the press on a near daily basis, and reporters hung on their every word as they said they were "desperately worried about the slide to a single currency" in Europe. Tony Blair's hair was all right, one of them noted, "but we don't agree with his tax policies." By March, John Major's Chancellor of the Exchequer was quoting them in his speeches, riffing to the audiences, "I'll tell you what I want, what I really want . . . healthy sustainable growth and rising living standards for the next five years."

Their most repeated quip was that Margaret Thatcher was their hero and role model—"the first ever Spice Girl." Thatcher responded by adding them to her Christmas-card list. The Tories quickly sought to claim the girls as mascots who might achieve the improbable and make Major seem way cool, and their media strategy room was reportedly adorned with Spice Girls posters. Tony Blair, for his part, claimed that "Wannabe" was one of the records he'd most want if stranded on a desert island. A Labor MP invited them to join him for a tour of Parliament. There was actually a brouhaha over whom they would vote for. After a record number of women—101—were elected to Parliament in May, reporters asked the group if they felt that their "girl power" message had contributed to this female sweep. "This was the sort of cultural obeisance that only the Beatles have ever really managed to secure," noted the *Guardian*.

And not since New Kids on the Block has a group been so vilified for being inauthentic, manufactured, and determined to pander to the most exploitable desires of preteen girls. The backlash was quick—there were the usual columns asserting that the Spice Girls were nothing more than the malleable creation of Svengali-type males, and others denouncing their music as having less substance than cotton candy. By April, there was the SpiceSlap Web page, in which the heads of the girls popped out of holes and your task was to slap as many of them as quickly as possible back into oblivion. *Advertising Age* reported that by the end of the month, the page had gotten over 170,000 hits.

Ever since the success of girl-group music in the early '60s, music that adolescent girls adore has been dismissed by music critics as inauthentic, overly commercialized trash. *The Rolling Stone History of Rock & Roll*, referring presumably to such luminescent achievements as "Will You Still Love Me Tomorrow," "Nowhere to Run," and "Be My Baby," put it this way: "The female group of the early 1960s served to drive the concept of art completely away from rock 'n' roll . . . this genre represents the low point in the history of rock 'n' roll." Real rock 'n' roll must be "authentic"—meaning it features instrumental virtuosity, original songwriting, social criticism, and a stance of anger and/or alienation. We are not talking fizzy pop euphoria here. Thank Pearl Jam, Nirvana, Counting Crows, Rage Against the Machine. Male standards of performance have usually defined what is truly "genuine."

But while the music industry—and music criticism—remain male dominated, female performers from Chrissie Hynde to Tori Amos to Salt-n-Pepa have achieved both commercial success and critical respect. So it's not just serious boys with whom the Spice Girls are unfavorably compared. It's the whole new spate of serious girls, many of them part of or inspired by the riot girl movement of several years ago. The explosion of feminism-inspired rock, rap, pop—even country—music means that Spice Girls lyrics like "Come a little closer baby, get it on, get it on" seem like drivel compared with songs about date rape, abortion, and the ongoing devaluation of women in society.

And male critics are not the only ones who have dissed the Girls. Feminists like Andi Zeisler have blasted their "Mattel-doll approach" in which "their saccharine image is being peddled under the auspices of female advancement." Zeisler argues that when "giggly things whose strings are pulled by their male managers" utter pro-female sentiments, it makes feminism seem vacuous and preposterous. By posing as political, they devalue politics.

In other words, it's pretty effortless, and irresistible, to dismiss these girls as nothing more than the Bay City Rollers in drag. After all, they are the most recent female singers to insist on having it both ways—on being sex objects while simultaneously critiquing patriarchal ways of looking at and thinking about young women. They swear, they smoke, they drink, they undress men with their eyes, and they goosed Prince Charles at a spring benefit in Manchester. They wear Wonderbras, bustiers, microminis and fuckme pumps. They try to look like Barbie and sound like Gloria Steinem. "Don't rely on your sexuality, but don't be afraid of it," they advise succinctly. "Girl power," they say, "is when . . . you and your mates reply to wolf whistles by shouting 'Get your arse out.' . . . You don't wait around for him to call. . . . You believe in yourself."

Madonna, of course, in the early years, with her black bra straps and "Boy Toy" belt, was a champ at this, and thousands of teenage wannabes, grateful for her claim that female sexual energy was nothing to be ashamed of, helped make her a millionaire. But it was precisely because her earliest fans were adolescent girls that Madonna was initially dismissed as a flash in the pan even though critics were not far off the mark when they described her as sounding, as one of them put it, "like a chipmunk on helium."

Despite all the huffing and puffing of adults, one way or the other, it doesn't matter much what we think of the Spice Girls. What matters is what they mean to their preteen fans. When adolescent girls flock to a group, they are telling us plenty about how they experience the transition to womanhood in a society in which boys are still very much on top. Girls today are being urged, simultaneously, to be independent, assertive, and achievement oriented, yet also demure, attractive, soft-spoken, fifteen pounds underweight, and deferential to men.

They are told that if they aren't sexy, they are nothing, but that their sexuality is dangerous to them and threatening to much of the rest of society. Boys are supposed to want them, but they aren't supposed to want boys back—thirty years after the women's movement began, the term "slut" is alive and well. The loss of self-esteem that all too many teenage girls suffer—when they learn to silence themselves, to censor their real desires and aspirations—has kept Mary Pipher's *Reviving Ophelia* (advice on how to help girls survive adolescence in a "girl-hostile" environment) on the bestseller list for more than two years. So along come five feisty, outspoken, attractive young women making bouncy dance music who assure girls that these contradictions can be finessed—that they can be, simultaneously, attractive to boys yet independent, tough, and strong—and, whammo, platinum records and a new wannabe movement.

What might singing a song like "Wannabe" at the top of your lungs when you're ten years old, while reading liner notes such as "She Who Dares Wins" and "Silence Is Golden but Shouting Is Fun," mean for feminist politics ten years from now? Especially when, in just a few years, these same girls will be ready for the likes of Sleater-Kinney, Liz Phair, Melissa Etheridge, and even some golden oldies by Laura Nyro or Annie Lennox. Of course, we don't know, and music, by itself, can hardly make history.

Right now, popular music is probably the most girl-friendly medium going. The movies remain dominated by hard-body, big-gun action films; the news media either ignore or trivialize issues of central importance to young women; and most TV programming aimed at teenage girls features skinny, poreless women who screw up at work and obsess about dating. Fashion magazines, despite their sometimes quasi-feminist politics, publish multipage spreads that insist girls should be preoccupied with one thing: "How to Get a Better Butt, Fast!"

But in their rooms with their boom boxes, whether they're listening to bubble gum or punk, teenage girls can imagine a world where they can have love and respect, where boys desire them but won't mess with them. So while it's easy as pie to hold a group like the Spice Girls in contempt, we should be wary when music embraced by preteen girls is ridiculed. These girls are telling us that they want a voice, that they want someone to take them seriously, that they want to be worldly wise and optimistic at the same time. The Spice Girls tell them that feminism is necessary and fun. Hey, when I was ten we had "I Wanna Be Bobby's Girl." Crass commercial calculation and all, the Spice Girls are a decided improvement.

REVIEW QUESTIONS

1. As Douglas indicates, the debate over the Spice Girls centers around their claim to be "girl power" for the '90s. What is your take? Can women who inconspicuously boast sex appeal also to be a positive force in gaining greater equality for women?
2. When considering the impact of the Spice Girls, does it matter that most of their audience is young girls?
3. Are there other entertainment choices (music groups, television programs, movies) that echo the same message as the Spice Girls—that is, strong women embodied in "Wonderbras, bare thighs, pouty lips, and top-of-the-head ponytails?" Is this happening elsewhere?
4. One of the controversies surrounding this band is that even though critics generally pan their music, record sales are astronomical. What explains this paradox? Is it possible that much of their success is due to the political message they preach, or is something else at work? Can you think of other times when this has occurred?

4 / Race and College Sports: A Long Way to Go

RICHARD E. LAPCHICK

As America confronts one racial crisis after another in the 1990s, the expectation remains that sports, more than fifty years after Jackie Robinson broke baseball's color barrier, can lead the way. College sports, in particular, has been portrayed as a beacon for democracy and equal opportunity.

This perception is taking place at a time when 75 percent of high school students indicated to public opinion analyst Lou Harris that they had seen or heard a racial act with violent overtones either very often or somewhat often in the previous twelve months. In all, 54 percent of African-American high school students reported that they had been a victim of a racial incident.[1]

One in three students said that they would openly join in a confrontation against another racial or religious group if they agreed with the instigators. Another 17 percent, although they would not join, said they would feel that the victims deserved what they got.[2]

According to Harris, the nation's leading opinion analyst, too many of our children have learned how to hate. He concluded that

> America faces a critical situation. Our findings show that racial and religious harassment and violence are now commonplace among our young people rather than the exception. Far from being concentrated in any one area, confrontations occur in every region of the country and in all types of communities.[3]

One of the most hallowed assumptions about race and sports is that athletic contact between blacks and whites will favorably change racial perceptions. However, for this change to take place, coaches must be committed to helping guide players' social relations. The *Racism and Violence in American High Schools* survey conducted by Louis Harris for Northeastern University in 1993 showed that 70 percent of high school students reported that they had become friends with someone from a different racial or ethnic group through playing sports. Among blacks, a 77 percent majority reported this result; the comparable majority was 68 percent among whites and 79 percent among Hispanics. That, indeed, was encouraging news.

BLACK STUDENT-ATHLETES ON PREDOMINANTLY WHITE CAMPUSES

However, on predominantly white campuses, as in corporate boardrooms, the atmosphere naturally reflects the dominant white culture. Most campuses are not equal meeting grounds for white and black students, whether from urban or rural America.

American public opinion of college sports reached its nadir in the mid 1980s. In an attempt to create meaningful reform, many measures were passed. Among them were Propositions 48, 42, and 16. The wide-ranging debate and protest against Proposition 42 placed the issue of race among the central ethical issues in college sports in the 1990s. Proposition 42 would have prevented athletes who did not achieve certain academic standards from receiving a scholarship. The new debate over Proposition 16 in 1994–95 has again raised the racial specter in college sports to a new level.

The American Institutes for Research (AIR) produced a study for the National Collegiate Athletic Association (NCAA) in 1989 suggesting that there are low academic expectations for black athletes. Only 31 percent of the black athletes surveyed for the AIR study indicated that their coaches encouraged good grades. The study also suggested that black student-athletes are not receiving the education promised by colleges in that they graduate at a significantly lower rate than do whites. They have few black coaches or faculty members on whom to model themselves. All of this is drawing public attention and pressure. The Reverend Jesse Jackson founded the Rainbow Commission for Fairness in Athletics to change such imbalances.

Although less than 6 percent of all students at Division I-A institutions are black, 60 percent of the men's basketball players, 37 percent of the women's basketball players, and 42 percent of the football players at those schools are black.[4]

All colleges and universities have some form of "special admittance" program in which a designated percentage of students who do not meet the normal admission standards of the school are allowed to enroll. According to the NCAA, about 3 percent of all students enter as "special admits." Yet more than 20 percent of football and basketball players enter under such programs. Thus, many enter with the academic odds already stacked against them.

The 1989 NCAA-AIR study presented a wealth of data. Those familiar with college athletics were not surprised by the study's findings, which indicated that black athletes feel racially isolated on college campuses, are overrepresented in football and basketball, have high expectations of pro careers, and are uninvolved in other extracurricular activities. However, the results of the NCAA study stood in stark contrast to the findings published by the Women's Sports Foundation (1989). It was the first major study of minorities playing high school sports. It clearly established that in comparison to black nonathletes, black high school student-athletes feel better about themselves, are more involved in extracurricular activities other than sports, are more involved in the broader community, aspire to be community leaders, and have better grade point averages and standardized test scores. Almost all those results contradict the view that most of white society has about the black athlete.

According to Lou Harris and Associates (1993), it is apparent that most varsity athletes believe that their participation in high school team sports has helped them to become better students and citizens and to avoid drugs:

It is especially significant to note that the value of playing sports in all these areas was significantly higher for African-American student-athletes in particular and for football and basketball players in general. It merits considerable attention by colleges and universities where the experience of African-American student-athletes, as well as their football and basketball players, is significantly different and appears much more negative.[5]

The primary question that now must be asked is what happens to black athletes, and black students in general, between high school and college that seems to totally change how they perceive themselves. Among other things, many black students leave a high school that is either overwhelmingly black or at least partially integrated. If students are from an urban area, they leave behind a core of black teachers and coaches. If students live on campus or go to school away from home, they leave behind whatever positive support network existed in the community in which they were raised and possible black role models who are not exclusively athletes.

Students arrive at college to discover that the proportion of black students at Division I-A schools is approximately 6 percent. Furthermore, less than 2 percent of the faculty positions at colleges and universities are held by blacks. Finally, the athletic departments hire just a few more blacks than the number of blacks on the faculty and actually hire fewer blacks than do the professional sports teams.

A great deal of emphasis has been placed on racial discrimination in professional sports, especially in the hiring practices of professional franchises. In fact, a great deal of the research done at the Center for the Study of Sport in Society is devoted to the publication of the annual *Racial Report Card*. However, a look at the number of available employment positions in our colleges and universities indicates that it is less likely for blacks to be hired in higher education than in professional sports.

Although the militancy and struggle of the 1960s and 1970s have reduced the negative self-perceptions of most young blacks, the stereotypes—and all the taboos that go with them—still exist for many whites. White and black athletes can meet on campus carrying a great deal of racial baggage. Their prejudices won't automatically evaporate with their sweat as they play together on a team. The key to racial harmony on a team is the attitude and leadership of the coach.

Student-athletes must be committed to equality and clearly demonstrate this to the team. The history of young athletes, and students in general, makes it an uphill task. Chances are that competition at the high school level bred some animosity; usually, white teams play against black teams, reflecting urban residential housing patterns. There is virtually no playground competition between blacks and whites because few dare to leave their neighborhoods.

On a college team, blacks and whites compete for playing time, while in the society at large, black and white workers compete for jobs, public housing, and even welfare. A primary difference is that whites are apt to accept blacks on the team because they will help the team win more games and perhaps get the white athletes more exposure.

It is easy for white athletes, no matter what their racial attitudes, to accept blacks on their teams for two other reasons. First, they need not have any social contact with black teammates. Sports at which blacks dominate are not sports like golf, tennis, and swimming where socializing is almost a requirement for competition. Players need not mingle after basketball, baseball, or football. More important, black male players need not mingle with white women after those games. Housing on campus, and social discrimination through fraternities and sororities, further isolates black athletes. Whether in high school or college, the black student-athlete faces special problems as an athlete, a student, and a member of the campus community.

Most of white society believed we were on the road to progress until Al Campanis and Jimmy "the Greek" Snyder made us challenge our perceptions. Their statements on national television that blacks and whites are physically and mentally different were repugnant to much of the country and led to widespread self-examination. Like many whites who accept black dominance in sports, Campanis believed that blacks had less intellectual capacity. It makes things seem simple to people like Campanis: Blacks sure can play, but they can't organize or manage affairs or lead whites. Marge Schott (owner of the Cincinnati Reds baseball team), speaking in private, reopened the wounds in 1992 when her remarks about blacks and Jews again stunned the world of sports.

Many people wouldn't see much to contradict in this view if they looked to society at large. In 1995, white men and women were twice as likely as black men to hold executive, administrative, and managerial positions. At the same time, blacks were twice as likely as whites to hold positions of manual labor. Decades of viewing this pattern could easily reinforce the Campanis viewpoint: Whites are intelligent and blacks are physically powerful.

After fifty years of trying to determine the genetic superiority of blacks as athletes, science has proved little. Culture, class, and environment still tell us the most. Instead of developing theories about why African Americans excel in sports, perhaps more time will now be spent on their achievements in human rights, medicine, law, science, the arts, and education who overcame the attitudes and institutions of whites to excel in fields where brains dictate the champions.

COACHES: A STUDY IN BLACK AND WHITE

The coach becomes the black student-athlete's main contact, and the court or playing field frequently becomes the home where he or she is most comfortable. Nonetheless, some black athletes feel that their white coaches discriminate against them and that their academic advisers give them different counseling. This may reflect a general distrust of whites or a strong perception that racism is the cause of certain events. Even well-intentioned acts can be interpreted by blacks as being racially motivated.

Over the years, black student-athletes have made a series of similar complaints irrespective of their campus location: subtle racism evidenced in different treatment during recruitment, poor academic advice, harsh discipline, positional segregation on the playing field and social segregation off it, blame for situations for which they are not responsible. There are also complaints of overt racism: racial abuse, blacks being benched in games more quickly than whites, marginal whites being kept on the bench while only blacks who play are retained, summer jobs for whites and good jobs for their wives.

To say that most or even many white coaches are racist is a great exaggeration. But most white coaches were raised with white values in a white culture. The norm for them is what is important for a white society.

Stereotypes of the Black Athlete

If white coaches accept stereotypical images of what black society is and what kind of people it produces, they may believe that blacks are less motivated, less disciplined, less intelligent (53 percent of all whites believe blacks are less intelligent), and more physically gifted. They may think that all blacks are raised in a culture bombarded by drugs, violence, and sexuality, and that they are more comfortable with other blacks.

They might believe those characteristics are a product of society or simply that they are the way God chose to make them. They might recognize themselves as racist, disliking blacks because of perceived negative traits. More than likely, however, they view themselves as coaches trying to help. In either case, if they act on these images, their black players are victimized.

In one of the most important scandals of the 1980s, Memphis State, a 1985 NCAA Final Four participant, fell into disgrace. There were many allegations about the improprieties of the school and its coach, Dana Kirk. One that could not be disputed was the fact that twelve years had gone by without Memphis State's graduating a single black basketball player. Like several other urban institutions, Memphis State built a winning program with the talents of fine black athletes. The fact that none had graduated brought back memories of Texas Western's NCAA championship team, which failed to graduate a single starter, all of whom were black. But this went on at Memphis State for more than a decade. The National Association for the Advancement of Colored People (NAACP) sued the school. Publicity finally led to the dismissal of Kirk. Indications are that Larry Finch, who replaced Kirk, has run a clean program. Perhaps the fact that Finch is black has resulted in a different approach to black players. In 1995, Memphis State had one of the nation's most open-minded and progressive presidents in Lane Rawlings.

I do not mean to single out Memphis State. In the ten years since Dana Kirk was fired, I have been on more than seventy-five campuses. The pattern is frequently similar: The academic profile of black football and basketball players and their treatment as students is different from whites, and their graduation rate is lower.

Positional Segregation in College

The issue of positional segregation in college is becoming less of a factor. For years, whites played the "thinking positions." The controlling position in baseball is the pitcher; in football, it is the quarterback. Everyone loves the smooth, ball-handling guard in basketball. These are the glamour positions that fans and the press focus on. These have largely been white positions. College baseball still poses the greatest problem at all positions, as fewer and fewer blacks play college baseball. Less than 3 percent of Division I-A college baseball players are black.

However, in a major shift in college football, large numbers of black quarterbacks have been leading their teams since the late 1980s. Between 1960 and 1986, only seven black quarterbacks were among the top ten candidates for the Heisman Trophy, and none finished higher than fourth. In 1987, 1988, and 1989, black quarterbacks Don McPherson (Syracuse), Rodney Peete (University of Southern California), Darien Hagan (Colorado), Reggie Slack (Auburn), Tony Rice (Notre Dame), Stevie Thompson (Oklahoma), and Major Harris (West Virginia) all finished among the top ten vote getters. In 1989, Andre Ware (Houston) became the first black quarterback to win the award. Florida State's Charlie Ward won it in 1993. In 1994, Nebraska won the national championship with a dramatic Orange Bowl victory behind the leadership of quarterback Tommie Frazier. Coach Osborne inserted Frazier into the starting lineup after Frazier missed nearly the entire season with a blood clot.

In basketball, more top point guards coming out of college are black. Recent stars such as Kenny Anderson, Tim Hardaway, Anfernee Hardaway, and Jason Kidd are just a few of the more prominent black point guards. Perhaps this bodes well for an end to positional segregation in college sports in the near future.

CAN BLACK ATHLETES SPEAK OUT?

The coach is the authority. Historically, athletes have rarely spoken out. This creates problems for all coaches who come up against an outspoken player. When the player is black and not a superstar, that player will often be let go. Only the superstars such as Bill Russell, Kareem Abdul-Jabbar, and Muhammad Ali remain secure because no one can afford to let them go. But even the greatest ones paid heavy prices for many years after their outspokenness.

Muhammad Ali, who refused to go into the army, knew that you had to be at the top to speak out if you were black. Ultimately, Ali had the money and influence to go all the way to the Supreme Court. Most blacks have neither the money nor the influence to make the system work.

In 1992, Craig Hodges spoke out about the Rodney King case in Los Angeles. Hodges was a great shooter but was a peripheral player on the

National Basketball Association (NBA) championship team, the Chicago Bulls. He had won the three-point contest at the NBA All-Star Game. After his remarks, he was cut by the Bulls—and no team picked him up.

Tommy Harper's case is also instructive. His contract was not renewed by the Boston Red Sox in December 1985. The Red Sox said he was let go because he was not doing a good job as special assistant to the general manager. Harper, however, charged that he was fired because he spoke out against racist practices by the Red Sox. Earlier in 1985, he said that the Sox allowed white players to receive passes to the whites-only Elks Club in Winter Haven, Florida, where they held spring training. (The Sox later stopped the tradition.) Harper sued and the Equal Employment Opportunity Commission ruled that the firing was a retaliatory action against Harper because he spoke out against discrimination. It took him awhile to get back into baseball. He is currently a coach for the Montreal Expos.

There are positive examples as well. It did not go unnoticed that when a group of black athletes at Auburn asked the president of the university to get a Confederate flag removed from a dormitory, it was removed. In 1987, the Pittsburgh basketball team wore ribbons as a protest against their school's investments in South Africa. In 1990, black athletes at the University of Texas at Austin led a protest against racism on campus. They had even been encouraged by members of the athletic department. Whether or not this will become a trend is hard to see, but the positive and widespread media coverage of their actions stood in dramatic contrast to early reactions to Russell, Ali, and Abdul-Jabbar.

In 1969, fourteen black players on the University of Wyoming football team informed the athletic department of their intentions to wear black armbands during an upcoming game against Brigham Young University. The players' intent was to bring attention to the doctrinal position of the Church of Latter Day Saints that prevented blacks from holding the priesthood. After hearing of the players' plan, Wyoming's head football coach cited a long-standing team policy that prevented players from engaging in protests of any kind. When the players showed up at his office wearing the armbands just one day before the game, the coach interpreted their actions as defiance of the rule and a direct threat to his authority. He summarily dismissed all fourteen players from the football team.

Although this incident remained a sore spot in the history of Wyoming athletics for nearly twenty-four years, the university held ceremonies to honor the players on September 24, 1993. The event was the result of the African American Studies Department working in conjunction with the school's administration to recognize the former players, signaling a new era in communication between student-athletes and the administration.

INTERRACIAL DATING AND SEXUAL STEREOTYPES

The image of the black male involved with sex and violence took a profound turn in 1994 after O. J. Simpson was charged with a brutal double murder.

Looking beyond the horror of the murders, the case once again brought out the fact that interracial dating is still a volatile issue in the 1990s. There is no question that it is far more common in the mid-1990s than it was in 1970 or even 1980 when Howie Evans, then a black assistant coach at Fordham and a columnist for the *Amsterdam News,* told me of when he used to work at a black community center in New York. Recruiters from predominantly white southern schools would come there to recruit black women for their schools. Those coaches seemed to think that they understood the powerful sexual drives of black men, so they went out to get them some "safe" women friends from the North.

When I talk to black athletes after a lecture, I try to ask them about this. It doesn't matter where I am—Los Angeles, Denver, New York, Nashville, or Norfolk—almost everyone says there is pressure, now usually very subtle, not to date white women. It doesn't matter how big the star is.

Black athletes also tell me that the assumption on campus is that they want white women more than black women. Not that blacks say they do but that whites believe they do. If a white student wants to sleep with a coed, that's part of college life in our times. If a black student wants to do the same, that's the primal animal working out his natural instincts. Stereotypes of blacks in the media are, of course, perpetuated by the virtually all-white sports media.

THE OPTIONS FOR BLACK ATHLETES IN CHOOSING A COLLEGE

The effects of the actions of white coaches who act on stereotypical images of black athletes are not dissimilar. Study after study has shown the devastating consequences to a person's psyche. As long as the act is perceived as being racially motivated—even if it is a well-intentioned act—the end result is the same.

Black student-athletes with professional aspirations seem to have three choices, none of which are equal. They can choose to attend a historically black college, a predominantly white school with a black head coach, or a predominantly white school with a white head coach.

So what should black athletes do? Should they attend a historically black college? After all, black colleges have turned out great pro athletes for years. But black college athletic programs started to decline when the white schools began to integrate. They don't have million-dollar booster clubs to compete with white schools to get star black athletes. Division I-A schools also offer the lure of bowl games, television coverage, and a "good education."

NBA Players Association Director Charles Grantham told me that the black athlete who wants to turn pro has little realistic choice. "Exposure on TV means the scouts will see you and, if they like you, a higher position in the draft. That means more money, much more money."[6]

The Southwestern Athletic Conference, which included Grambling,

Jackson State, and Southern, used to provide thirty-five to forty players a year to the National Football League (NFL) in the early 1970s. By the 1990s, the numbers were between six to ten in a big year.

Grambling's Eddie Robinson is the winningest coach in college history and has sent more players to the NFL than any coach. Could Eddie Robinson coach at Michigan or in the NFL? He has never had the opportunity to turn down a Division I-A job. Eddie Robinson is black; he became a coach before white institutions were ready for him.

Playing for a black coach at a predominantly white institution is another option for the black student-athlete. Many of today's black players would like to attend schools that have black coaches. For Division I basketball players, that amounts to forty-five schools, excluding the sixteen historically black institutions. The NCAA has 302 Division I schools with approximately thirteen players per basketball team. Therefore, of the 3,926 slots for men's basketball players, approximately 793 fall under black basketball coaches.[7] The slots are far fewer in college football where there were only five black head coaches at the Division I level at the close of the 1994 season. Finally, in Division I college baseball, there is not a single black manager.[8] (See Table 4.1.)

The NCAA's 1994 Men's Final Four featured teams with a total of fifty-four players; twenty-nine were black (54 percent), twenty-four were white (44 percent), and one was Hispanic. On the other hand, alongside the court there were thirty-nine coaches; 85 percent were white. There was not a single person of color on any of the four teams' medical staffs. The fifteen athletic directors and associate athletic directors were all white. Of the fifty-four basketball administrators, only five were black (9 percent). Of the 186 basketball support staff positions, whites occupied 174 (94 percent).

Even the media covering the game were overwhelmingly white. Twelve of the thirteen local radio and television broadcasters were white as well as 145 of the 150 local newspaper reporters.[9]

The 1995 National Championship game in football, played at the Orange Bowl, was no different. Table 4.2 depicts the combined racial break-

Table 4.1 / Percentage of Black Employees in NCAA Member Institutions

Member Institution	Black Employees (percentage)
Athletic Administration	6.2
Athletic Directors	3.6
Associate Athletic Directors	4.5
Assistant Athletic Directors	4.9
Head Coaches	3.9
Revenue-Sports Head Coaches	12.9
Assistant Head Coaches	9.8

Source: National Collegiate Athletic Association (1994).

down of the University of Nebraska and University of Miami football programs. Although nearly 63 percent of the players were black, 100 percent of the presidents, athletic directors, head coaches, associate athletic directors, sports information directors, and medical staff were white.

There are many potential jobs available for blacks in coaching and in athletic departments. There are 906 NCAA members in all divisions, with an average of 15.8 teams per school.[10] That amounts to 14,315 teams. The National Association of Intercollegiate Athletics (NAIA) has 391 members with an average of 9.5 teams per school. That's another 3,715 teams. With an average of 2.5 coaches per team, college sports has approximately 45,075 coaching jobs. That excludes junior and community colleges.

When so very few coaching positions are held by black Americans, there should be little wonder that black student-athletes feel isolated on campus. Pressure needs to be placed here to change these percentages. The coaches are available—the Black Coaches Association has three thousand members. If there is to be a more promising future for the black student-athlete, then more black coaches and assistants will have to be hired.

Table 4.2 / 1995 College Football National Championships: Racial Breakdown of Participants

Presidents/Chancellors[a]			Sports Information Directors		
White	3	(100%)	White	2	(100%)
Total	3		Total	2	
Athletic Directors			Assistant Coaches		
White	2	(100%)	White	29	(78%)
Total	2		Black	7	(19%)
			Latino	1	(3%)
			Total	37	
Head Coaches			Medical Staff		
White	2	(100%)	White	18	(100%)
Total	2		Total	18	
Associate Athletic Directors			Nonplaying Staff		
White	5	(100%)	White	167	(89%)
Total	5		Black	16	(8.5%)
			Latino	5	(2.5%)
			Total	188	
Players					
White	49	(36%)			
Black	85	(62.5%)			
Latino	2	(1.5%)			
Total	136				

[a]The University of Nebraska has both a president and a chancellor.
Source: Rainbow Commission for Fairness in Athletics, January 1995.

How do present-day black coaches fare? In 1985, Nolan Richardson was hired by Arkansas and became the Southwest Conference's first black head basketball coach. When his first two teams lost thirty games, Arkansas newspapers wrote him off. When he led the team to the Final Four in 1990, Richardson was elevated to sainthood in the Arkansas media. When Arkansas won the 1994 National Championship, Richardson was clearly a star in the state. People were saying that his presence, and especially his success, was leading to improved race relations in northern Arkansas.

Georgetown's John Thompson made many people angry when he became the first black coach to win a national championship in 1984. This was especially true of some media figures who said he was arrogant and abrasive and kept his team insulated from the public. They said his team was overly aggressive. The intensity of the attack varied but was prolonged over a decade. His personal leadership as the outspoken elder statesman of America's black coaches has enhanced his status in the black community and alienated many in the white community.

Thompson was breaking all the molds shaped by a stereotyping public. First, he was a big winner with a lot of black recruits coming to an increasingly multicultural campus. Second, these black players comprised not a freewheeling, footloose team but, rather, one of the more disciplined teams in the country. Even more important, at a time of great negative publicity concerning the academic abuse of college athletes, Thompson's players had one of the highest graduation rates in America. Was there some jealousy involved in the attacks? Didn't these same writers call aggressive white teams "hustling teams"? White coaches like John Wooden were called father figures when they kept the press at arm's length from their teams.

Even if you accept the fact that Thompson's style was a tough one for the public to grapple with, this still doesn't explain the degree of the attacks against him. The racial issue seemed, once again, to be a factor. Although several national writers wrote balanced pieces on John Thompson and Georgetown, too many others clearly showed us how far we have to go.

For now, most black student-athletes are maintained because they might be steered into easier courses. They are less likely to get a degree. With prevailing stereotypes, some coaches will make assumptions about them they would never make about whites. Socially, they will be in an alien world, segregated in student housing, off-campus housing, and on road trips. Increasingly, they will be forced to withdraw into the safer athletic subculture, becoming isolated from both black and white nonathletes.

The odds are surely not in favor of black student-athletes. If, after enduring all these problems, they don't get a degree, then why do they subject themselves to all of this in the first place? The answer is simple. They assume that sports is their way out of poverty. How prevalent is this belief? The NCAA AIR study of black college athletes showed that in 1989, approximately 45 percent of black basketball and football players at predominantly white schools thought they would make the pros. Less than 1 percent will. The Northeastern University study conducted by Lou Harris in 1993 showed that 51 percent of black high school student-athletes think they can make the pros.

Sports have been promoted as the hope of black people. But too often that hope is empty. If black athletes do not emphasize their studies, they will slip farther and farther toward the bottomless pit of functional illiteracy. Black athletes become involved in a cycle that trades away their education for the promise of stardom, a promise that is very unlikely to ever pan out. A black high school student has a better chance of becoming a doctor or an attorney than of becoming a professional athlete. But those civic role models are not as visible as black athletes. For black high school students, the professional athlete seems like the best model.

Unfortunately, some schools "pass" certain student-athletes to the next level without regard to academic achievement. They are conditioned to believe that academic work is not as necessary as working on their bodies. The promise of the pros is the shared dream, no matter how unrealistic.

The media is now reporting more on the problems. The NCAA has paid far greater attention to the racial issue in college sports. In the last ten years, things have gotten markedly better for black student-athletes. Their graduation rates have improved by more than 10 percent. The number of black coaches has increased. Public pressure for change, especially that coming from Reverend Jackson's Rainbow Commission for Fairness in Athletics, has finally been sustained over time.

Nonetheless, college sports has a long way to go before it fulfills its promise as a beacon of democracy and equal opportunity.

REVIEW QUESTIONS

1. Lapchick notes that, historically, white athletes have occupied the controlling positions in baseball (the pitcher), in football (the quarterback), and in basketball (the guard). Recently, however, black athletes have increasingly occupied these spots. What political implications do you think this pattern has—both in the past and in the future?

2. Many would argue that perceptions of the black athlete are different from those of the white athlete; the black athlete is seen as an "animal" while the white athlete is perceived as "aggressive." Would you agree? In what ways are these images created and maintained?

3. Lapchick suggests that the sports arena is seen as an area where individuals of different races have equal opportunities. Yet, as he indicates, black student athletes face discriminatory practices both on and off the field. What changes, in your opinion, need to be made for the reality to be transformed into the ideal?

4. Discrimination in sports seems to be part of the overall college atmosphere in which black students are isolated academically and socially. Lapchick notes that coaches who understand the concerns of

black student athletes are often able to make a difference. What else
can be done to address the concerns of the black student-athlete?

5. Clearly, there is a power differential in sports; there are very few
black coaches. How are the minority athletes who play under white
coaches affected? Do you think the reverse also applies—that is, for
white athletes who play under black coaches?

Notes

1. Louis Harris & Associates, Inc. *Project TEAMWORK Responds: Racism and Violence in American High Schools* (Boston: Center for the Study of Sport in Society, 1993).

2. Ibid.

3. Ibid.

4. National Collegiate Athletic Association, *1994 NCAA Division I Graduation Rates Report* (Overland Park, Kans.: National Collegiate Athletic Association, June 1994).

5. Quotation taken from unpublished data from the 1993 Louis Harris survey. Available from the Center for the Study of Sport in Society, 360 Huntington Ave., 161 CP, Boston, Mass. 02115.

6. Stanley Johnson of the NCAA, interview by the author, January 31, 1993.

7. Deb Kruger of the Black Coaches Association, interview by the author, February 1995.

8. Ibid.

9. See the April 1994 press release from the Rainbow Commission for Fairness in Athletics. Available from the National Rainbow Coalition, P.O. Box 27385, Washington, D.C. 20005. Data for Table 4.2 available from the National Rainbow Coalition, P.O. Box 27385, Washington D.C. 20005.

10. Phyllis Ton, NCAA spokesperson, interview by the author, January 25, 1995.

5 / Logo or Libel? Chief Wahoo, Multiculturalism, and the Politics of Sports Mascots

NEIL A. ENGELHART

The peculiar evil of silencing the expression of an opinion is that it is robbing the human race. . . . If the opinion is right, they are deprived of the opportunity of exchanging error for truth; if wrong, they lose, what is almost as great a benefit, the clearer perception and livelier impression of truth, produced by its collision with error.[1]

J. S. MILL

"There aren't a lot of us, and the issues we push aren't always heard by the majority population," says Clark Hosick of the Native American Cultural Center in Cleveland.[2] Hosick was speaking of the Cleveland Indians baseball team's failure to change their name and their Chief Wahoo logo in 1993, when they planned to move into their current home at Jacobs Field. "The Wahoo issue was something all Indians felt very strongly about," said another activist, "but we are so small in number, they didn't listen."[3]

Many Native Americans have been powerfully offended by the common practice of giving sports teams Indian-derived names and mascots, yet they have had difficulty impressing the importance of this issue on the majority of Americans. Many Americans view the practice as mere symbolism, not intended to offend, and harmless fun. The isolation of Native American voices was most powerfully symbolized by a single protester, Aaron Two Elk, who stood outside Atlanta-Fulton County stadium with handmade cardboard signs during the Atlanta Braves' 1991 season.

Why do symbols such as an Indian name or mascot provoke such strong feelings? Do we need to take such protests seriously when they come from such a small minority? When such a large majority finds the practice fun, are we obligated to desist from it? Does the displeasure of a few necessarily override the pleasure of the many?

One of the most fundamental facts of human cognition is that it is symbolic in nature. Language, for instance, is an entirely symbolic means of communication. We also construct and use a wide variety of physical objects as symbols—from religious symbols such as the crucifix and the Star of David, to secular ones like road signs, to political symbols such as party mascots and national flags.

Symbols become politically significant when they are used to organize people and to motivate them to act collectively. National anthems and flags, for instance, are used to represent the emotional commitment citizens have to their country. They can therefore be useful for mobilizing people to act patriotically, to the extreme of motivating soldiers to risk their lives for their country.[4]

Not every one has the same attitude toward the same symbols, however. Cultures are diverse, and because of this diversity, symbols may have different meanings for different people. A swastika, for instance, has a very different meaning for a skinhead than for a holocaust survivor. Symbols that appear perfectly innocuous and completely nonpolitical to some people may appear highly political and offensive to others.

Symbols are used and reproduced because they have meaning. This meaning is not inherent in the symbols, however. Meaning is something we learn from other members of our community. It is therefore cultural in nature—it is part of the vast amount of commonly shared information people teach to each other.

A person's physical appearance is also symbolic in nature. People in positions of leadership commonly dress in suits, which are symbolic of authority. Long white coats are worn by doctors and lab workers as emblems of cleanliness and sterility. The robes and hoods of Ku Klux Klan members are as meaningful as their equally symbolic practice of burning crosses.

Race can become symbolically encoded in the same way that clothing or other objects can. This kind of symbolism is particularly problematic because people cannot choose or change their race in the same way that they can choose or change their clothing. The symbolic meaning of race is ascribed to people regardless of who they are and what they are really like, and regardless of their preferences. The symbolism can have a powerful role in shaping the identity of people.

The meaning of race is also culturally shaped, and members of minority communities may feel that they have no power to construct their own identity as a result. The most powerful or numerous group will inevitably have the greatest impact on the commonly shared culture of the community. If some members of this majority community harbor racist attitudes, it may create a cultural context in which race can always be interpreted in a pejorative way.

In such a context, any reference to a minority group is automatically suspect as having either racist intent, or at least being subject to racist interpretation. As an illustration of this kind of problem, consider the following description of the TV show *Miami Vice:*

> The "good guys" on the show are vice squad members Crockett and Tubbs. They are partners, but rather unequal ones. Their relationship involves a play of racial dominance and subordination more subtle but no less demeaning that the one between the Lone Ranger and Tonto. During the 1984–1986 seasons, the black cop Tubbs consistently acted overly emotional; he appeared irrational, hence inferior. His white partner, Crockett, consistently restrained and guided him; he appeared rational, hence superior. During the 1986–1987 season, the locus of irrationality shifted from Tubbs to Crockett. But this time when the

white cop acted crazed, his black partner nurtured him. This minidrama was a displaced version of the relationship between a nanny (Tubbs) and her master's child (Crockett). Despite the reversal in the locus of irrationality, the lines of dominance and subordination between the two partners remained constant.[5]

Miami Vice was probably not intended to be overtly racist. This is beside the point, though. In the context of a racist society, there are always cultural resources available to give a racist interpretation to virtually any interaction between people of different races. The show did not generate its own interpretation: it used symbols and situations that could be given racist interpretations, given the context of racism from which they drew their meaning. This made it virtually impossible to have dramatic tension between the characters without creating a plausible racist interpretation.

Symbols that draw on the symbolism of race are thus potentially very touchy, particularly when employed by people not of that race. Even if there is no overt racist intent, they may be interpretable in a racist way. At the very least they may recall a history of oppression that the minority group would prefer to leave behind. Furthermore, they may be vulnerable to the charge that the majority group is once again trying to define the identity of the minority for them, once again perpetuating stereotypes. All of these charges have been leveled against Indian sports mascots.

MASCOTS

For sports fans and teams mascots are not political in nature. They symbolize team spirit. For teams they provide a logo and a valuable merchandising trademark. For fans they symbolize the entertainment they derive from watching a game and identifying with a team. They are fun and are certainly not meant to harm or insult anyone else.

Most mascots are unproblematic in this respect. Mascots are generally chosen to represent something about the team and its fans. In other words, they are generally chosen because they already have meaning, and the team wishes to attach that meaning to themselves—to make it a part of their identity. This is why fierce and indomitable animals such as tigers and lions are common mascots. Not all such mascots are meant to represent a fighting spirit, however; some are chosen ironically. The University of California, Santa Cruz, has the banana slug as its mascot—a common animal on campus, but also one which as a mascot indicates a rather low valuation of team sports. Similarly, the New York University Violets represent the university's emphasis on academics over athletics. In professional sports, when non-fierce animals are used as mascots or team names, they are usually birds, which symbolize speed, grace, and beauty—for instance the St. Louis Cardinals, Baltimore Orioles, or Seattle Seahawks.

Animal mascots—say, tigers or leopards—are unlikely to offend anyone. This is true even in deeply ironic, even tragic circumstances—such as the

University of California, Berkeley, using the now-extinct golden bear as its mascot, and keeping a stuffed specimen in its student union.

Other mascots symbolize some characteristic of the city or school where the team is located. These are often represented by objects, such as the Detroit Pistons. They may also be quite abstract—the Philadelphia Phillies or the Oakland Athletics. Sometimes teams are named for groups of people who were important to an area's history—the Dallas Cowboys, Boston Celtics, or New York Yankees.

In most cases naming teams after real people is not derogatory. The whole point is to pick a mascot and name of which the team can be proud. In addition to being offensive, a name like the Sambos or the Krauts would be ludicrous. Those terms are purely derogatory, and as such lack the association with power, skill, or local pride that one would normally want in a name. The names that teams pick are ordinarily free of such associations.[6] In mainstream American culture there is no racist context in which to interpret a name like the Yankees or the Padres.

Indian Mascots

This is not true for the many teams named after Indians, however. Indians are unique among the set of commonly used team mascots. They are a group of real people, able therefore to organize themselves, and they have been victims of discrimination. They have both the capacity to object to stereotyped images of themselves, and good reasons to do so. Animals cannot object, and Cowboys or Mariners—groups that have not suffered widespread discrimination—do not have any reason to do so.

For many—but not all—Native Americans, Indian mascots are offensive. They claim that these mascots play on stereotypes of Indians as wild, savage, animal-like creatures, and that they help perpetuate these stereotypes. Because they are seen as offensive, mascots have become symbols around which these groups have mobilized protests—in others words, they have become political.

This is a development that makes no sense to most fans. For them, these mascots are simply fun—they have no serious content and are not meant to offend. For Indians, however, they have come to mean something very different: they are symbols of a long history of oppression and racism. This makes them political, because racism and oppression are themselves political issues.

The cultural context within which Indian mascots occur is crucial to understanding the problem. One might argue that naming a team after Native Americans is a sign of respect, homage to the original inhabitants of what is now the United States. One might even point out that mascots are a positive thing, that the power and skill mascots are supposed to symbolize should be empowering to American Indians.

Many Native Americans do not feel this way. They understand the use of Native American mascots through the lens of a long history of oppression by whites, one which continues today. White settlers displaced Indians from their homes, killed vast numbers of them and have denied basic civil and economic rights to those who remain. They have justified these actions by developing a number of derogatory stereotypes of Indians—as vicious, wild people akin to animals, as habitual drunkards, as lazy, foolish and naïve.[7]

The indictment of white America is clear: European settlers came and took their lands from the native population, killing many with disease, violence, and starvation. The descendants of those white settlers moved the surviving Native Americans onto reservations and subjected them to the power of Indian agents, the Bureau of Indian Affairs, and various philanthropic groups. These agencies attempted to solve problems of poverty and despair on the reservation by encouraging Indians to assimilate into the majority culture as workers and laborers, but stripped of their Indian identity.

An important part of this strategy was sending Indian children to boarding schools, where they were forced to dress like whites and speak English. They were forbidden to speak their native languages or engage in traditional practices, including Native American games.

Baseball became a part of their indoctrination into mainstream white ways. It was one of the few forms of exercise or entertainment in which boys at these schools were allowed to indulge. A good, American game, it was held to train the students in "self-control, purity, democracy, and obedience"—all traits Indians were held to lack—and to be "a good backing for any mental or industrial training."[8] As an American game about which many Indian boys were enthusiastic baseball became an important part of the acculturation program.

Many American Indians interpret such ostensibly philanthropic programs as being racist in nature. Patronizing at best, such projects necessarily devalue native cultures and therefore threaten the collective survival of those cultures. They represent yet another attempt by the white majority to define the identities of Indians for them.

While many other minority groups have made progress in blunting stereotypes and improving respect for their civil rights, many Native Americans see a history of steady decline.

> A basic and essential fact concerning American Indians is that the development of civil rights for them is in reverse order from other minorities in this country. Politically, other minorities started with nothing and attempted to gain a voice in the existing economic and political structure. Indians started with everything and have gradually lost much of what they had to an advancing alien civilization. . . . While other minorities have sought integration into the larger society, much of Indian society is motivated to retain its political and cultural separateness.[9]

Senator Ben Nighthorse Campbell echoes this sentiment: "Americans tend to put all minorities in the same bag. But there is a big difference with us. Everyone else came here to see what they could get. Indians were here and have had everything to lose."[10]

In this context, it is difficult for many Native Americans to accept any use of the term "Indian" by whites. The term inevitably taps into this long legacy of conquest and oppression that has defined their relationship with white culture. It recalls a history of attempts by whites to define Indian identity.

This context-bound quality of the relationship is crucial. Indians have become symbols in their own right, representing certain things in the community they share with whites and other races in the United States—but because of their lack of power in that community, they have no control over what exactly it is they represent. The stereotypes of the majority community are therefore extremely galling to many Native Americans, who feel that such stereotypes are an attempt to construct an identity for them. As a result many Indians are suspicious of any invocation of their name or cultures. This may be frustrating to non-Native Americans who are sympathetic and would like to help. Because of the context of racism, though, it may not be possible to help in any unambiguous way.

It is possible that any use of Indian names or symbols by whites, no matter how they are intended, can be interpreted as derogatory. The only way to guard against this is if Native Americans themselves are involved in the manufacture and use of these symbols—hence the common claim that only Native Americans have the right to determine how they are depicted publicly.[11]

For this reason, the complaint of many fans that Native American names are not meant to be offensive may be irrelevant. For those who protest such team names, that issue is only the tip of the iceberg. The real problem is a deeper core of racism that is part of American culture. Sports mascots simply provide a convenient and highly visible example of the deeper issue, but because of this visibility, they can act as a catalyst for collective action among Native Americans and a tool that can be used to attempt to educate and sensitize people.

Fans also often argue by reductio ad absurdum that if names like "Indians" is offensive, so should any name taken from any group of people, or for that matter anything real at all. *Boston Globe* columnist Michael Madden provides a typical example of this argument: "WASPs angry at the Yankees? Animal rights groups furious at the Tigers and Orioles and Bengals? The antismoking crowd angry at the aroma from the Phillies, the best cigar there was? The thermal-warming activists sensitive to the implications of the Heat? The church-state crowd furious at the Padres?"[12]

Like most arguments founded on a reductio ad absurdum, this line of reasoning is absurd. The difference between the extremities offered by Madden and protests over names like the Indians, the Braves, and the Redskins is clear: no one has actually been offended by the Yankees, Phillies, Heat, or Padres. There is no cultural context within which to interpret those names as offensive. Sensing the weakness of this argument, Madden tries another:

> I am Irish and there are two sports teams that make a gross caricature of the Irish tradition, the Celtics and Fighting Irish of Notre Dame. Each uses that little leprechaun as a symbol, a leprechaun often with red cheeks, and this symbol hints at stereotypes but describes nothing of the Irish. Yet, I have never been offended by it.[13]

Madden is on stronger ground here. The Irish have been victims of discrimination in America, particularly in the late nineteenth century. The red cheeks and raised fists of the Notre Dame mascot exploit derisive stereotypes of the Irish as chronic drunkards and brawlers that were common then.

Yet this has changed. The Irish in America are not victims of widespread discrimination any longer. As a group the Irish have been able to define their own identity and overcome those stereotypes. This is something that still eludes American Indians, and what makes the name and mascot issue so sensitive for them.

Furthermore, the standard of whether something is offensive must be whether somebody is actually offended by it. It simply adds further injury to the initial insult to tell someone they are not justified in being offended.[14] As the manager of a Washington, D.C. radio station said of their decision to stop broadcasting the name "Redskins" for a certain football team based in their city, "it is the minority group that determines what is offensive, regardless of what the majority wants."[15] To do otherwise is to show a profound lack of respect for those one has already injured.

Teams—especially professional teams—are very reluctant to change their names. They have considerable investment in their names and logos, which become valuable franchises for them. They also become imbued with a tradition and history with which fans identify. Professional teams are notoriously reluctant to change their nicknames when they move, although the name may now seem inappropriate, even ludicrous. When the Lakers moved from Minnesota, the Land of Ten Thousand Lakes, to the deserts of Southern California, they became the L. A. Lakers. When the New Orleans Jazz moved to the more staid environment Salt Lake City, they too retained their name, becoming the Utah Jazz.

The issue therefore becomes even more problematic, because teams sporting names which some people find offensive are unwilling to change even after they have been made aware of the problem. Such teams can appear not only racist, because of their name, but also insensitive, even callous, because of their unwillingness to change.

A CASE STUDY: CHIEF WAHOO

"Indians" and Indian-derived names are among the most popular in baseball. I focus on the Cleveland Indians and the mascot, Chief Wahoo, in part because they have a stronger defense than many other teams. The name is not so obviously offensive as, say, the Washington Redskins or the tomahawk-chopping Atlanta Braves, and even has some justification in the team's history. This makes it a conservative case: if the name "Indians" is offensive in this case, it must be all the more so in others where there is less justification for the name and mascot of a team.

The Cleveland Indians have been the target of Native American protests in recent years. Native American groups have protested the name and the logo at Indians games, and attempted to persuade the team to change both when they moved to their new home at Jacobs Field in 1994.[16]

The argument against Chief Wahoo and the Indians name is straightforward: They promote stereotyped images of Indians as bloodthirsty warriors and are part of a tradition of white domination of Indians which has included depriving them of their lands, civil rights, collective identity, and even their survival.

The Cleveland Indians respond that they are trying to honor Native Americans, and that the name is justified by team history. Because of the various Indian school programs discussed above, there were a large number of Native American pro and semipro players in the early days of the sport. There were even a few semipro All-Indian teams at the turn of the century using Native American names that "capitalized on the stereotype of the Indian as a picturesque, colorful curiosity."[17] One of these early Native American players, possibly the first to play professional baseball, was Louis Sockalexis. He played for Cleveland from 1897 to 1899, and the team is supposedly named after him.[18]

In professional baseball's early years team nicknames changed often. When Sockalexis played for Cleveland, they were known as the Spiders, because of several tall, thin players. Between 1901 and 1913 they were known first as the Blues, because of their blue uniforms, and then as the Broncos, because "Blues" was not felt to be forceful enough, and finally as the Naps, in honor of player-manager Napoleon Lajoie. In 1914, Lajoie left the team and a new name was needed. A fan suggested "Indians," in honor of Sockalexis.[19]

The Chief Wahoo logo dates back to the 1920s. The first versions were relatively tame: conventional, serious Indian heads in red with feathered war bonnets.[20] In the 1940s *Cleveland Plain Dealer* cartoonist Fred Reinert created the basic design of the new Chief Wahoo—a cartoonish head with red (originally yellow) skin whose main features are a feather headband and an enormous, goofy grin.[21]

The Cleveland Indians organization insists that their name is not offensive because of its historical connection to Louis Sockalexis. In fact, they claim that they are honoring Sockalexis' memory with their name, and that some Native American groups have expressed their appreciation for this. They furthermore insist that Chief Wahoo is meant to be a logo and nothing more, and is not meant to offend anyone.[22]

The Cleveland Indians also claim that they are sensitive to Native American sentiments on this issue. A spokesman repeatedly said that they recognized there are two sides to the issue, and that they try to use Chief Wahoo in a restrained and sensitive way. This means using on the Indian head logo, without ever animating it, giving it a voice, or depicting Chief Wahoo with a body.[23] This is because they do not want people to mistake their logo for a depiction of an actual Native American. They do not use Native American paraphernalia (e.g., drums, tepees, war whoops, and so on), nor do they have a Native American mascot on the field during games.[24] Furthermore, they claim they do not play on words associated with Native Americans, such as "warpath"—although it must be noted that they do in fact use the word "tribe" quite freely to refer to the team.[25]

If the Indians name, and Chief Wahoo in particular, are so objectionable, why not simply abandon them? When the team moved to Jacobs Field, the *Cleveland Plain Dealer* ran an article suggesting it might be a good time to get rid of Chief Wahoo, which the paper referred to as "the American Indian equivalent of Little Black Sambo."[26] According to an Indians spokesman, the team received tens of thousands of letters urging them not to change their name or logo, and only a couple of hundred in favor of such a change.[27] They claim that this justifies their decision not to change either their name or logo, arguing that such a change would upset fans in a world in which change already comes too easily and traditions are not respected. Of course, for Native Americans the whole point is that there is a tradition of American racism which needs to be changed.

The Cleveland Indians organization and their fans hold that the team's name and logo represent baseball, not racism. The team's news release on this issue says that "We believe that when people look at our logo, they think of Cleveland Indians baseball. . . . People think of great players and great moments in baseball history."[28] Most fans seem to agree that the logo represents a baseball tradition, not an insult.[29]

The question, then, is whether something can be insulting even if it is not intended in that way. Furthermore, if something is offensive, do we have an obligation to remove the source of offense once it is brought to our attention? Even if something that offends a few is a source of pleasure and a symbol of fun for many more?

MULTICULTURALISM

Diverse societies have a particular problem: people from a variety of different groups live together, employing the same institutions and many of the same symbols, while fundamentally disagreeing about their meaning. A symbol like Chief Wahoo can therefore mean different things to different people. This means that sometimes one group may unintentionally use or treat such a symbol in ways which members of another group find inappropriate or offensive.

This is not ignorance—or at least, not simple ignorance. Cleveland Indians fans do not consider themselves ignorant of the meaning of Chief

Wahoo. They know exactly what he represents: fun, entertainment, and team spirit. When they cheer the Indians, wear baseball caps with the Chief Wahoo logo, and refer to the team he represents as the Tribe, they are engaging in good, clean fun which removes them from the ordinary cares and concerns of their daily lives. The suggestion that Chief Wahoo is racist, or even political, is bound to strike such people as mean-spirited.

Similarly, Native Americans who object to Chief Wahoo also know exactly what he represents. He symbolizes racist stereotypes associated with a long history of oppression, a chilling reminder of the vicious way they and their ancestors were treated by European immigrants and their descendants. He caricatures Indians and reduces them to objects of scorn. Chief Wahoo is therefore far from innocent, and it is grossly offensive and deeply callous of the Cleveland team to use both his image and the name "Indians."

The problem here is not one of ignorance. Both sides know exactly what Chief Wahoo means—to them. The problem is that what they know about him is deeply, fundamentally incompatible. The real problem then is getting both sides to recognize the other's position and to take it seriously.

Multicultural politics is sometimes referred to as a politics of recognition. It requires recognizing other groups as important, as legitimate members of a community deserving of respect. This respect is due despite—or perhaps because of—the fact that some groups have historically been marginalized and oppressed in the past.

Majority members of a community can sometimes feel threatened by such politics, which can degenerate into shrill condemnation of the majority and an insistence that any behavior displayed by an oppressed minority should be tolerated. This is an impoverished version of multiculturalism, though.

What is really important about multicultural politics is that it forces us to collectively recognize the diverse people who are members of the community in which we live. As Susan Wolf puts it, "the politics of recognition urge us not just to make efforts to recognize the other more accurately—to recognize those people and those cultures that occupy the world in addition to ourselves—it urges us to take a closer, less selective look at who is sharing the cities, the libraries, the schools we call our own."[30]

This more accurate recognition of the communities we live in is important because it forces us to treat each other with the respect on which stable political life is built. Lack of recognition leads to a lack of respect, which in addition to being morally problematic, also tends to create resentment, conflict, and violence. Recognition of the divergent meanings of Chief Wahoo and symbols like him will not only help us become better people—it will also help us build a stronger community.

REVIEW QUESTIONS

1. Engelhart notes that symbols which refer to particular races are touchy, especially when they are used by people not of that race. What political implications are inherent in the use of sports mascots that refer to "Indians"? Does the use of these mascots work to define the identity of certain groups?

2. Are sports franchises justified in using these mascots if discontinuing their use would mean decreased profits and inconvenience? Or should the voice of the minority in this instance override the concerns of the owners—and indeed most fans? Does the entertainment value outweigh the cultural significance of the act?

3. Engelhart notes that the Cleveland Indians organization insists that their name is not offensive, but that it pays homage to Louis Sockalexis. Do you think the use of Chief Wahoo is justified on these grounds?

4. As noted, one of the goals of multiculturalism is for the majority to recognize the interests and concerns of other groups. In your opinion, does the recognition of the diverse meanings attached to Chief Wahoo serve this goal, or is further action needed?

5. Do you think there is a significant difference in the use of mascots such as the Celtics and mascots such as the Braves?

Notes

1. John Stuart Mill, "On Liberty," in *Selected Writings of John Stuart Mill,* ed. Maurice Coming (New York: Mentor, 1968), pp. 135–136.

2. Quoted in Paul Shepard, "Indians Blame Lack of Clout for Wahoo Decision," *Cleveland Plain Dealer,* July 11, 1993, p. B2.

3. Juanita Helphrey, quoted in ibid.

4. Theodore Herzl, founder of the modern Zionist movement, once said that "with a flag one can do anything, even lead a people into the promised land." Quoted in David Kertzer, *Ritual, Politics and Power* (New Haven, Conn.: Yale University Press, 1988), p. 174.

5. Renato Rosaldo, *Culture and Truth* (Boston: Beacon, 1989), pp. 212–213.

6. One bizarre exception to the rule is the name of the Pekin Community High School (Illinois) team, the Chinks. Clearly racist and lacking the usual sense of power associated with a mascot, the name was apparently derived from the town's name, an old romanization of Peking/Beijing. The Education Department's Office of Civil Rights ruled in 1979 that this name was not a violation of civil rights laws, because there was no evidence that it caused the school to discriminate against Asians. Lynn Schnaiberg, "Indian Mascot Does Not Run Afoul of Rights Law, O. C. R. Says," *Education Week,* August 26, 1995, p. 26.

7. For a review of the impact of racism on American Indians, see Joseph E Trimble, "Stereotypical Images, American Indians and Prejudice," in *Eliminating Racism: Profiles in Controversy,* eds. Phyllis A. Katz and Dalmas A. Taylor (New York: Plenum Press, 1988).

8. Harold Seymour, *Baseball Vol III: The People's Game* (New York: Oxford University Press, 1990), p. 382. Industrialists at the turn of the century organized baseball teams among their workers for similar reasons; it was thought to help reinforce them against the blandishments of socialists.

9. U.S. Commission on Civil Rights, *Indian Tribes: A Continuing Quest for Survival* (Washington, D.C.: U.S. Government Printing Office, 1981), pp. 32–33.

10. Ben Nighthorse Campbell, quoted in Paul Shepard, "Indians Blame Lack of Clout for Wahoo Decision," *Cleveland Plain Dealer,* July 11, 1993, p. B2.

11. Native American groups often use the very names and symbols they consider offensive when employed by non-Indians. The American Indian Movement, for instance, in addition to

using the term Indian in its name, refers to activists as "warriors," and uses peace pipes and drums in its meetings. All of these things would be found objectionable if used by a non-Indian organization. See AIM, "The American Indian Movement," at <http://www.dickshovel .com/aimhist2.html> (originally from *Indian Nation*, 3:1 [April 1976]).

12. Michael Madden, "What's In a Name? A Lot of Controversy," *Boston Globe*, October 17, 1991, p. 65.

13. Ibid

14. Indeed, such arguments are most often heard where the offender has failed to understand why his or her act was offensive to someone else.

15. Michael Douglass, quoted in Tim Giago, "Mascot Issue Will Not Go Away, and Neither Will Indian People," *Editor and Publisher*, June 20, 1992, p. 7.

16. Bob DiBiasio, Cleveland Indians spokesman, telephone interview by author, September 17, 1997.

17. Seymour, *The People's Game*, p. 392.

18. Ibid., p. 393. In the early, less institutionalized days of baseball, the distinctions between college summer games, semipro, and professional ball were less clear than they are now, so defining whether a player was a professional or not was more difficult. It was precisely this ambiguity that led to another great Native American athlete, Jim Thorpe, being stripped of his Olympic medals.

19. Cleveland Indians, "Name/Logo issue," undated news release.

20. Sockalexis was a Penobscot Indian from Maine, whose ancestors did not participate in the Northern Plains Indian tradition of the war bonnet.

21. Indians spokesman Bob DiBiasio makes a point of calling the Chief Wahoo logo a caricature rather than a cartoon, because of the implication that a cartoon might be meant to poke fun. Bob DiBiasio, telephone interview.

22. Ibid.

23. Cleveland Indians, "Name/Logo Issue." In fact, there is a Chief Wahoo doll with a body available for sale through the team's Web site at <www.indians.com> (1997). The team does not receive income directly from merchandising clothing, baseball cards, etc., with the Chief Wahoo logo. Royalties from such merchandising for all major-league baseball teams are paid into a central fund which is then divided evenly among the teams. While the Cleveland Indians do benefit from such merchandising, it is indirect and shared among all the major-league teams. Andrew Zimbalist, *Baseball and Billions* (New York: Basic Books, 1992), pp. 57–59.

24. The official Cleveland mascot, in the sense of a live figure designed to stir up support and excitement in the crowd while the game is in progress, is a generic furry creature called Slider.

25. Other instances in which this rule is not strictly followed pop up occasionally, such as entitling a news release "Smoke Signals" (release date August 15, 1997).

26. Bill Livingston, "Insensitivity Lives On in Wahoo," *Cleveland Plain Dealer*, July 1, 1993, p. E1.

27. DiBiasio, telephone interview. Richard Jacobs was quoted as saying that "95 percent of non-American Indian fans wanted to keep the team logo." Livingston, "Insensitivity."

28. Cleveland Indians, "Name/Logo Issue."

29. Bob DiBiasio, telephone interview.

30. Susan Wolf, "Comment," in *Multiculturalism: Examining the Politics of Recognition*, ed. Amy Guttman (Princeton, N.J.: Princeton University Press, 1994), p. 85.

6 / Number One with a Bullet: Songs of Violence Are Part of America's Folk Tradition

DAVID HERSHEY-WEBB

When rock and blues musician Eric Clapton was honored with six Grammys, there were no cries of outrage from the law-enforcement community. Wasn't this the same Eric Clapton whose big hit a number of years ago was a song about killing a cop?

While black rapper Ice-T's song "Cop Killer" has been relegated to the Orwellian dustheap after protests by police officers' organizations and former Vice President Dan Quayle, white pop star Clapton's "I Shot the Sheriff" (written by reggae legend Bob Marley) has escaped condemnation.

Perhaps Clapton's hit was spared because the killer "didn't shoot the deputy" or because he swore, "it was in self-defense?" (Don't they all?) Or was the pressure to pull "Cop Killer," while ignoring other songs (and countless movies) that contain similar messages, another reflection of the racial bias that Ice-T and other rappers denounce in the legal system? The National Black Police Officers Association thought so and opposed the threatened boycott that led to the song's demise.

While the censors have their fingers poised over the erase button, there are a number of other songs by white nonrap artists that might deserve deletion for either glamorizing crime or undermining people's faith in the criminal justice system. Following the logic of the opponents of "Cop Killer," removing these songs from record catalogs and songbooks would be a significant contribution toward restoring respect for law enforcement in an increasingly violent society and may also bring down the crime rate. Similar treatment of white and black recording artists would also demonstrate society's commitment to equal justice before the law.

Woody Guthrie is probably the best-known American folksinger. He has had a deep influence on songwriters from Bob Dylan to Bruce Springsteen. His classic "This Land Is Your Land" has become something of an unofficial

---

Editor's Note: Los Angeles rapper Ice-T released the album *Body Count* in the spring of 1992. It was an instant hit, selling over 300,000 copies by mid-summer. One of the songs, "Cop Killer," was extremely controversial. The character in the song is angry over police brutality, saying he is " 'bout to dust some cop off." The chorus adds: "die, pigs, die." Scores of law enforcement organizations voiced their disapproval, arguing that the song encouraged violence against police and they called for a national boycott. A number of record stores agreed and pulled it from their shelves. With falling sales and mounting public pressure, Ice-T called upon Time Warner to stop the album's distribution. It was re-released without "Cop Killer."

national anthem. Like Ice-T, however, Guthrie also wrote a song about killing a police officer, called "Pretty Boy Floyd." In the song Pretty Boy is riding into town when

> *A deputy sheriff approached him in a manner rather rude,*
> *Using vulgar words of anger,*
> *And his wife, she overheard.*

> *Pretty Boy grabbed a log chain,*
> *And the deputy grabbed a gun,*
> *And in the fight that followed,*
> *He laid the deputy down.*

After the deputy has been killed—unlike Clapton's or Marley's protagonist, Pretty Boy did "kill the deputy"—Guthrie proceeds to turn Pretty Boy into a hero in a way that surpasses Ice-T's cop killer. Pretty Boy's life on the lam is filled with acts of generosity toward the poor. He pays a "starvin' farmer's mortgage," and leaves a "Christmas dinner for a family on relief." Guthrie's final two stanzas suggest that those with the law on their side cause more suffering than those who break the law:

> *Now as through this world I ramble,*
> *I see lots of funny men,*
> *Some will rob you with a six-gun,*
> *And some with a fountain pen.*

> *But as through this life you travel,*
> *And as through this life you roam,*
> *You won't never see an outlaw*
> *Drive a family from their home.*

"Pretty Boy Floyd" is available on any number of recordings by various artists. Shouldn't law enforcement officials be concerned about a song in which a deputy sheriff is killed simply for using "vulgar words in anger" and which suggests that such outlaws are heroes?

Bob Dylan was Woody Guthrie's biggest fan, in his early days self-consciously patterning himself after the folksinger. Dylan has written a number of songs about crime that display a deep distrust of the fairness of the legal system. "The Death of Emmett Till" is about the acquittal of two brothers for the torture and killing of a black youth in Mississippi. Dylan writes that "On the jury there were men who helped the brothers commit this awful crime/And so this trial was a mockery, but nobody seemed to mind."

The alleged frame-up of former boxing champion Rubin "Hurricane" Carter on a murder charge is the subject of another Dylan song. "Hurricane" helped bring the case to the public eye. Dylan sings:

. . . If you're black you might as well not show up on the street
'Less you wanna draw the heat.

. . . The trial was a pig-circus, he never had a chance.

. . . The DA said he was the one who did the deed,
And the all-white jury agreed.

And, recalling Guthrie's "Pretty Boy Floyd":

Now all the criminals in their coats and their ties
Are free to drink martinis and watch the sun rise
While Rubin sits like Buddha in a ten-foot cell,
An innocent man in living hell.

Dylan's songs are not calls to lawless violence like "Cop Killer," or seem-ing justifications of lawlessness, like "Pretty Boy Floyd," but aren't they just as dangerous? Don't they evoke in the listener a contempt toward the legal system that could easily lead to lawbreaking? The implicit message is the same in all of these protest songs—if the system is not fair, why play by the rules? What this means in the case of "Cop Killer" is that if police brutality will not be punished under the law, its victims will seek retribution on their own.

Guthrie and Dylan are not the only folksingers who treat criminals in a sympathetic manner. Killers of one kind or another abound in traditional folk music, suggesting that folk music is one of the primary causes of the high murder rate in this country.

Traditional folk songs do not overtly criticize the injustice of the legal system. Instead, like the movies, they perpetuate a myth of the outlaw as an American hero. The well-known folk ballad "Jesse James" is about a "lad" who "killed many a man." Like Pretty Boy Floyd, he had a philanthropic streak. "He took from the rich and gave to the poor." The ballad portrays him as a popular figure, recognizing his bravery and denouncing the "dirty little coward" who killed him. How many schoolchildren have been exposed to this and other folk songs that make a killer appear heroic?

Unlike Pretty Boy and Jesse James, "Stagolee" was no friend of the poor. He was simply a "bad man" who shot Billy de Lyons because "he stole his Stetson hat." Still, there is something alluring about the killer who spent "one hundred dollars just to buy him a suit of clothes." Could this song, in some small way, be responsible for the numerous homicides that have been committed because someone desired expensive sneakers?

Some of the most violent folk songs involve "crimes of passion." Given the widespread occurrence of domestic violence in society today, these songs are ripe for depublishing. Their particular insidiousness stems from the fact that they tend to be sung in a sweet, lilting manner that contrasts sharply with the macabre details of the story.

In "Bank of the Ohio," a folk song from the early 1900s, the jilted lover sings of his victim whom he took "by her lily-white hand":

> *I dragged her down to the riverbank,*
> *There I pushed her in to drown*
> *And I watched her as she floated down.*
>
> *. . . I murdered the only girl I love*
> *Because she would not marry me.*

"Knoxville Girl" is even more vivid:

> *She fell down on her bended knees,*
> *For mercy she did cry;*
> *Oh, Willy dear, don't kill me here,*
> *I'm unprepared to die;*
> *She never spoke one other word;*
> *I only beat her more,*
> *Until the ground around me*
> *With her blood did flow.*

The tension between the sweetness of the melody and the luridness of the crime is perhaps one of the reasons why Mike Seeger of the New Lost City Ramblers writes that when he sang the song to college students in the early 1960s "it always brought forth laughs."

While the victims in crimes-of-passion songs are usually women, one of the most famous ballads, "Frankie and Johnny," is about a woman who kills her man because "he is doing her wrong." Bob Dylan sings another version of this song, called "Frankie and Albert," on his latest recording.

Like folk music, modern country music (sung almost exclusively by white people, for white people) has also had its share of celebrated outlaws. In Johnny Cash's "Folsom Prison Blues" the singer says he "shot a man in Reno/Just to watch him die." How many senseless murders were inspired by that line? Cash not only made a hit out of this bouncy tune about a killer, he also cultivated the outlaw image, dressing in black and singing in prisons. How would the law enforcement establishment greet the news of Ice-T performing "Cop Killer" at San Quentin?

Another country music legend, Merle Haggard, whose "Okie from Muskogee" and "Fighting Side of Me" made him the darling of the love-it-or-leave-it crowd during the Vietnam War, launched his career with crime songs. Haggard's hits "Lonesome Fugitive," "Branded Man," "Mama Tried," "Sing Me Back Home," and "The Ballad of Bonnie and Clyde" are all songs that evoke sympathy for the perpetrators of crime.

Cash and Haggard's success with crime songs set the stage for a group in the 1970s, made up of Willie Nelson, Waylon Jennings, and others, which called itself the Outlaws. Their album *Wanted: The Outlaws* was the first country album to sell over a million copies. One of Jennings's big hits was "Ladies Love Outlaws." How many men have been drawn into a life of crime after listening to this song?

Is there something that distinguishes these songs from "Cop Killer," that argues for their being spared, apart from the fact that the singers (and usually the listeners) are white? Only two of them ("I Shot the Sheriff" and "Pretty Boy Floyd") deal explicitly with the killing of an officer of the law. It might be argued that it is the heinousness of the crime that separates an acceptable song from an unacceptable song. But is killing a man "just to watch him die," or drowning a woman in a river, really that much more palatable than murdering a police officer?

Another significant difference is that in most folk and country songs the killer is either paying the price for his deed ("Folsom Prison Blues," "Mama Tried," "Stagolee," "Banks of the Ohio," and "Knoxville Girl") or has been killed himself ("Jesse James"). Haggard's "Lonesome Fugitive" and Clapton's sheriff killer are both on the run. It could be argued, therefore, that these songs act as a deterrent, rather than encouraging crime. "Cop Killer" is quite different in this respect. The killer hasn't been caught or convicted. But that's because he hasn't killed anybody, either; he's only threatening to. Is the listener to believe that if he carries out his threat he's going to get away?

Does it matter if the killer gets away or not? The romance of the outlaw and the gangster is so deeply embedded in American culture that the distinction between a criminal who pays the price for his deed and one who gets away may not be so important. Either way, immortality has been achieved in a song.

Probably what sets "Cop Killer" apart from even the protest folk songs is the intensity and directness of the anger expressed. There is no question that this is a profoundly disturbing song. "I'm out to dust some cops off" is a long way from "I shot the sheriff." There is also no pretense of self-defense: Ice-T's cop killer is looking for retaliation. It is hard to argue that the character in the song is not advocating the killing of police.

If the anger is more extreme than in other protest songs, it is because the wrongs that have provoked such anger are more extreme. Ice-T is not concerned, like Woody Guthrie, with people being driven from their homes, or even, like Bob Dylan, with the conviction of an innocent man or the acquittal of a racist murderer.

Ice-T's anger stems from the unpunished and unjustified beating and killing of numerous African Americans by the police. ("Fuck the police/For Rodney King/Fuck the police/For my dead homeys.") It's hard to imagine a more effective expression of such anger than this song.

In the interests of law and order, and equal justice, the most prudent course of action may be to purge from the past, as well as the present, all those songs (and movies) that might encourage lawless behavior. Self-censorship by Ice-T, in response to the threatened boycott, was a good first step, but only a first step. The only reasonable alternative to this approach would be to allow "Cop Killer" to take its place alongside the legion of crime songs in the American songbook. A couple of slight changes might help—sing it as a country song and have the killer end up "stuck in Folsom Prison."

REVIEW QUESTIONS

1. Can entertainment provoke a certain action in a viewer or listener? Does the repetition of particular messages over time have the power to shape individual attitudes and beliefs? The author of this chapter notes that "killers" abound in folk music. Do you believe that folk songs have the capacity to produce a certain result, or do folk songs and rap songs merely reflect reality?

2. Is it your belief that songs like Ice-T's "Cop Killer" differ from songs by, say, Bob Dylan or Johnny Cash? If so, in what ways?

3. What can account for the adverse reaction to "Cop Killer" when songs which glorify other problems in society, such as domestic violence, have not received such attention? Could it be that police officers have the power to speak out against such lyrics, while other out-of-power groups, such as women, are not similarly positioned?

4. Do you agree with Hershey-Webb that self-censorship a good first step? Is it a good idea to purge all songs that encourage lawless behavior, or should we focus our attention on the social conditions that promote the creation of such lyrics?

7 / Aunt Jemima, the Frito Bandito, and Crazy Horse: Selling Stereotypes American Style

MARILYN KERN-FOXWORTH

From the turn of the century to the present day, multiracial groups have been used in American advertising. Some of the characters were so visible and so accepted that they became American icons. In fact, during certain eras in history, it became difficult to go through a single day without using one of these memorable products featuring an Asian, an African American, a Native American, or a Latino as its trademark. Yet advertisers chose to paint this mosaic collection in the worst, most hideous manner imaginable. The smiling black maid served up a generous dose of southern hospitality, while the hot-blooded nefarious Mexican stole the hearts of all and the savage Indian tempted consumers with his wild and uncontrollable idiosyncrasies. These images were personified in the form of such notable characters as Aunt Jemima, the Frito Bandito and Crazy Horse.

Although several companies abandoned advertising campaigns as they came to the recognition that such distorted images tended to perpetuate harmful stereotypes, many companies continue to manufacture and use advertising schemes that portray multicultural groups in a derogatory manner. This paper examines several of these pejorative advertisements and the impact they might have on our political culture and attitudes about people of color.

AUNT JEMIMA AND OTHER AFRICAN-AMERICAN STEREOTYPES

One of the most pervasive and stereotypical advertising characters is Aunt Jemima. Born out of the dreams and aspirations of two local businessmen in Joplin, Missouri, Aunt Jemima had her beginnings in 1889. It was a historical occasion for three reasons: (1) Aunt Jemima, the first ready-made pancake mix, ushered in the first convenience product; (2) it was the first product to use a real individual to personify its logo; and (3) the Aunt Jemima owners were the first to promote the idea of giving away a free product to entice sales. Invited to have breakfast with millions of families all over the world for over a century, she has been woven into mainstream American culture.

Her phenomenal success can be traced to her various owners who have methodically changed her appearance as societal issues and racial tensions have dictated. Making her debut at the 1893 World's Fair Exposition held in Chicago, she was a hit with consumers. One writer offered this account as an explanation of her instantaneous success: "Aunt Jemima's appeal as a product representation combined nostalgia for lifelong black servitude with modern convenience. Just add a dixie cupful of water to the pancake mix and presto, access to soul food no longer required integration."

During the Civil Rights Movement, the heightened era of black nationalism, Aunt Jemima's appearance was transformed. Losing fifty pounds and trading in her checkered bandanna for a contemporary headband, she came to resemble an executive secretary more so than the slave mammy that she had portrayed for decades. Aunt Jemima received another makeover, on her 100th birthday, in 1989. The headband was traded in for soft, gray-streaked hair; to make her more a woman of the '90s, she was given pearl earrings and a dainty lace collar. Now all that is reminiscent of the once pleasingly plump, always smiling, plantation-conditioned, consummate servant Aunt Jemima is her effervescent smile and her name. And Quaker Oats is not likely to relinquish the name without a fight; it is a name brand that sells approximately $300 million of Quaker Oats' total $5.3 billion in annual sales.

Despite the success of Aunt Jemima as an advertising mechanism, many have found the way the image has worked to define black womanhood to be deplorable. The resentment harbored by blacks against the trademark became apparent when Quaker Oats launched a national television advertising campaign in 1994 for its Aunt Jemima Lite Syrup which featured Gladys Knight. "For some consumers, there's no amount of makeover that would sufficiently offset the stereotypes associated with the name and the picture," remarks Ken Smikle, publisher of Target Market News, a Chicago-based newsletter covering black consumer marketing. He continues, stating that "there's no way that Gladys Knight as spokesperson eliminates the pain that black women feel when they see that racist label on the box."

The resentment felt by blacks toward advertising strategies did not end with Aunt Jemima, however. Through the years other companies have been plagued with charges of insensitivity and outright racism.

General Motors and Chrysler: Running into Trouble

During the Civil Rights Movement in 1964, General Motors threatened to withdraw its sponsorship of the popular Western television series *Bonanza* if an episode featured an African-American guest star. Pressure from NBC and public condemnation mounted, and the automobile dealer reversed its position. Nonetheless, as late as 1968, Chrysler expressed reservations about its sponsorship of *Petula,* a variety show, because the program's star, British singer Petula Clark, held the arm of Harry Belafonte, a black singer who appeared as a guest on the show. "Chrysler deemed it far too intimate a pose to appear on camera."[1]

Ganging Up on Crime: Evanston Faces a Dilemma

The town of Evanston, Illinois, found itself embroiled in a controversy when it sanctioned an anti-gang advertising campaign which included a television advertisement along with posters designed to help stop black-on-black crime. The advertisement was a pro bono project of the Leo Burnett Advertising Agency under the direction of Tom Reilly, a vice president at the agency. The thirty-second spot, authorized by the Evanston Human Relations Commission, titled "An Interview with a Klansman," opens with a neo-Nazi skinhead saluting and an announcer saying, "If they were giving medals for killing black people, this guy would win a bronze." The picture then shifts to a hooded Ku Klux Klansman, the announcer saying, "This guy, a silver." Finally, the camera pans to a young man who appears to be a gang member. "But this guy would win the gold. If you're in a gang, you're not a brother. You're a traitor." The commercial closes with the Klansman saying, "Right on, black brother. Right on!" The announcer cites chilling statistics noting that while the Klan had murdered at least twenty African Americans since 1960, eighty-five African Americans in Chicago in 1991 alone were killed by street gang members.

Evanston became aware that a problem was brewing when a screening of the commercial was disrupted by protesters. One of the staunchest critics was Rochelle Washington, one of four black members of Evanston's eighteen-member city council. When it was screened by the city's Human Services Committee, she stormed out of the meeting room, slamming the door for extra emphasis. Later she commented, "I think our kids brood and let things pile up inside themselves, instead of letting them out. This ad isn't saying, 'Come in and let me help you.' It is pushing them farther away."[2] Other opponents of the campaign included the Consolidated Committee of Concerned Black Men. The committee released a written statement claiming that the ads feed into mainstream America's stereotypes that all "black males are either gang members, criminals, or at least suspects."

Owen Thomas, the Evanston Commission's executive director and an African American, rebutted critics by saying, "We want the gang members to wake up and think of what they're doing to our future doctors, lawyers, and policemen of America. We feel strongly this is the right thing to do regardless of how painful it may be."

Conversely Speaking: Sneaking Up on Controversy

Converse, the renowned shoe manufacturer, created a stir in 1993 when it marketed a basketball sneaker called Run 'N Gun. The controversy centered around the implications the name had relative to inner-city youths. Though the phrase generally refers to a fast-breaking style of basketball, in light of the rampant gun-related killings occurring in inner-city neighborhoods, it was criticized as an insensitive marketing scheme. Retailing for $80 a pair, the name was maligned because high-priced sneakers serve as a status symbol among inner-city youths. In fact, many killings and assaults have been linked to attempts to acquire the high-priced sneakers at "discount prices."

One of the campaign's most outspoken critics, Georgette Watson, executive director of the Governor's Alliance Against Drugs in Massachusetts, lambasted the decision to call the shoe by such an offensive name and said, "Marketers have no sensitivity toward what is happening in the inner city." Officials at Converse cried foul for being singled out, noting that other shoe companies had introduced products with names that might be considered inflammatory, such as Shooter, Assault, Marauder, Air Magnum Force, and Slasher. Nonetheless, to appease critics, Gilbert Ford, president of Converse, said that the Run 'N Gun name would not appear on the shoe or in commercials. In those instances, the shoe would be referred to as a "running basketball shoe."

Sprinting toward Stereotypes

Sprint experienced an unpleasant reaction following the release of its July 1995 Central Telephone Directory in Las Vegas. The illustration, which was selected by a panel of judges from 1,500 entries by local schoolchildren and which then appeared on the cover 750,000 local phone books, was the work of a Cheyenne High School eleventh grader. The illustration, which pictured four people of different races in the process of planting trees and picking up litter, showed a young black girl on her knees in the dirt. The girl was depicted with a frown on her face and wearing an unflattering hairstyle reminiscent of a piccaninny during times of slavery.

Barbara Robinson, a retired attorney who writes a weekly column in the *Las Vegas Review-Journal*, said the hair, as depicted in the sketch, was an early 1900s stereotype. Robinson said she found the cover racially insensitive, politically incorrect, and downright ignorant.[3] State Senator Joe Neal (D-North Las Vegas) also criticized the cover: "This illustration sends a subtle message to the population that you ain't nothin'. I don't know if you ever heard the term 'mud people' but that's the subtle message behind this illustration."[4] Lucille Bryant added, "I am humiliated by that picture. We have struggled long and hard to change the image of blacks Americans from the stereotypes of yesteryear. Our children should not be embarrassed by this type of thing. They do not get down in the dirt at others feet."[5] One of the most vocal and visible critics of the picture, Marzette Lewis of Westside Action Alliance Korps—Uplifiting People (WAAK-UP), observed that the little girl looked like a space alien, an anteater. Lewis and others requested that the company make a public apology, recall all 750,000 phone books, and replace them with more suitable covers.

Dru Silver, public relations manager for Sprint, responded to the request in an open letter to the community, stating that the company genuinely apologized to all residents who were upset by the cover. The letter also stated that cultural diversity is a priority at Sprint: ". . . [W]hat the company has learned in recent weeks will be reflected in next year's contest."[6]

Can They Afford the Embarrassment?

Ford Motor Company emerged with egg on its face in early 1996 when it deliberately superimposed white faces on photos of its black and South

Asian workers during a marketing campaign in Europe. The deception was discovered when several black, Indian, and Pakistani workers in Britain, who had posed for the photograph along with their white counterparts, saw a reprint in a company brochure. To their dismay, they all had "become white." The photograph contained their bodies and clothes, but with white heads and faces.

In reporting the incident, the *Wall Street Journal* noted that the act of removing dark-skinned people from an advertisement to reflect the makeup of its target market highlighted the dilemma faced by multinational companies that advertise in different markets around the world.[7] Commenting on the snafu, Lewis Blackwell, editor of *Creative Review* in London, said "It was the wrong decision in political correctness terms, but a right one in marketing terms. At the end of the day, the majority of people in Poland are white." Most of the advertisers in Poland were in agreement. Wolfgan Ulrich, managing director at Grey Advertising remarked that in nearly three years of advertising experience in Poland, he could not remember a single advertisement that contained a black person. Nonetheless, Ford's advertising agency, WPR Group's Ogilvy & Mather Worldwide in London, altered the photos for a second advertising campaign in Poland.

Counting Black Jelly Beans at Texaco

In 1996, another corporation found itself ensnared in a public relations fiasco drawn along racial lines. Texaco Corporation was put on the hot seat after tape recordings surfaced in which top executives at the company were found making derogatory and discriminatory statements about its multi-ethnic employees. Network broadcast news and magazine programs aired footage of Texaco officials calling black employees "black jelly beans" and smirking about the possibility of blacks reaching the higher echelons of employment at Texaco.

Shortly thereafter, in the wake of a widely publicized settlement of a racial discrimination lawsuit by black employees, the company hired black-owned Uniworld Group Advertising to produce corporate image messages aimed at blacks and Hispanics. A spokesperson for Texaco commented that the purpose of hiring Uniworld was to develop a "nationwide corporate ad campaign that will communicate the company's pledge to make Texaco a model of workplace opportunity for all men and women." The resulting campaign included print ads, mostly carried in African-American and Latino magazines and weekly newspapers, which emphasized company efforts to abolish discrimination and demonstrate its commitment to multi-ethnic suppliers. One magazine advertisement featured a red-suited black female CEO of a black-owned financial firm stating, "How you act in a crisis shows your true character. Texaco stood by us during an incredibly tough time."[8]

A segment in a newspaper advertisement signed by Peter Bijour, Texaco's Chairman and CEO, read:

> Texaco is facing a vital challenge. It's broader than any specific words and larger than any lawsuit. We are committed to begin meeting this challenge swiftly

through specific programs with concrete goals and measurable timetables. Our responsibility is to eradicate discriminatory behavior wherever and however it surfaces within our company. Our challenge is to make Texaco a limitless opportunity for all men and women. Our goal is to broaden economic access to Texaco for women and minorities and to increase the positive impact our investments can have in communities across America. We have started down this road by reaching out to prominent minority and religious leaders to explore ways to make Texaco a model of diversity and workplace equality.[9]

Texaco's message strategy, its selection of media, and its hiring of a black agency were harshly criticized by marketing industry insiders. Thomas Burrell, of black-owned Burrell Communications, which had initially been offered the Texaco assignment stated, "They can't project a positive image of the company until the company has a positive image to project." Critics highlighted the limitations of advertising to change the tarnished image of Texaco. Dick Tobin, president of Miami-based Strategy Research Corporation claimed, "Unless they have a whole lot of success stories that testify to their current and past history of positive relations with blacks and other minorities . . . advertising is not going to help them."[10] Observers also criticized Texaco's strategy of placing the ads only in ethnic publications, rather than in general-interest media as well. One Chicago advertising agency CEO asserted that "most people" were alarmed by racist remarks made by Texaco executives and that Texaco's response to the crisis deserved a broader audience.[11] Jonathan Saidel, a Philadelphia comptroller whose city pension fund voted to sell off its shares of Texaco stock in protest of the company's actions, called the creation of a message solely for multiethnic audiences as "patronizing."[12]

Some industry observers also greeted Texaco's decision to hire Uniworld with skepticism, suggesting that the decision was motivated only by the company's newfound commitment to using multiethnic advertising agencies. However, there was some support for the selection of the black-owned agency. Vince Cullers, owner of one of the oldest black-owned agencies, asserted, "They might be making a mistake not to allow the African-American agencies to get involved because the company's image is wrapped up in a racially charged debate."

THE FRITO BANDITO AND OTHER LATINO IMAGES

During the 1960s, no advertising figure in the Latino community made more of an indelible impression on mainstream, middle America than the corn chip–snatching Frito Bandito. The Frito Bandito, a mustached cartoon-like Mexican bandit clad in an oversized sombrero and armed with a six-gun and a sinister smile, made a habit of stealing Fritos corn chips from unsuspecting victims. Bullet-riddled wanted posters were an essential part of this elaborate advertising campaign that featured Mexicans as cunning, clever, and sneaky thieves. A highly recognizable and visible symbol, the Bandito could be seen in American living rooms on television commercials featuring rambunctious youngsters who joyfully swiped corn chips. After biting into the stolen corn chips, "Mexican" style mustaches would appear on their innocent little faces.

The Frito Bandito became a well-known advertising caricature and the Frito-Lay Corporation, owner of the product, experienced high sales volume. Though Frito-Lay laughed all the way to the bank, many Latinos, civil rights activists, and organizations objected to the campaign. They argued that the character reinforced the stereotype of the Mexican bandit—of Mexicans as "mustached thieves." In 1970, after carefully staged protests, threatened boycotts, and the refusal of some television stations to air the offensive cartoon character, Frito-Lay withdrew the campaign.

Airing out Arrid

A little more than ten years later, a band of hard-riding, nefarious-looking Mexican bandits were to appear again. The ride is called to a halt by the obese, sombrero-wearing, mustached leader, who upon coming to a screeching stop, reaches into his saddlebag for a small can of Arrid spray deodorant, lifts up his underarm and sprays. At this time, listeners can hear a voice, "If it works for him, it will work for you." For many, this reinforced a stereotype that Mexicans reek of terrible body odor and smell worse than others. Needless to say, the ad campaign, produced by Liggett & Meyers, was not well-received by the Latino community.

Another commercial by Liggett & Meyers for L&M cigarettes featured Paco, a lazy Latino who never "feenishes" anything, not even the revolution he is supposed to be fighting. Of course, Latinos were livid at such a blatant stereotypical representation. A spokesperson for the company defended the commercial, stating "Paco is a warm, sympathetic, and lovable character with whom most of us can identify because he has a little of all of us in him, that is, our tendency to procrastinate at times."

Crazy Horse and Other Native American Stereotypes

Hornell Brewing Company did not realize the fervor it would generate when it decided to name a beer after Crazy Horse. The beer, sold in forty-ounce bottles, featured a Native American in headdress, and the text referred to "blue-clay pony soldiers" and "a land where the wailful winds whisper of Sitting Bull, Crazy Horse, and Custer." Opposition to the name was spearheaded by Big Crow, the Sioux warrior's grandnephew. But he was not alone; many other Native Americans also found the label objectionable to the legacy of Crazy Horse. Their criticism was fueled by the fact that Native Americans suffer an alcoholism rate up to six times that of the general population. What is more, the incidence of fetal alcohol syndrome is nearly twenty times greater among Native Americans. A Sioux tribal judge said naming a beer after Crazy Horse was tantamount to "naming a police baton after Rodney King."

The issue resulted in Congress voting to ban the label in 1992. The beer owners fought back arguing that the ban infringed on their right to free speech. Citing the existence of Thunderbird wine and Chief Osk Kosh Red Lager, a federal judge agreed with the owners and declared the ban unconstitutional.

Budweiser Sells Stereotypes Overseas

Native Americans were livid when they learned that Anheuser-Busch was using beer-guzzling American Indians to sell Budweiser in Britain. The ad, dubbed "Pale Rider," was created by London-based Omni Group's DDB Needham Worldwide Communications unit. The advertisement followed a truck driver for a company called Chieftain Cement who finds himself in a dim bar patronized by a crowd of American Indians. The bartender, a silver-haired Indian, is shocked by the man's ghostly pale face, which is covered with cement dust. So the driver dunks his head in a barrel of water, washing the dust away and revealing that he is an Indian. The camera zooms in as he gulps down a bottle of Budweiser.

Budweiser and marketing experts in America were convinced that the advertisements had become a cult hit in Britain, where consumers are apparently unaware of negative stereotypes about Indians and alcohol. "The campaign is Budweiser's most popular ever in Britain, raising brand awareness to an all-time high, prompting viewers to request photos of the main actor and boosting the popularity of the theme music. According to Peter Jackson, marketing director for the U.K. and Ireland, "In the U. K., there aren't any inappropriate or stereotypical images of Native Americans."

Nonetheless, Indian advocacy groups and advertising experts saw the ads as insensitive to the problem of alcoholism among Native Americans. Reacting to the uproar, the *Wall Street Journal* posed several telling questions: Should multinational companies be held to the same standards of ethics and taste abroad as they are at home? Does it make a difference if images that are offensive in one culture are benign in the market where the ads are shown? Allyson Stewart-Allen, director of International Marketing Partners, a London consulting firm, sums up the issue in this manner: "You should assume you have a multiethnic client base these days. We're in a global marketplace. Ads like those are totally naive and offensive." Ultimately, offensive ads shown in foreign countries filter back.

COLORIZING ADVERTISING:
A TWENTY-FIRST CENTURY IMPERATIVE

Images play a pivotal role in socializing those exposed to them. It should come as no surprise that some of the most potent and indelible images are those that have come to us by way of advertising in magazines, television, radio, newspapers, and other forms of mass communicating. Jean Kilbourne, researcher of sexist advertising, has speculated that we see or hear approximately two thousand advertising messages daily. Some estimates also have gone as high as sixteen thousand messages daily.

Advertising, which serves the purpose of introducing us to products, services, and ideas for trade and sale in the marketplace, also help individuals develop a self construct of who they are. Advertisements are, in fact, a deciding factor in helping us determine our places in our homes, our offices, our communities, and in society. We might say that the best ads are designed to hook consumers by reaching into their psyches and grabbing them where they live. Advertisements tell us who we're supposed to be and what we're supposed to value.

It seems that so long as people continue to be exposed to thousands of advertising images daily, advertising will remain an influential factor in helping people determine who they are, what they should be and what they should do. What are the ramifications of these images if they are distorted, negative, pejorative, condescending, patronizing, and offensive? What are the consequences if such portrayals are overtly stereotypical? What are the consequences if certain groups are omitted from advertising?

The images promulgated through characters of the likes of Aunt Jemima, the Frito Bandito, and Crazy Horse have had a devastating psychological effect on African Americans, Latinos, and Native Americans. Marketing campaigns like these that so skillfully targeted all consumers have become codependents and enablers in deflating the self-esteem and aspirations of people of color for decades. Can you imagine how difficult it must be to feel good about yourself when there are products on shelves that show blacks wanting to be white, that depict Asians eating rats, and that portray black children as gator bait, Latinos as bandits, and Native Americans as savages?

The advertising campaigns presented in this chapter also have had a detrimental effect on whites, who, because of their exposure to such demeaning portrayals, have cognitively processed these images as true reflections of reality. Over the years, stereotypes have laid the foundation for slavery, the Ku Klux Klan, segregation, Jim Crow laws, the principle of "separate but equal," Proposition 209, institutionalized racism, and, in so doing, have created a dichotomized, polarized, schizophrenic United States, an America that is anything but "united." Ann DuCille writes in *Skin Game*, "Despite the ease with which the pronoun 'we' has slipped from the lips of politicians and poets alike, the United States has never had an easy time living up to its professed plurality." Though stereotypes of people of color have existed in America for nearly four hundred years and, thus, prior to television and radio advertising, it is evident that advertising campaigns which play on long-standing, harmful stereotypes only exacerbate the situation.

To rectify this situation there must be more images presented of African Americans, Asians, Native Americans, and Latinos in advertising. The advertisements presented of multiethnic groups must be positive and sensitive. To accomplish this, it is imperative that more people of color become high-level managers within the advertising industry. More people of color must become entrepreneurs and start their own advertising agencies. And maybe once all of this is accomplished, the Aunt Jemimas, Frito Banditos, and Crazy Horses will be given a proper burial and never surface again.

REVIEW QUESTIONS

1. What is the effect of advertising that does not regularly present images of minority groups and which, when it does, portrays these groups in a negative light? Is advertising that uses stereotypical images simply "part of the fun" of entertainment? Or does the repetition of these stereotypes have a greater impact and actually work to reinforce racist sentiments?

2. Do you believe that advertisers should be able to use images to sell their products even if they reinforce stereotypes of certain groups? Or do you believe that advertisers have a responsibility to be sensitive to those who might be offended?

3. Are images such as these contextual and therefore culture-bound? Or should advertisers realize that we are in a global marketplace? Should companies like Ford and Anheuser-Busch be forced to change advertising in foreign countries even if the consumers will not be likely to perceive the racist subtleties behind their advertisements?

4. Kern-Foxworth's piece cites examples of popular images in advertising that use race as their primary focus. Can you think of other images that are used in advertising that play on gender or class stereotypes?

Notes

1. Fred McDonald, *Blacks and White TV* (Chicago: Nelson Hall, 1992).
2. Clarence Page, "Taking the Glamour out of Gang Life," *Chicago Tribune*, August 12, 1992, sec. 15.
3. "Las Vegas Spring Telephone Directory Cover Offends Residents; Incites Action," *Jet*, August 28, 1995, pp. 14–15.
4. Bob Schemeligian, "Sprint Apologizes for Cover," *Las Vegas Sun*, August 11, 1995.
5. Bob Schemeligian, "Action Planned against Sprint for Directory Cover," *Las Vegas Sun*, August 10, 1995.
6. Ibid.
7. Tara Parker-Pope, "British Budweiser Ads Rankle American Indians," *Wall Street Journal*, July 16, 1996, pp. B1, B5.
8. *Black Enterprise*, June 1997, p. 231.
9. *Michigan Chronicle*, November 26, 1996, p. 8A.
10. Sally Beatty, "Texaco Agency Has a Tough Task Ahead," *Wall Street Journal*, November 22, 1996, p. B8.
11. Sally Beatty, "Texaco's Effort to Repair Image Comes under Fire After First Ad," *Wall Street Journal*, November 27, 1996, p. B2.
12. Ibid.

8 / Affluent Class and Corporate Brass in the Make-Believe Media

MICHAEL PARENTI

Despite the widely publicized notion that just about everyone in the United States (except for a few millionaires and beggars) is "middle class," there are marked differences among us in income, status, education, and lifestyle. But class is not just a matter of these demographic differences. More important is the way class acts as a force of power and wealth. Thus, there are the rich and powerful, those who own and exercise a preponderate control over the command positions within corporations, banks, industries, communications systems, and the media. Class power permeates our economic, political, military, educational, and cultural institutions. The realities of class are omnipresent in our society, ingrained in our everyday experience, helping to shape the quality of our lives. Yet people are taught not to think in class terms. And references to class power are often dismissed as conspiracy theory or Marxist ideological mouthing.

Increasingly, attention is given in our media and public life to just about every subject one might imagine. Even racism and sexism, while insufficiently confronted, are at least recognized as bigotries, certainly more so today than in earlier generations. But *class* bigotry continues to be an unchallenged and unperceived form of prejudice. The realities of class power and class oppression remain largely a forbidden topic. The expressions of class bigotry in our literature and textbooks, in our institutions and daily lives, and in our films and television shows go unexamined. Class is the colossal reality right before our eyes that we Americans are trained not to see.

ESCAPING CLASS

If the make-believe media are "escapist," it is in large part because they have long downplayed or avoided altogether the harsh realities of racial, gender, and class oppression. For many decades, through the magic of the entertainment industry, racial oppression was transmogrified into a happy-go-lucky tap dance routine. Women's oppression was reduced to love problems or the difficulties that arose when women strayed from traditional roles and ventured into a man's world. The economic injustices of capitalism were dismissed as just a matter of "hard times." Instead of dramatizing the class dimensions of political power, the media gave us morality plays about the personal venalities of individual politicians. To quote one critic:

For the most part the movies continued to reiterate in the talkies of the 1930s the familiar, threadbare themes of the silent 1920s: that the rich, too, had their troubles, and were not to be envied; that a woman's life, however useful, acquired meaning only in romance; . . . that the ills of existence were mostly moral ills; that the cure for these ills lay in preserving an unquenchable optimism and a sense of good-neighborliness. The mores of Hollywood remained more or less the same in spite of the Depression.[1]

In the Frank Capra films of the '30s and '40s, America is a nation of small towns and modest but comfortable homes, inhabited by ordinary but sometimes heroic folks who try to set aright any greedy or snobbish individual. Capra's *It's a Wonderful Life* (1946), frequently replayed on television at Christmastime, gives us the character of George Bailey, who spends most of his life lending a helping hand to folks in his town. George makes a populist speech before the financial tycoons of the town. Think about the little people, he says, who built this community with their hard work. They don't have big sums of dough to shell out. The building and loan institution gives them a chance to own a home. It's the only alternative to living in one of the slums that the evil banker, Mr. Potter, owns. Potter, the "cruelest, richest man in town," knows it all too well and he wants to close the building and loan. But the other moneybags on the board are touched by George's plea and they vote Potter down, if you can believe it. In violation of all market imperatives, they decide to float the building and loan even though it's in the red (for having been too soft with people who were down on their luck). They then appoint George as its executive officer.

But the building and loan falls on hard times. Potter tightens the screws and denies George financial aid, telling him to get help from "the riff-raff you love so much." George wishes he was dead and for a short while, with the aid of his guardian angel, he gets his wish and sees what the community he loves would have been like if he hadn't been there: a tacky, tawdry, heartless, rundown town with honky-tonks and strip joints, dominated completely by Potter. George realizes that one person can make a difference. In the final scene, the hometown folks come through for George. The same crowd that previously had been besieging the building and loan to get their money out now congregate spontaneously in George's living room to sing Christmas carols and empty their pockets of thousands of dollars (where did they get all that money?) in order to bail out George and save the building and loan, so grateful are they for all he has done.

It's a Wonderful Life tells us that there are bad greedy business people like Potter, the monopolist banker, who operate on the imperative of "accumulate, accumulate, accumulate," and good business people like George Bailey who are the purveyors of good works and faith and want what is best for ordinary folks. It is vintage Capra, a fairy tale.

In Capra's *Mr. Smith Goes to Washington* (1939), the decent, honest senator refuses to play ball with cynical, corrupt malefactors. Good meets evil but evil is still personal and never systemic. "The evil of [Capra's] corrupt characters never rubbed off on the institutions they controlled or the social and economic system that shaped their behavior and allowed them to succeed."[2] Probably the most influential director of his time, Capra created the kind of mythical, celluloid America that Ronald Reagan was still selling us in the 1980s.

To gladden the troubled spirits of people gripped in the Great Depression, Hollywood in the '30s also created Shirley Temple, the adorable song-and-dance imp. In *Bright Eyes, Curly Top, Dimples,* and *Poor Little Rich Girl,* Shirley plays the loveable little child who heals other people's lives. She teaches us not to hate the rich; they are just grumpy old people whom nobody loves. She softens their hearts and transforms them into warm, caring folks. Shirley also helps friendless servants, blacks, and hoboes. She dispenses love and affection to all who need her. Happiness is a matter of having the right attitude. The Depression is just a silly thing that should not be taken seriously. Anyone can be an old sourpuss about malnutrition and unemployment, but under Shirley's spell we learn to sing away our poverty and dance away our despair.[3]

The Academy Award–winning *The Best Years of Our Lives* (1946) tells us that small-town America is the best place to be. The affluent bank officer, a returning veteran, pals around with two other veterans, ordinary working guys, one of whom gets romantically involved with the banker's daughter. Early in the film, the three men drive past the fire station, the diner, and the ballpark, places which they supposedly share in common: one town, one class of people. The women are maternal and caring, except for one wife with loose morals, who refused to be domesticated and is not worthy of audience sympathy, as the film makes clear.[4]

Films about small-town America depict a society taken straight from a Normal Rockwell painting. Class is not a factor of life because everyone is middle-class. Ethnicity is not a factor because everyone is a white Anglo-Saxon Protestant, except perhaps for the black maid and the Latino delivery boy. Sexism is not an issue because women know their place.

Forty years after *The Best Years of Our Lives* not all that much had changed. *Down and Out in Beverly Hills* (1986) gives us a class view that fits the Reaganite mythology. It tells us that the homeless "choose" street poverty as a preferred lifestyle. A street person works his way into a nouveau-riche household, manipulates all the family members, and steals the hearts of the rich man's wife, daughter, and maid. Needless to say, he prefers this rip-off life to honest hard work, even refusing a management job in the rich man's factory. In somewhat similar fashion, an African-American homeless friend of his refuses a sandwich offered in a restaurant, preferring to steal some food from the same restaurant. The film lets us know that you just can't be nice to these lowlifes. It also tells us that the rich are not to be envied for they are bored and unhappy. In search of diversion, the rich man goes slumming with the bum and has the time of his life, partying with the indigents, learning to beg and eat garbage, "It was great!" he says. *Down and Out in Beverly Hills* transforms the desperate plight of the homeless into a diverting escapade. It panders to class prejudices by portraying the poor as little more than lazy predators.

TRAUMA IN SOAPVILLE

Soon after conquering America, television gave us the soap opera, a dramatic form carried over from daytime radio. Relatively inexpensive to produce, yet commanding large audiences and high advertising revenues, the afternoon soaps provide the networks with more profits than does prime-time television. Here is a make-believe society devoid of politico-economic oppression, inhabited mostly by white, economically well-off, professionals (lawyers, doctors, architects, and business executives and their families) who spend their waking hours wrestling with a never-ending succession of personal crises. Relatively few Latinos, African Americans, and Asians and even fewer blue-collar workers appear as principals.[5] Soap characters have little to say about the struggles of working people, the injustice of the tax system, the price-gouging of consumers, the destruction of neighborhoods, the impossible cost of housing and rents due to realty speculation and landlord greed, the undemocratic powers of corporations, and the fast-buck desecration of our environment—dramatic issues that affect us directly and personally.

In Soapville there are seldom any class differences and certainly no class conflict. All behavior is seen as morally motivated. The woman from the wrong side of town who schemes and lies to get a man and the man who schemes and lies to get a job are seen simply as evil people.

The afflictions of the elderly are another neglected theme. Emphasis is on relatively youthful persons, those considered to be at the top of the hill, not over it. Occasionally an attractively greying older individual or couple who are in perfect health and financially secure appears as part of the family montage. But the special travails of the aged rarely figure significantly.[6]

Motherhood is lauded, yet children are in scarce supply in Soapville. Pregnancies are numerous but so are miscarriages and stillbirths; however, abortions are unheard of. The little ones who survive childbirth often do so with their paternity in question. They are kidnapped and fought over in custody battles. But once the controversy is resolved, they usually are conveniently killed in accidents, die of rare diseases, or just drop out of sight. In this way, the adult characters are less limited in the number of times they might marry, divorce, switch partners, have mental breakdowns, disappear, engage in money schemes, and plot murder. The fortunate few kids who escape all dangers grow up at a supernatural rate, are shipped off to school, and are only occasionally referred to in adult conversation. In no time, they suddenly reappear almost full-grown to become a source of family conflict and to start romances of their own.[7]

The few social problems that make their way into soap scripts, such as alcoholism, drug addiction, unemployment, and crime, are reduced to purely personal phenomena. People are victimized by aberrant mishaps or by other ill-willed people and never by socioeconomic and political injustices. In time, virtuous individuals rectify the situation and sometimes even reform evildoers.

Reality gives us millions of isolated, lonely people living in congested, automobile-dominated, crime-ridden urban sprawls. Soapville gives us a secure, comfortable, small-town community that resembles an extended family, filled with concerned people who drop by to chat and who give themselves totally to each other's troubled affairs, defending their friends from treacherous interlopers.

Reality gives us overworked, sleep-starved, single mothers who spend long hours toiling at underpaid jobs, raising children, and doing household chores while worrying about how they are going to make ends meet. The soaps give us mostly well-heeled, childless women—wives and lovers—who sometimes have careers of their own but who in any case, seldom worry about grocery bills, tuition costs, mortgage payments, and old-age retirement. Their waking hours, like those of their men, are consumed by endless rounds of romance, seduction, and interpersonal conspiracies. These experiences are acted out in comfortable upper-middle-class living rooms, bedrooms, kitchens, or executive offices by beautifully groomed people, who, even if just lounging about the house, look as if they are prepared for a photo session with a fashion magazine.

But one should not think that life is easy in Soapville. It is a series of perpetual catastrophes. Characters are forever contracting fatal illnesses; dying in accidents; attempting and sometimes succeeding at suicides; being blackmailed, murdered, raped, or kidnapped; going insane; suffering amnesia; developing split personalities; falling victim to nefarious financial schemes; and—judging from the accidental pregnancy rate—engaging in sexual encounters without the slightest knowledge of modern birth control techniques. Here are some examples covering only one week (May 22–26, 1989):

On *Another World,* Cass accuses Nicole of killing Jason; Gwen constantly reminds Evan that Rachel killed his mother; Evan admits to Rachel that he wanted to get revenge against her, but has changed his mind; after walking out on Vicki, Jamie decided to have blood tests to see if he is Steven's father.

On *Guiding Light,* Sonni is arrested on kidnapping charges; Reva realizes that Sonni is innocent of the charge; Josh is devastated when the police fish Rose's body out of the lake; Roger and Alan fight over a gun in the church organ loft during Phillip's wedding ceremony; Alan gets the drop on Roger then threatens to blow up the church if Roger doesn't reveal his true identity to everyone; Alan shoots Roger when he tries to get rid of the bomb; just as Phillip is about to say "I do," he is shot by a stray bullet; and, of course, Meredith and Rick are still at odds because she is carrying Phillip's baby.

On *Days of Our Lives,* Tom urges Robin to tell Mike that Mike is the father of her infant son; Marcus is upset that he can find no record of his own birth; Roman regains consciousness and tells Abe that he is sure he was shot by Cal;

Adam kisses Kimberly, who tells him she loves Shane; Alfred kidnaps Shane and admits sending threatening letters to Kimberly to get her and Shane to leave town.[8]

Just ordinary moments in the lives of ordinary people.

The soaps teach us that individuals cannot join together to work toward a harmonious, collective solution of difficulties. Indeed, the message is that interpersonal contact *causes* rather than solves difficulties. The picture is of a bourgeois society composed of clashing, throbbing egos, devoid of common social and political goals, caught up in an interminable succession of treacheries, seductions, crimes, and monumental mishaps.

On the rare occasions when explicitly political material is worked into the script, it is not likely to be very edifying. Thus in 1983 during the Reagan era, one story line on *General Hospital* involved a scientist, Dr. Putnam, whose education was financed by the "Party," a secret sinister political organization. He was under the dictatorial control of a "Party" agent who herself was under the command of "Comrade Grigory." This comrade, it turns out, was part of a mysterious international spy ring in the service of a foreign power. Facing repeated commands from Party agents such as: "The Party demands you do this!" Dr. Putnam had no choice but to obey. He engaged in acts of espionage and murder on behalf of his superiors, in a script that was little more than an anticommunist caricature.[9]

While issues regarding class power remain untouched, the 1980s did see the incorporation of various contemporary cultural themes into soap scripts—in that superficial co-optive way designed to contain rather than activate an issue. Thus, without ever actually challenging existing social arrangements, the soaps can come away seeming very relevant by touching upon subjects such as gender roles, rape, incest, spouse abuse, homosexuality, and AIDS. But, again these things are usually presented as personal problems to be tackled by personal means.

Sometimes these cultural issues are accorded broader treatment. In 1988, *All My Children* was the first soap opera to feature a lesbian as a major character and the first to have the show's characters grapple—as a community—with prejudice against homosexuals. This same soap also portrayed a community effort to educate people about AIDS and to protect an AIDS victim, in this case a working-class single mother, from vigilante harassment.[10]

These exceptions aside, the political text of the soaps has not changed much in forty years. "The nuclear family, motherhood, heterosexual monogamy, and capitalism are permanent, unquestioned norms. Abortion is still forbidden. Characters are either 'good' or 'bad' from birth, and their moral condition has no relation to their class of work."[11]

THE RISE OF THE "OIL OPERAS"

During the early 1980s, a novel variation of the soap opera emerged, geared to prime-time evening viewers instead of the afternoon audience, appearing weekly instead of daily. Shows like *Dallas, Dynasty, Falcon Crest,* and *Flamingo Road* are set in the South or West and focus on the big business and domestic struggles of corporate patriarchal families. The leading characters are business moguls, usually oil barons, who manifest a single-minded dedication to lust, wealth, and power. Whether pursuing money or women, they are ruthlessly self-serving, betraying little need for companionship and affection. They plot and scheme in their palatial homes, private planes, executive suites, and swank resorts, tended to by small armies of disciplined and devoted servants.

There are few if any virtuous lead characters. One usually must choose between "bad guys" and "worse guys." Occasionally, a somewhat less venal character might agonize for a moment, as when Bobby Ewing of *Dallas* gets drunk and groans: "There must be a way to run Ewing Oil without lying and cheating." He is quickly proven wrong by his older brother, the notorious J.R.[12] The oil operas pretty much do away with questions of social conscience. There are no moral values as such, only instrumental values which either work or don't work in advancing one to still greater heights of wealth and corporate power. Bribery, blackmail, fraud, corruption—no tactic is too reprehensible if it works.

Occasionally, a female power monger like Alexis in *Dynasty* might fight her way into this man's world of high finance—thus, letting us know that, given the chance, a woman can be as determinedly rotten as any man. More often, however, women are just one of the properties that the moguls fight over and acquire. Although set in places like Dallas and Denver, the oil operas have few Latinos, blacks, or working-class whites. When such characters do appear, they have no interests apart from the rich employers to whom they're bound.

The oil operas are not intended to incite resentment against the rich. If anything, they invite the audience to enter vicariously into a lavish world. In the absence of any specific statements to the contrary, these soaps promote implicit acceptance and even enjoyment of the wild and wicked doings of the rich and powerful, those who reduce sex, family, land, career, and most other things to property acquisitions.

None of these tycoons do any productive work; they are too busy skimming the cream. "This is a world where the tables and floors are always cleaned, the food is always cooked, the mansions are always built and maintained in just the right way—and the oil is pumped out of the ground at a steady rate. All taken completely for granted."[13] Missing from the picture are the working people who do the work that enables the oil barons to live the way they do.

BENIGN BOSSES AND BAD BOSSES

For decades, the make-believe media have represented the socioeconomic power of our society as being in good hands. With some exceptions, the Establishment figures who preside over the businesses and other institutions come across as dedicated, fair-minded, and deserving of our trust, rarely racist or sexist, and not apt to pursue policies that hurt the poor and the powerless while favoring the rich and powerful.

Of course, bad apples come along occasionally, those who play ruthlessly and violate the established rules. In the case of the oil operas, as just noted, such venal tycoons are elevated to a kind of amoral hero status. In most instances these undesirables are set straight by more scrupulous individuals or are likely to meet a deservedly unfortunate end. Whatever the outcome, their evil is seen as being personal to them rather than representative of the business system and other institutions from which they draw their power.

Then there are the *good* business people, who sometimes are indifferent to other people's troubles only because they are so preoccupied with their own business affairs. Once they are properly apprised of the problem, they are "capable of legendary generosity and humanity."[14] A rare species in real life, these selfless types have been around for quite a while in the make-believe media. In *The Devil and Miss Jones* (1940), for instance, a crusty mogul poses as a clerk in his own department store in order to ferret out union organizers. However, he is soon won over to his employees' cause and becomes a caring, sharing kind of boss.

Equally unlikely is Frank Capra's *Mr. Deeds Goes to Town* (1936). Longfellow Deeds inherits $20 million and decides to give it all away to needy people. He comes across as an admirable, humane person, one of the loveable, nurturing rich. In *Million Dollar Baby* (1941) a wealthy lady takes a fancy to a young working woman and gives her a million dollars. The sudden acquisition of so much money causes strains between the young heroine and her penniless but proud boyfriend (Ronald Reagan). In the final scene, she solves everything by dashing about town, tossing away her entire fortune to passersby, who happily grab at the fluttering dollars. The message: wealth is best left to the wealthy; not only does money fail to guarantee happiness, it seems to cause unhappiness when placed in the hands of ordinary folks; no use resenting the rich; the best things in life are free.

Money is given away more sedately and systematically in *The Millionaire,* a television series that ran through much of the 1950s (updated and redone in 1978 as a made-for-TV movie). Through a trusted assistant, a never-seen millionaire hands out million-dollar cashier's checks to people of modest means. The acquisition of such funds changes the lives of the characters, sometimes in ironic ways, since they often don't know how to make the best of their bounty.

A wealthy elderly lady in *Christmas Eve* (1986) hands out money to the poor with the assistance of her chauffeur. As proof of her eccentricity she gives cash and does not even bother to get receipts for tax deductions. At one point she is arrested for interfering with a police round-up of street people. When her embarrassed son ("It's in all the newspapers") comes to bail her out, she won't go unless all her poor friends go, so he has to bail out all of them. She also refuses to go along with her high-powered son who wants to swing a lucrative business deal involving a new housing complex. No, she says, we won't build a new complex until we have a place for the poor people living there now. "That's the way your father did it"—which makes one wonder how father managed to get so rich investing in real estate. Stories about generous millionaires almost never focus on the less-than-generous ways they or their families accumulated and sustained their fortunes.

The best thing for workers is to cooperate fully with a benign management so that together they might ward off foreign competitors. Such is the message in *Gung Ho* (1986), an otherwise lightweight movie about a Japanese company that reopens a shuttered auto plant in the United States. The conflict between labor and management turns out to be only a *cultural* one. The workers don't take their morning exercises seriously the way Japanese workers do. Worse still, they goof around on the assembly line. Finally, when it becomes a matter of produce or perish, they learn to work hard as a compliant team under management's guidance, performing their tasks and even their exercises with a rigorous martial-arts dedication. The plant stays open; no unions are in sight; no mention is made of the profits that go to the owners; workers and bosses hug each other; everyone is happy.

The inventive, independent entrepreneur who tilts against corporate giants is the theme of *Tucker: The Man and His Dream* (1988), directed by Francis Ford Coppola. Far superior to the usual Hollywood fare, this film draws from the real-life story of the Michigan small businessman who dreamed of building the car of the future in the 1940s with safety and per-formance features that were reluctantly adopted decades later by the same giant automakers who originally resisted him. Seeing Tucker as a threat to their market, the automotive cartel and its political allies destroy him. His steel supplies are cut off; he is placed under surveillance by the FBI, attacked by a Michigan senator and by an unsympathetic business-owned press, and hit with trumped-up charges by the Securities and Exchange Commission. During the course of events, Tucker gets in a few telling lines, as when he notes that the big guys "don't give a damn about people; all they care about is profits. They're guilty of criminal negligence."

But like other promising films, *Tucker* goes only so far. Thus, Tucker's enemies—Ford, General Motors, and Chrysler—are never mentioned by name, being evasively referred to only as "the Big Three" or "Detroit."[15] (Presumably, the "Big Three" are identifiable to most people, though one young viewer with whom I attended this movie wondered if Toyota was included among them.) Nor do the corporate conspirators arrayed against Tucker ever appear on the screen to tell us exactly why their oligopolistic interests require that he be crushed.

In a final courtroom speech, Tucker irrelevantly blames his troubles on a red-tape society created by "bureaucrats." Today Benjamin Franklin would need a permit to fly his kite, he quips. In fact, the government bureaucrats who do appear in the film helpfully provide Tucker with a large surplus war plant for his auto-building—at no cost and with a minimum of red tape.

Tucker also irrelevantly blames his troubles on the fact that "we" have a self-inflated view of ourselves as a nation because "we" invented the atomic bomb and are now resting on our laurels. He says not a word about the business oligopoly that is actually destroying him. Instead, we get a preachment on the need to return to the purer private enterprise system of the small entrepreneur, free of irksome government regulations. No right-wing libertarian could ask for more.

Special attention should be given to Oliver Stone's *Wall Street* (1987). Though a good film, it illustrates better than most "antibusiness" movies the limits of a liberal critique. The main character, inside trader and cut-throat corporate raider Gordon Gekko (Michael Douglas) represents *bad* Wall Street. In Gekko's world, no room exists for fair play or friendship; as he tells young Bud, a would-be protégé: "If you want a friend, buy a dog." Leading a takeover fight at a stockholders meeting, he declares: "Greed is good, greed is right. Greed works." Turning to Bud, Gekko delivers one of the rarest commentaries one is likely to hear on the big screen:

> Capitalism at its finest. The richest one percent of the country owns half our country's wealth, five trillion dollars. One-third of that comes from hard work; two-thirds from inheritance, interest on interest accumulating—and from what I do: stock and real-estate speculation. It's bullshit: You got 90 percent of the American public out there with little or no net worth. I create nothing. I *own*. We make the rules, pal. The news, war, peace, famine, upheaval, the price of a paper clip—we pick that rabbit out of the hat while everybody sits out there wondering how the hell we did it. You're not naïve enough to think we're living in a democracy, are you, Buddy? It's the free market and you're part of it.

But closer scrutiny reveals that this is not a Marxist film. Counterposed to Gekko's *bad* Wall Street is *good* Wall Street, embodied in Lou, the crusty old broker, one of those who create the "one-third" of investor wealth that supposedly "comes from hard work." Lou puts a fatherly arm around Bud's shoulder and warns him against playing fast with illegal insider information:

> There are no shortcuts, son. Quick-buck artists come and go with every bull market. The steady players make it through the bear markets. You're part of something here, Bud. The money you make for people creates science and research jobs. Don't sell that out.

The film accepts the capitalist mythology that Wall Street's money is "created" by the investors and speculators who gamble with it, rather than by those who actually work at the "science and research jobs" and other occupations. We are being asked to believe that *good* Wall Street serves the nation, not itself. Bad guys like Gekko are at fault, not the system that produced them.

In the end, the Securities and Exchange Commission steps in and arrests Bud for insider trading and nabs the evil Gekko. Crime does not pay, not even on Wall Street, at least not if it's a crime against other financial interests. This is Gekko's sin: he is bilking other investors. While the film leaves us with the impression that the SEC protects the public interest, it really protects the corporate speculators from each other—on occasion.

The wicked businessman is not an unfamiliar character in the make-believe media. George Gerbner, dean of the Annenberg School of Communications at the University of Pennsylvania, reports that "good" business characters in prime-time television outnumber the "bad" ones by two to one. In contrast, the ratio for doctors was sixteen to one and for police twelve to one.[16] So while the image of business people is more positive than negative, it is less positive than other establishment professions. Perhaps this is a concession to popular sentiment, specifically the resentment felt toward the tycoons who treat the productive forces of society as just so many gaming pieces in the contest for self-enrichment.

To the extent it exists, the media critique of the business world goes only so far. Consider the classic *Citizen Kane* (1941), which was based on the life of press mogul William Randolph Hearst. The film's twenty-six-year-old star, director, and coauthor Orson Welles produced a movie that was exceptional more for its dramatic composition, narrative structure, and camera techniques than for its politics. In fact, the film's political theme was the usual Hollywood fare: power corrupts and money does not bring happiness.[17]

At its best, the mainstream entertainment industry tiptoes up toward the truth but never quite embraces it. From *Citizen Kane* to *Wall Street*, the focus is on the ruthlessness of individual moneybags. Their wrongful ways are not born of the system in which they operate but are personal to them. "If television is unkind to businessmen," notes Gitlin, who could also be describing Hollywood, "it is scarcely unkind to the values of a business civilization. Capitalism and the consumer society come out largely uncontested."[18]

While the media teach us that money does not bring happiness and often makes us miserable, we should remind ourselves that in real life the rich live quite well. Very few of them voluntarily give up their fortunes so that they might pursue the deeper satisfactions of putting in a ten-hour day driving a taxi or plucking chickens in a poultry plant. One need only recall the candid remark made in 1984 by Barbara Bush, wife of then–Vice President George Bush, that she and her husband were not ashamed of being rich; they enjoyed their wealth.

At the very least, even if money does not guarantee happiness, it certainly makes life much easier; it makes it easier to deal with adversities or to escape altogether the many kinds of unhappinesses caused by not having enough money for one's needs. Money creates the best possible life chances in a capitalist society, providing privileged opportunities for professional success and for comfortable living in spacious homes; the best schooling; diverse and advantageous social contacts; superior access to political careers, power, and favored treatment by government and the law; greater opportunities for travel, leisure, and recreation; the finest health and therapeutic care; quality retirement conditions; and a host of other services that are not readily accessible to those of lesser means and not available at all to the poorest among us.

Money can raise persons of limited talent and inferior intelligence to remarkable heights. As the career of Vice President Dan Quayle demonstrates, money can magically transform the mediocre into the meteoric. When portraying the luxurious world of the rich, the make-believe media say little about all this. Instead, we are fed images of generous millionaires, amorous playboys, embattled tycoons, and bored heiresses.

REVIEW QUESTIONS

1. In your opinion, should films which offer an unrealistic portrayal of the rich be viewed as a sort of propaganda, works that justify a capitalistic system? Perhaps these films should be viewed purely in terms of their entertainment value. After all, the public may wish to escape and to not be reminded of the everyday struggles of working and of the injustices of the tax system. So what's the big deal?

2. Parenti suggests most movies and television portray not only class relations unrealistically, but familial relations as well. Adult characters in soap operas, for example, are not limited by the burdens of parenting and the concerns of the elderly are seldom addressed. What effect might this have on society and on politics?

3. Can the mainstream entertainment industry be criticized for not quite embracing reality?

Notes

1. P. H. Melling, "The Mind of the Mob: Hollywood and Popular Culture in the 1930s," in *Cinema, Politics and Society in America,* eds. Philip Davies and Brian Neve (New York: St. Martin's Press, 1981), p. 24.

2. Leonard Quart, "Frank Capra and the Popular Front," in *American Media and Mass Culture,* ed. Donald Lazere (Berkeley: University of California Press, 1987), pp. 178–79.

3. Charles Eckert, "Shirley Temple and the House of Rockefeller," in Lazere, *American Media,* pp. 172, 177.

4. Ralph Willett, "The Nation in Crisis: Hollywood's Response to the 1940s," in Davies and Neve (eds.), *Cinema, Politics, and Society,* pp. 72–73.

5. Bradley Greenberg, et. al., "The Soaps: What's On and Who Cares?" *Journal of Broadcasting* 26 (Spring 1982): pp. 519–535.

6. Michael Intintoli, *Taking Soaps Seriously* (New York: Praeger, 1986).

7. Rose Rubin Rivera, "The World of Afternoon Soap Operas," *World Magazine,* February 17, 1983, pp. 12–13.

8. Adapted from Nancy Reichardt's weekly "Soap" synopis, *Washington Post,* May 28, 1989.

9. Fred Blair, "Soap Watchers Beware," *Daily World,* October 8, 1983.

10. Elayne Rapping, "Soap Operas Lead the Way as Pop Culture Tackles AIDs," *Guardian,* April 6, 1988, p. 17.

11. Elayne Rapping, "Looking Inside Soap Operas' Bubbles," *Guardian,* August 22, 1984, p. 21.

12. Elayne Rapping, "Dallas: Capitalism's Heroes," *Guardian,* February 11, 1981.

13. Paul Wilcox, "Three Jeers for the Ruling Class," *Workers World,* February 6, 1981.

14. Les Brown, *Television: The Business behind the Box* (New York: Harcourt, Brace, Jovanovich, 1971), p. 309.

15. Ford is mentioned once in a neutral context.

16. Gerbner's report is referred to in Todd Gitlin, *Inside Prime Time* (New York: Pantheon, 1983), p. 268.

17. Terry Christensen, *Reel Politics* (New York: Basil Blackwell, 1987), p. 58.

18. Gitlin, *Inside Prime Time*, p. 59.

9 / There He Is, Miss America: Howard Stern's Deconstruction of Media Images

NICK GILLESPIE

For reasons that are clear—if not at all convincing—the media mostly loathe Howard Stern, the New York–based radio and TV personality who just happens to be the country's greatest living satirist. Stern is, of course, hugely popular with wide segments of the American people: His daily drive-time radio show airs in about two dozen markets across the country and usually captures top or near-top ratings; his nightly show on cable's E! network is among that channel's most popular features; his first book, *Private Parts* (1993), was a chart-topper and his second, *Miss America,* is the fastest-selling title in its publisher's history; his *Rotten New Year's Eve,* aired on December 31, 1993, remains the highest-grossing non-sports event in pay-per-view history; the movie version of *Private Parts* made over $40 million in the United States during its 1997 theatrical run.

But critics—whose moralistic pronouncements are typically not burdened by familiarity with Stern's broadcast or written work—take a quick peek at the man and his shtick and cluck their tongues, convinced that here is just one more example of *Vulgarity über Alles.*[1] "Because he continues to embrace the qualities of a child splashing in sewage, Stern still belongs among those icons of depravity who make their living pandering to humanity's basest instincts," proclaims Al Martinez of the *Los Angeles Times,* who dubs Stern the "king of excrement." Stern's popularity, Martinez cryptically warns, "ought to tell us something about ourselves in an age that fawns over what it loves and blows up what it hates."[2] For Alan Ehrenhalt, the executive editor of *Governing* magazine, Stern is the terminus of a debased economic system that dares give people choice. Writing in the *New York Times,* Ehrenhalt invokes Stern as the horror child of laissez-faire economics: "The tyranny of the market . . . has destroyed the loyalty of corporations to their communities; customers to their neighborhood merchants; athletes to their local teams; teams to their cities. The market has given us Howard Stern."[3] "Stern is no satirist, a latter-day Jonathan Swift making 'a modest proposal,'" contends ex-Reagan administration staffer Linda Chavez in *USA Today.* "He incites nastiness, crudity, and effrontery . . . Stern has made millions with this trash. . . . [M]aybe [we] can shame the media executives who give Stern a platform." Echoing the *Times*'s Martinez, Chavez asks, "What does it say about the state of our popular culture that radio shock-jock

Howard Stern can replace Colin Powell as the best-selling author in America?"[4]

Short answer: It means things are pretty damn swell.

Contrary to Chavez, Stern is indeed a latter-day Jonathan Swift—and not just because he is nasty, crude, and scatological (go read *Gulliver's Travels* some time). There is a quasi-political message to be gleaned from Stern's inspired rants and ramblings, one that is particularly relevant to a media-saturated, market-based society. In the tradition of folks such as Mark Twain and Lenny Bruce, Stern's search-and-destroy hijinks puncture the pretensions of all manner of fakes and phonies.[5] He relentlessly and systematically debunks the self-congratulatory fictions we tell about ourselves. He is particularly brilliant at deconstructing the pat, clichéd narratives that actors, politicians, and other public figures spin to their own advantage. In an age of overweening celebrity, that alone should make him a national treasure.

No wonder, then, that the media dislike him. They crave good "stories"—tight little tales that assume predictable, easily recognized shapes and reinforce already-held notions. But in this sense, Stern is resolutely antistory, reveling in the mismatch between perception and reality, between what we say and what we do. He delights in pointing out just how large that gap often is. (That's also one of the reasons why he is such a great interviewer of celebrities—he gets them to step out of their well-rehearsed raps.) Stern's popularity is an indication that many people maintain a healthy skepticism toward the machinations of hucksters of all stripes.

And it's worth pointing out that despite his open obsession with strippers, lesbians, and sexual fantasies, such musings are a minor part of his act. Stern is, in fact, a moralist whose teachings could hardly be more traditional. The secret of life, he wrote in *Private Parts,* is simple: "You wake up in the morning. You eat a little breakfast, maybe read the newspaper. If you're lucky enough, you're married. You yell at your wife, you make up with your wife. If your testicles feel all right, you bang your wife. You watch a video you rented or maybe you go out to the movies. . . . That's life. If you have kids, you live with the kids. You don't move out on your wife. . . . That's the secret of life."[6] Indeed, what drives him insane is the degree to which people get let off the moral hook.

As his superb *Miss America* (1995) makes abundantly clear, Stern goes about his business with a child's sense of discovery, outrage, and insistence. Consider his comments on the Kennedy family in a chapter titled "The Fruit Doesn't Fall Far from the Scumbag." "The Kennedy men bother me enough," writes Stern, "but the idolization of the Kennedy women makes me berserk. People always get pissed off when I blast the Kennedy women, but they should thank me for the hypocrisies that I point out.

"Let's start with Rose Kennedy: What kind of role model is that? Here's a woman who buried her head in the sand and sat idly by while her husband fucked every Hollywood bimbo on two feet. The whoremeister General Joe

Kennedy would even bring home Hollywood starlets to sit at the dining-room table with the whole family while Rose Kennedy kept her stupid mouth shut. . . . [T]his woman should be ashamed of herself. No wonder her sons grew up and couldn't keep it in their pants. Just remember: The fruit doesn't fall far from the scumbag."[7]

In "An Open Letter to All the Third Generation Kennedys (Except for my friend, Arnold Schwarzenegger)," Stern adds, "You don't know what it's like to grow up in the real world, to actually have to work for a living. . . . My grandfather wasn't a criminal who passed down his money to a series of leeches who are so nonproductive that they've just about pissed away the family fortune. . . . My uncle never drowned a poor young woman and got away with it. My aunt never married an old Greek just so she could raid his coffers. My uncles never gang-banged Marilyn Monroe."[8] This is powerful, outrageous, irreverent stuff—all the more so because it is essentially (if not quite literally) true.

While Stern might have the energy level of a child, however, it's wrong to think that he is an unsophisticated observer. The chapter in *Miss America* detailing Stern's clandestine meeting with Michael Jackson demonstrates that the "shock jock" possesses a pretty sharp mind. In 1994, after Jackson had settled a child-molestation charge out of court and married Lisa Marie Presley, his agent contacted Stern. In a meeting at Dolly Parton's Manhattan apartment, Jackson's agent spun out a scenario in which Stern, who had mercilessly lampooned Jackson for years, would champion the singer and lead a "spontaneous" demonstration in the "streets" supporting Jackson.

As the agent unveiled the absurd plan, Stern kept sneaking peeks at Jackson, who sat silently in the room, his face slathered with thick white makeup, his nose covered in dirty, unraveling surgical tape. Stern paints a portrait of a literally dissolving image: "It is getting hot and every few minutes Michael is wiping his face . . . and now there are big black smudge marks running all over it. . . . [His agent] keeps talking like Michael is normal. . . . I want to stand up and call 911: Come quick, we've got a melting Michael Jackson on Dolly Parton's chair. Over!"[9]

Stern, of course, turned down the offer to be part of Jackson's public relations rehab team. And his critique of Diane Sawyer, who later aired a puff piece interview with Jackson and Lisa Marie, is nothing short of devastating. Sawyer, he says, is "just Sally Jesse Raphael with better skin and hair." Her interview was "candy-cane journalism."[10]

"The interview was pathetic," writes Stern. "She did everything but beg the audience to take to the streets for MJ. . . . And then I realized that the son of a bitch even got the masses into the streets for him. Of course, he had to pay them, but take a look at that stupid movie trailer that . . . ran during the show. The streets are lined with weeping fans. They're holding up signs saying KING OF POP. And here comes Michael, like a conquering monarch. He's got the gay militia outfit on, with the hockey shinguards, and he marches into town, surrounded by troops, waving, blowing kisses. The camera is pulled back so you can't see the melting face. It's a perfect world."

But even as "everybody falls into line," Stern notes that "Michael's record sales go into the toilet. Why? Well, partly it's just that the music sucks, and partly it's the nasty smell of those charges, charges that linger in the public's mind because there are questions that were never answered."[11]

Even Stern's most seemingly juvenile antics reveal a contempt for glossy, prefabricated images. For instance, one of the most popular—and pillo-ried—parts of Stern's radio program involves his sending his crony "Stuttering John" out to interview celebrities. As he did in *Private Parts,* Stern devotes a chapter to John's misadventures in *Miss America.* "To me," writes Stern, "John has the scariest job imaginable. He has to approach celebrities and, armed only with a microphone and a list of cleverly engi-neered questions that we write, verbally terrorize them into revealing their true essence to the world. . . . Morton Downey Jr. overturned a table and threw John to the floor. . . . Eric Bogosian grabbed him and slammed his head up against a wall. . . . Lou Reed put his hands around John's neck, try-ing to strangle him. . . . Raquel Welch whacked him right in the nose" after he asked her, "Are they drooping yet?"[12]

What is brilliant about the bit is that it catches off guard celebrities who thrive on presenting a seamless image to the public—it is guerilla theater at its best. The results can be simultaneously tactless, hilarious, and subversive, as when John showed up at a fund-raiser for pediatric AIDS put together by a group of "supermodels" going by the vainglorious name of DISHES (Determined, Involved Supermodels Helping to End Suffering). In the mid-dle of a speech by Cindy Crawford, John interrupted with the question, "Hey, Cindy, do models take vomiting lessons?"[13] Such a query disrupts equally the sanctimony of the event and the glossy image of models, whose figures and faces belie widespread eating disorders among their ranks.

In the same vein, Stern devotes a chapter to "the unleashing of the mad phone stalkers," fans of his program who harass other radio and TV pro-grams with fake calls. Highlights include calls to the *Today* show with Ross Perot as a guest ("Mr. Perot," queried the caller, "Have you ever had the desire to mindmeld with Howard Stern's penis?"), to CNN's *Sonya Live* during the World Trade Center bombing (posing as a worker trapped in the building, a caller attributed the explosion to one of Stern's farts), to local Oklahoma TV in the wake of the Oklahoma City bombing (impersonating Rep. Frank Lucas, a caller told viewers that the suspects were Islamic men and "one of them was believed to be Howard Stern"). "I'm of the opinion," writes Stern, "that disaster calls actually play a worthwhile function. They point out what idiots run our media." "What's amazing" he continues, "is that these genius phone artists can go right on the air . . . and no one even bothers to check them out."[14]

The ultimate coup came when a caller got through to Peter Jennings of ABC News during the conclusion of O.J. Simpson's Bronco chase. While Simpson's truck was parked outside his Brentwood home, the caller got on by posing as one of Simpson's neighbors. The caller, as Stern tells it, "slipped into a thick black dialect that made Kingfish seem like a Rhodes scholar," complete with observations along the lines of "Oh, my Lord, this is quite tenses" and "Now lookee here, [O.J.] look very upset. I don' know what gon' be doin'." While such shenanigans are in undeniably bad taste, Stern correctly points out, as with Stuttering John's questions, that the media get what they deserve: "If Jennings wasn't a wooden Indian, he would have realized that this guy is a fake. First of all, his dialect was obviously phony. Second, a shucking and jiving black man is obviously not O.J.'s neighbor. All Jennings could see was his exclusive!"[15]

Stern's account of his abortive 1994 run for governor of New York on the Libertarian Party ticket similarly illustrates his penchant for discombobulating standard procedure. In *Miss America*, he recounts how he came clean to the electorate at the press conference announcing his candidacy: "I've got a few faults: I'm forty years old and I masturbate. Maybe I talk about sex too much. I don't think that's a horrible thing. But I'll tell you what my assets are. I am totally honest. There will be no backroom dealings on this. Everything will be done on the radio. I'm embarrassed I'm so honest. Who else would admit to the size of his genitals being under two inches? . . . So I'm saying that I'm an honest person—and I have the hair to be the governor."[16]

Stern's campaign—which included a photo-op at an upstate strip club called Goldfinger's—was a ferocious parody of the political process, right up to its anticlimactic end, when he dropped out because he couldn't get a waiver from financial disclosure laws (he notes that his lawyers even filed a challenge against the rules). At his farewell press conference, Stern spoke after being introduced by a man who "suffered from throat cancer and . . . could only speak through his voice kazoo." Stern relates his criticism of disclosure laws: "I want you to know that I spend twenty-five hours a week telling you all the most intimate details of my life. Name another candidate who gives you such disclosure. Has Mario Cuomo ever told you the size of his penis? Has he talked about the stains on his underpants and burying those underpants in his backyard when he was young? And this guy Pataki [whom Stern would later endorse], has he ever shown you his face on camera, much less his ass at the MTV Music Video Awards?"[17]

To be sure, this kind of humor is not for all tastes. But it is remarkably consistent and Stern, like all great satirists, rarely forgets to train his guns on himself and his image. "There are those in my audience who think I'm busy going to parties and socializing with celebrity friends," writes Stern in a chapter on cybersex. "But the pathetic fact is, I sit in my basement . . . and seldom emerge except for meals."[18]

Stern's attempts at scoring on the Internet are no more successful than his pitiful, premarital attempts were in the real world. "If you're ugly, if you're deformed, and married for twenty years, this is the place for you. Here on Prodigy chat I'm a single, Brad Pitt look-alike," he says. But alas, that's only one more illusion that fades away. After striking out with a potential cybermate, Stern notes: "Well, a major theory of mine had just been shot down. For forty-one years I had always believed that I was one of those guys who had a great personality but women never noticed me because of my ugly face. Turns out, not only am I ugly, but I have a dip-shit personality." And even when he finally does find cybermates, the sex turns out to be less than perfect—typing and masturbating don't really work well together and he has a bit of a performance problem ("I prematurely ejaculate *even* with computer sex").[19]

True to form, Stern must completely tear apart the image: He eventually brings "Rubberbaby," a cyberlover who had described herself as a Janine Turner lookalike into his radio studio. "Rubberbaby shattered my illusions. . . . My dear sweet vixen was . . . well, she was a housewife on fucking crutches. She wasn't ugly, but she wasn't exactly a fantasy woman. . . . The way she was hopping around the studio on one leg to give me a hug wasn't exactly filling me with fantasies," writes Stern, who swears he will not "use the computer for sexual purposes, ever again."[20]

Although Stern's unending demolition of public and private narratives strikes some as nihilistic, cruel, and perverse, it seems to me that it is absolutely an appropriate response to the world in which we live. When Stern asks, say, Woody Allen pal Dick Cavett, "Do you have any daughters I can bang?", he isn't simply going for a cheap laugh. He is driving home the point that when everyone is constantly trading in self-serving visions of goods, services, and themselves, the only proper response is to insist on honesty. It is Stern's willingness to stand by that fundamental truth that energizes his satire and binds him to his considerable audience.

REVIEW QUESTIONS

1. Gillespie suggests Howard Stern should be praised for using outrageous means to portray reality. Do you believe Stern's work should be appreciated for revealing social commentary, or dismissed because of its vulgarity?
2. Why do you think some—especially politicians and those in the media—object to Stern's commentary? Are his musings simply offensive or do they reveal a reality that some do not wish known?
3. Do you agree with those (like Alan Ehrenhalt) who assert Stern is essentially a product of our economic market? After all, he is extremely popular. Or is he, as the author suggests, an innovator?
4. Howard Stern is clearly outrageous and, to some, offensive. Why, in your opinion, does Stern enjoy so much success in our culture? Does he reflect popular culture, or does his morning program help to shape it?

Notes

1. This is not to say Stern has had no defenders in the media. Especially during the publicity for the film *Private Parts* (which received mostly positive reviews), Stern rode a wave of good press, though one that often made a distinction between Stern's radio and film personas. For an example, see David Edelstein's review in *Slate*.

For reasons that will become clear, it is interesting to note that among the harshest critics of the film version of *Private Parts* were Stern's regular listeners. As one longtime, New

York-based fan put it to me in a personal communication, "When I saw Stern promoting the movie as a 'love story' on the same morning talk shows he used to abuse all the time, I thought, 'what a sellout.'"

2. Al Martinez, "The King of All He Perceives," *Los Angeles Times,* December 5, 1995, Southland ed., p. B3.

3. Alan Ehrenhalt, "No Conservatives Need Apply," *New York Times,* November 19, 1995, late ed., p. 15.

4. Linda Chavez, "Shock Jock: Trash Talk, Trash Book," *USA Today,* November 22, 1995, final ed., p. 15A.

5. Stern has often been compared to Lenny Bruce, the controversial comedian who died of a drug overdose in 1966. (Interestingly, Stern's first date with his eventual wife of twenty-plus years, Alison, included going to see the Dustin Hoffman movie, *Lenny,* about the comedian.) Beyond an emphasis on sexual material and "blue" language, both performers exhibit a strong sense of indignation at what they view as societal hypocrisy. (Both performers have also run afoul of obscenity laws.) The following passage from *Private Parts,* in which Stern discusses being fined by the Federal Communications Commission for "patently offensive" remarks, is highly reminiscent of Bruce: "I live and work in a community where priests rape young boys, where pit bulls chew through kids' heads, where you get shot in your car, where an angry black mob stabbed a Hasidic Jew and the mayor turned his back, where crack runs free like River Ganges, and where movie directors fuck their wives' daughters. *Now you tell me what I should talk about on the radio!!*" (emphasis in original).

6. Howard Stern, *Private Parts* (New York: Simon and Schuster, 1993), p. 80.

7. Howard Stern, *Miss America* (New York: HarperCollins, 1995), p. 234.

8. Ibid., pp. 235–236.

9. Ibid., pp. 78–79.

10. Ibid., pp. 85–86.

11. Ibid., pp. 87–88.

12. Ibid., pp. 359–366.

13. Ibid., p. 363.

14. Ibid., pp. 386–399.

15. Ibid., pp. 403–405.

16. Ibid., p. 326.

17. The last reference is to Stern's role as a presenter at MTV's annual awards show in 1991. Stern appeared in a revealing costume as "Fartman," a parodic superhero character (with obvious powers) originated on his radio show. At the awards ceremony, Stern even managed to disgust the rock 'n' roll crowd, which normally glories in shocking social conventions. After his appearance, he writes in *Private Parts,* "I was walking around [backstage] and people were like nauseated. I went out and posed for all these pictures, and they made every newspaper, with my disgusting ass and belly sticking out. Then there was all this debate . . . as to whether or not I should have done this, how it was such a terrible, terrible thing, how it brought a complete lack of decorum to the MTV awards. I'm going, 'Excuse me. Decorum? This is MT Fucking V!'" (p. 257).

18. Stern, *Private Parts,* p. 12.

19. Ibid., pp. 20–25.

20. Ibid., p. 47.

10 / Popular Populism: Political Messages in Country Music Lyrics

JIMMIE N. ROGERS and STEPHEN A. SMITH

A generation ago, before most of today's college undergraduates were born, President Richard Nixon and his political coconspirators appeared to think that all country music fans were "patriotic, red-blooded, all-American vote fodder for conservative Republicans."[1] Nixon appeared onstage at the Grand Ole Opry and said that country music "comes from the heart of America. It talks about family. It talks about religion. And as we all know, country music radiates a love of this nation, a patriotism. . . . Country music . . . make[s] America a better country."[2] Facing the suspicions raised by the Watergate scandal and the folk and rock anthems of antiwar protest music, the Republicans found country music's growing popularity providing "the trend that gave Nixon his mandate," for they thought it was indicative of "the nation clarifying basic premises—home, job, faith—after a dangerous and anarchic decade when music was preeminently the tool of the radicals."[3]

Even today, the pundits still claim that country music is "much more clearly about core American values than anything coming out of Seattle or New York." An article published in the *New Republic* during the 1996 election argued, "Just as rock 'n' roll foreshadowed many of the changes in gender and race relations that followed in the 1960s, country music today—with its suburban, middle-aged themes of family and renewal—may be the clearest reflection of many of the anxieties and aspirations that have just begun to bubble to the surface in American political life." The contemporary popularity of country music, the author contended, provides "one of the most vivid examples of America's reigning backlash against its own culturally liberal past.

Perhaps this overstates the case, suggests another columnist for the *Des Moines Register.* "This mistakenly assumes that the baby boom—entrenched in the suburbs and getting increasingly conservative—has embraced country music because it reflects the generation's newfound values, . . . when in fact the explanation may be no more complicated than the fact country tends to be easier on aging ears than rock and (God forbid) hip-hop."[4] Country music fans in New York City also seemed to disagree with the premise as they protested, "You don't have to be shaped by the conservative values and politics of the South to enjoy country music."[5]

COUNTRY MUSIC AND POLITICS

The relationship between politics and music has a long tradition in the United States. James Madison noted in 1828 the popular aphorism that any country might be governed at the will of one who had the exclusive privilege of furnishing its popular songs. Contemporary politicians, too, have understood the political implications of the nexus between lyrical narrative and the resulting construction of social reality.

One young congressional staffer recently explained, "There's a lot of political themes and good wisdom that goes with country music. It helps in the job I do now."[6] The relationship is symbiotic. Roy Acuff, Jimmy Swann, and Jimmie Davis thought so too, and each attempted to parlay their country music stardom into political power by running for governor, and Senator Fred Thompson (Republican-Tenn.), a leading critic of political fund-raising, helped himself to $170,000 in campaign contributions during a gathering featuring Tammy Wynette, Lorrie Morgan, and Hank Williams, Jr. at Nashville's Wildhorse Saloon.[7] Country music stars were also active in 1992 and 1996 "Rock the Vote" media campaigns to encourage voter registration.

The size of the country music audience makes it particularly worthy of attention by politicians and political analysts. More than 43 million listeners tune in to country radio each week, making it the furthest-reaching format, according to Interep's new qualitative profile of the country radio audience. With a weekly cume of 43.5 million, country tops adult contemporary (36.4 million), news/talk (31.3 million), oldies (20.9 million), and every other format.[8] With 2,642 radio stations now programming country music, it has become the dominant radio format in the United States, reaching 20 million more people a week than its closest competitor, adult contemporary. By 1993, country radio had become the top-rated format in fifty-five of the nation's top one hundred cities, including Baltimore, Buffalo, Milwaukee, Seattle, San Diego and Washington, D.C.[9] The Eagle Group's 1996 *State of Country Radio* analysis revealed that 66 percent of respondents said they listen to country "often," as opposed to "sometimes." Respondents who said they listen to country one to three hours a day were up from 29 percent to 36 percent this year.[10] Further confirming the growing importance of the message, sales of country records quadrupled between 1989 and 1996.[11]

The demographics of the country music audience also makes them more important politically, because they share many of the same characteristics of those most likely to vote. Country fans are more educated than either adult contemporary or rock audiences. According to the *Simmons Study of Media and Markets,* 36 percent of country music fans have a postgraduate degree, as compared to 30 percent for adult contemporary and only 22 percent for rock. They are also wealthier. Forty percent of individuals with annual incomes over $40,000 listen to country music, as do a third of individuals who earn over $100,000 a year.[12] According to Interep's profile of country listeners, 94 percent are white, 81 percent have a high school-level education or better, 72 percent own a home, 69 percent are employed full or part time, 64 percent are married, and 62 percent have a household income of $30,000 or more. Also, 71 percent of country listeners are in the 18–49 demographic and 65 percent are in the 25–54 demo.[13]

Country music lyrics often express certain political sentiments; however, like beauty, truth, and pornography, the country music message means different things to different people, and its interpretation has often escaped precise measurement even by scholars and critics who have applied the tools available in our various disciplines. Casual observers often assume that Merle Haggard's "Okie from Muskogee"[14] is the quintessential political statement of country music. Even some journals and books have advanced articles with such suggestive titles as "Country Music: The Ballad of the Silent Majority."[15]

The diversity of themes in recorded country lyrics is so broad that one can find examples to support almost any hypothesis or conclusion by selectively searching and choosing certain titles. In this chapter we focus attention on those songs popular enough to appear on the top fifty charts from 1960 to 1997 and those songs successful enough to make the weekly charts. Since country music is still primarily a musical message delivered on singles and individual album tracks over radio, we contend that these communication artifacts contain the messages which have the greatest impact.

The range of themes found in the most popular country songs is somewhat narrow. Over 60 percent of the successful songs are about love relationships between adult men and women.[16] Most of the songs which are not about love are concerned with living as it is, should be, or could be. It is from this second group that we can discover the most widely accepted attitudes about social, economic, and political events in this country. That is, through these narratives about life, we can better understand the political ideology of country music.

Our findings suggest that the political philosophy presented in country music was found to be much more *libertarian* (a philosophy that asserts minimal governmental activity) than suggested by either previous studies. We argue that libertarian politics and populist economics (policies that aid the working class) are the values most frequently articulated in country music lyrics and that the rejection of authoritarianism, institutional structures, and even, at times, the "American Dream," is so pervasive as to border on anarchism. One critic aptly dubbed this "the no-nonsense populist politics most country musicians unreflectively espouse."[17]

A Vehicle for Racists Messages?

Several early studies suggested that country music, as a convenient vehicle which reflected southern social norms, was a popular outlet for the expression of white racism.[18] While one can cite "under-the-counter" records with limited sales or a few "put-on" albums such as those by Kinky Friedman to support that view, this analysis of the lyrics of the most popular commercial country music revealed something quite different. Indeed, while not one song reflecting racist attitudes appeared on the annual charts of the top fifty singles, there were numerous songs with varying commercial success that reflected an interracial understanding that has developed from shared personal experiences and a class affinity. Bobby Goldsboro and Tanya Tucker each recorded in 1974 Bobby Braddock's "I Believe the South Is Gonna Rise Again," which posits a vision of interracial harmony much like that found in Martin Luther King, Jr.'s "I Have A Dream" oration. Other examples of this emerging genre are Tony Joe White's "Willie and Laura Mae Jones," Johnny Russell's "Catfish John," Kenny Rogers' version of "Reuben James," and Tony Booth's version of "Irma Jackson."

The most significant finding of the present study in the area of race relations is the discovery of only five songs on the annual top fifty charts that make specific references to racial minorities. Johnny Cash's "The Ballad of Ira Hayes" expresses sympathy for the plight of an Indian who was among the heroes of Iwo Jima, but who died a broken, forgotten man. In the more upbeat hit "America," Waylon Jennings declares that all his brothers are black and white and yellow. He also insists that the red man has a right to expect "a little from you" and then chastises America to "promise and then follow through."

It may be, as suggested by Tony Joe White in "Willie and Laura Mae Jones," that the people depicted in most country songs are so busy trying to survive they have little time to worry about the color of other people's skin; it might be that they perceive themselves as a minority group in contemporary America and recognize shared discrimination with other minorities; or it may be that radio station managers have been concerned about minority challenges to their FCC licenses. Whatever the cause, racism cannot be said to be a major theme among the songs which achieved commercial success, and country music cannot be said to create or reinforce racism among its audience.

Law and Politics: Anarchy on the Airwaves

After hearing Merle Haggard's "Okie from Muskogee" and "The Fightin' Side of Me" some critics once suggested that the country music message is a lyric version of "My country, right or wrong" and have stereotyped the music and the audience as the epitome of the reactionary forces of "law and order." On the other hand, Merle Haggard's Okie anthem still results in heated arguments over its central message, almost thirty years after it first hit the charts.

Numerous songs about prison life indicate that violation of the law is a rather common practice in the mythic reality of the world of country music. Respect for or obedience to the law is not one of the major themes, and the opposition ranges from a song which expresses a benign disrespect for a city ordinance (Billy Edd Wheeler's "Ode to the Little Brown Shack Out Back") to one which advocates the active violation of laws such as speed limits, toll charges, weight limits, and ICC logs in C. W. McCall's number one hit, "Convoy."

Customary among recent songs which refer to the government and its actions is the theme that those who propose and enact the laws, even the "conservative" administration of Ronald Reagan, are viewed with skepticism and cynicism set to music. Hank Williams, Jr., in his song "I'm for Love," surveys the infighting among various levels of government, then observes that the people are "against the politicians, and the highway still ain't paved." In his satiric view of "The American Dream," Williams again focuses on the hypocrisy of politicians by describing Reagan's stated intention to control inflation and stop spending and then observes that the new tax increase is the biggest in history. The singer feels that the circular reasoning and behaviors of the politicians just leave the citizen in a hole.

Mac Davis, in "The Beer Drinking Song" also despairs over political solutions to the problems of the average citizen. He wants to know why the Social Security system is failing and asks "Where the hell's all the money we paid?" After the specific concern for a national problem he gets more universal in scope and reinforces Williams' "hole theory" by lamenting that "if the commies don't take us, Reganomics'll break us."

One reason that the dramatis populi in country music lyrics despair of political brawn is that they see the federal government as being insensitive to their needs. Another explanation for the apparent disregard for government authority is the perception that the statutes and the system unfairly discriminate against the average country music citizen—a theme not uncommon in the populist rhetoric of the nineteenth century. Jerry Reed's "She Got the Goldmine (And I Got the Shaft)" is an obvious indictment of the "justice" dispensed by the legal system. Reed explains that he intended to be reasonable following the breakup of a marriage and to divide the joint property equally, but the court entered an order that he felt was unfair. Similar sentiments about a stacked deck are also expressed by John Conlee in "Working Man," when he complains about a policeman's vigilance with a radar gun and a notice from the IRS telling him his taxes are "a big mess." He wonders, "is this the way the good life's supposed to be."

Guy Drake also expresses his opposition to government spending in "Welfare Cadillac," and the same theme continues to appear in more recent titles. Aaron Tippin sings the praises of the working man in "Working Man's Ph.D.," admitting that a "long hard day sure ain't much fun," but finding solace in the fact that "there ain't no shame in a job well done." Nonetheless, he suggests that a "few more people should be pulling their weight." Garth Brooks' "American Honky-Tonk Bar Association" is even more pointed, arguing that when "Uncle Sam dips in your pocket for most things you don't mind," but he is less than enthusiastic "when your dollar goes to all of those standin' in a welfare line."

However, not all country songs reject the social and economic programs of the New Deal era. In his 1961 hit "Po' Folks," Bill Anderson laments that his granddaddy's pension of $1.33 "was ten dollars less than the landlord wanted for rent" without any suggestion that $1.33 was too much money or a wasteful government expenditure. He further admits that the Salvation Army provided clothing for the family and "a man from the county came to cut our hair." Bob McDill's populistic "Song of the South" not only discussed participation in New Deal programs but also venerated them as a salvation from an unrewarding economic system. The songwriter described a situation that was rather typical for the times when he relates how a family was told that Wall Street fell. The family was "so damn poor we couldn't even tell." After they suffer sickness and the loss of the farm, the family moved to town. The father gets a job with the TVA after the move, and they are then able to survive.

In a commentary on more modern times, Charlie Daniels' "America, I Believe in You" laments people going hungry and living in the streets, because "in this land of plenty, this shouldn't be going on. We've got enough for everybody," he contends, if only we'd share. Hardly a Marxist, Daniels says he is "glad about the Berlin Wall," but when it comes to foreign loans, he thinks "charity begins at home." The Pirates of the Mississippi, in "A Street Man Named Desire," also explicated the plight of a worker who lost his job when the "assembly plant moved to Mexico." First he was evicted from his home, then his wife left him facing "these modern grapes of wrath."

ECONOMICS: "NOTHING BEHIND YOU, NOTHING IN SIGHT"

Although the lyrics of country music do not provide the listeners with any complex economic theory, they are not without a certain insight as to economic realities and the fact that "someone has been trickling-down on the working man." Ray Steven's "Workin' for the Japanese" has the singer admitting, "I ain't never read the *Wall Street Journal,* [and] I ain't got no Ph.D.," so that might be why the "trickle-down theory and the Laffer curve are just Greek to me." He is aware, however, that Sony, Toyota, and the other players in the global economic field have made the playing field less level for the average wage earner. Neither does the fact that many low-wage jobs are being sent to Mexico escape the Charlie Daniels in "America, I Believe in You." Daniels also responds to a Japanese business executive's calling "the working people in America were lazy and dumb" by pledging that in the future he won't buy anything unless it says "Made in the USA."

In their study, DiMaggio, Peterson, and Esco also suggested that the lyrics of country music bemoan the economic structure but fall short of rejecting the system and the American Dream of success through hard work. Three songs in their study seem to lend support to their thesis. Bill Anderson's "Laid Off" portrays the plight of a man and his wife who both lose their jobs on the same day, but says they will make it even though they will be on their knees asking the Lord to help while they are out of work. Clint Black's "One More Payment" is a more recent reflection of the same theme. Even though the singer realizes that his "mind's been on vacation" while his "body's been workin' overtime" and acknowledges that he is breaking his back to make the payments while fearing "that banker's bound to foreclose," he remains motivated by the thought that "one more payment and it's mine."

Merle Haggard's "If We Make It through December" tells of a man who "can't afford no Christmas" because, despite his diligent efforts and hard work, "got laid off down at the factory." Although he feels that "their timing's not the greatest in the world," he expresses hope for the future if his family can just make it through the winter. Haggard is less optimistic, however, in this 1969 hit, "Hungry Eyes," in which he concludes that "another class of people put us somewhere just below," and he laments that their prayers and hard work only brought a loss of courage.

Hopelessness is more clearly expressed in Charley Pride's "Down on the Farm." He bemoans the plight of farmers who "never thought of giving it up," but who are now "staring out a factory window, trying to understand it all." Despite their hard work, they discovered that "a way of life can be auctioned off," and despaired, "It was only the family farm, who really cares if its gone." Sadly, Pride acknowledges, "somebody's dreams are gone." As Hank Williams, Jr., sang of the situation, the "banker's against the farmers; the farmer's against the wall," and Chris LeDoux's "Cadillac Ranch" tells of a farm family's situation when both the well and the cow went dry. The next inevitable step was when a "banker came by the house one day [and] said he's gonna take the farm away."

John Conlee's version of "Nothing behind You, Nothing In Sight" is one of the finest and clearest statements of how working men and women feel about their plight. He tells of how all week he sells his time to a company that is interested only in using his body and cares nothing for his mind, and of the lack of hope generated when the worker knows that all his tomorrows will be just alike, that there is nothing behind you and nothing in sight "when the worries have stolen the dreams from your night." He describes the plight of a woman who works in the home from "daylight to midnight" with no monetary rewards, but astutely observes that "what she needs most is some time all her own." Another Conlee hit, "Working Man," echoes the same themes.

Conlee's songs leave little hope for improvement and offer no solutions, and McGuffey Lane's "Making A Living's Been Killing Me" also rejects the dream without satisfactorily resolving the dilemma. He is being underpaid for overtime work and the money he is paid cannot buy any peace of mind. The frustration is compounded when the foreman tells him that three hundred more will be laid off in the near future, when he will probably be waiting his turn in the unemployment line. Lane also introduces the element described earlier by others, that the people at the top of the ladder are becoming richer while those at the bottom that pay the taxes and have less than they need to survive. Several of the more recent songs observe the inequality of the economic structure in a tone that borders on an implicit declaration of the class struggle. Travis Tritt, in "Lord Have Mercy on the Working Man," asks, "Why's the rich man busy dancing, while the poor man pays the band." With equal resentment, Hal Ketchum's "Someplace Far Away" says, the dream "that makes a rich man money, ain't no dream at all."

Perhaps the best known song in this genre, due to its exposure as the theme song for a movie and a television series, is Dolly Parton's "9 to 5." While the visual adaptation suggested that the song was about secretaries in corporate offices, the lyrics are equally applicable to other occupations. Parton reinforces the idea that the worker is barely surviving and that the employers are always taking but seldom giving. Unlike the man in Conlee's song, she suggests that they do use the worker's mind, but do not give them credit for what they produce and that this will "drive you crazy if you let it." In "Hard Workin' Man" by Brooks and Dunn, the narrator complains, "I can't get ahead no matter how hard I try," and he echoes Parton's and Conlee's frustration that he "ain't nothin' but business from nine 'til five."

The lyrics of "9 to 5," like those cited earlier, attribute part of the blame to management ("They let you dream just to watch them shatter"); however, more fault is found with the system ("It's a rich man's game, no matter what they call it"). In general, the economic system is seen as being no more fair than the legal and political systems discussed earlier. Johnny Cash and his friends expressed no guilt or moral constraints when they decided to steal a Cadillac "One Piece at a Time," because the large and impersonal "GM wouldn't miss just one little piece." Furthermore, to sweeten his victory over the economic system, Cash's hero also delighted in the havoc created at the court house when it took the whole staff to type the sixty-pound title to his newly acquired vehicle.

Contrary to the conclusions of investigators who have focused on the alleged work ethic, considerable resentment toward the system is expressed in country music. In one song a man convicted of murder admits his failure in society and in his personal life, but proudly boasts, "I Never Picked Cotton." McGuffy Lane's hero in "Making a Living's Been Killing Me" decides to quit his job and go "where it don't make a damn what the boss man says."

More recently, Reba McEntire's "State of Grace" sings the praises of a woman who had worked at Wal-Mart for fifteen years. One day she looked up to see herself in the mirror working the checkout line and tore up her time card, cleaned out her bank account, and hit the road to find a life worth living. One music critic called the ballad *Thelma & Louise* without the ammo."[19]

The lyrics cited above seem to suggest that contemporary country music does actively question, in the traditional populist spirit, the fairness of the economic system. Other songs go even farther, questioning the underlying values of the American Dream itself. Loretta Lynn's "Success" discusses the damage done to a personal relationship by a husband's pursuit of the dream, and a related theme was also raised in the chorus of Hank Williams, Jr.'s "American Dream," where he questions whether we want or really need the dream because all it does is drive us crazy.

CONCLUSIONS: "LONG-HAIRED COUNTRY BOY"

An examination of those songs which received the widest attention and acceptance by the country music audience from 1960 through 1997 suggests that many of the stereotypes of the country music message should be revised. The most popular songs, when taken as a group, offer a message that conflicts with that discovered and reported by casual observers and in some previous studies.

The protagonist in most country songs is an individual seeking maximum freedom from any system, whether it be social, political, or economic. While they may not advocate the overthrow of any institution or system, there is little evidence to indicate they plan to suffer the resulting pain quitely. The freedom they seek is to get through life with few constraints on their personal freedom—a freedom only infrequently and grudgingly sacrificed even to a spouse or the immediate family. Outside of this close circle, there is little support for any type of formally recognized group or organization.

The fierce individualism portrayed may help to explain the lack of references to racial matters in the songs. Since the music is primarily one of personal relationships, there is seldom any comment on groups of individuals. The sorrow and joys highlighted are those applicable to any person regardless of race, creed, or color. There is no support for the claim of racism in commercially popular music and little, except that previously sighted material, which even refers to race.

The lyrics offer little support for any law, whether the law is generally perceived as for the public good or not. The characters portrayed in the songs resent being told what to do by anyone. A few songs support our national government, some (especially the songs expressing regional preferences) find satisfaction with particular political environments, and a few will support a political or governmental unit if it is attacked by outside forces. However, the primary emphasis is once again on the individual's exasperation with constraints levied by those outside the primary group.

If there is group identification, it is found in economic class consciousness. Many of the country music people encounter economic problems—problems ranging from those identified by Dolly Parton's "In the Good Days (When Times Were Bad)" and in Loretta Lynn's "Coal Miner's Daughter" which reflect on life in the past, to songs of the present which describe people working at menial and boring jobs in modern factories or going belly up on the farm. The important finding here is the emphasis on unsatisfactory working conditions and the fatalistic lack of faith in ever fulfilling the American Dream. It is in this area where we find the greatest interest in group identification—poor or hard-working folks. Poor-but-proud is a common theme, followed closely by poor-but-better. Several of the love songs contain the latter theme. A poor man, who lost a lover to a rich man, implies that he is probably a better sexual partner than the rich man in "The Door Is Always Open," and a woman who married a man for his money admits the poor man she deserted was a superior lover in "Satin Sheets."

Moreover, the theme of a class or group taking advantage of the poor is prevalent. The "us versus them" tactic so popular with politicians also finds favor in these messages. They often mention that they cannot identify with others outside their group. For instance, "Rednecks, White Socks, and Blue Ribbon Beer" suggests that these people described in the song are a little too noisy and loud to "fit in with that white-collar crowd."

Whatever the cause of the economic hardship, the solution is most often an individual one. "Busted" contains a reference to stealing for a living, but most are like the man found in Haggard's "Workin' Man Blues" who will keep his nose to the grindstone and drink a little beer with his friends on the weekend. Although Hank Williams, Jr., sings that "the union is against the workers working against their will" there is little support for organizing a union, for this would be the antithesis of individualism and represent the forfeiting of cherished freedoms. These lyric heroes would be just as unlikely to join the chamber of commerce, nor do they seem inclined to flock to the Ku Klux Klan or the local bass club, either.

These "AM-FM Anarchists" are individuals, and they prefer it that way. They covet few other lifestyles and will defend their way of life in some of the most fascinating verbal ways imaginable. They do not particularly care what others might think of the way they act, work, or spend their free time, and—perhaps ironically—they will go out of their way to tell the world how they feel. As Charlie Daniels said in "Long-Haired Country Boy," they are asking for nothing they cannot get on their own and if that is unsatisfactory to you then just leave them alone.

REVIEW QUESTIONS

1. In the Introduction of this book it is argued that our political culture places premium on individualism and minimal governmental inter-ference. The authors of this chapter suggest much the same. Is it fair to say, then, that country music is an accurate embodiment of our political culture? Was Richard Nixon on the mark with his comments at the Grand Ole Opry?

2. The authors suggest political leaders frequently adopt country music for their own uses—as a means of connecting with "average Americans." Given what we now know about the messages espoused

in country music, would this make sense? Much related, do the demographics of country music listeners have anything to do with its praise by politicians?

3. What might account for the popular perception that country music reflects racist sentiments and the "law and order" movement, even though there are songs which clearly indicate otherwise? Does it matter that country music is especially popular in the South?

4. Is country music different from other types of music in its overt treatment of economic themes and in its success in conveying economic class consciousness? Would it be fair to say that rap music does for African Americans what country music does for working class white Americans?

Notes

1. Frye Gaillard, "Sour Notes at the Grand Ole Opry," *Southern Voices*, May–June 1974, pp. 49–50

2. Richard M Nixon, "The Grand Ole Opry," *Weekly Compilation of Presidential Documents*, 10, 12, March 25, 1974, p. 333.

3. D. Keith Mano, "Going Country," *National Review*, January 18, 1974, p. 90.

4. Patrick Beach, "Is Country Our Culture?" *Des Moines Register*, February 8, 1996, p. 10.

5. Jeffrey M. Dine, Karen B. Dine, and Barry Langman, "Hank Williams, Garth Brooks," *New York Times Magazine*, November 17, 1996, p. 22.

6. Annys Shin, "Staff Profile: Matt M. Miller," *National Journal* 29 (May 10, 1997): p. 944.

7. Andrew Mollison, "Music, Politics, and Money," *Austin American-Statesman*, March 31, 1996, p. E1.

8. Phyllis Stark, "Study Shows That Country Radio Leads In Listeners," *Billboard*, March 22, 1997, p. 86.

9. Richard Leiby, "The Ballot of the Lovelorn Voter: Country Stars Join In Registration Effort," *Washington Post*, February 21, 1996, p. B1.

10. Chuck Taylor, "Country Radio Clamors for Calm: CRS Focuses on Solutions, Keeping Listeners," *Billboard*, March 22, 1997, p. 86.

11. Terry Teachout, "Country Music for the Uninitiated: Wailing: The Real-Life Story Can Be Loved Even by City Folks," *Sun* (Baltimore), April 20, 1997, p. 1F.

12. Richard Leiby, "The Ballot of The Lovelorn Voter," p. B1.

13. Phyllis Stark, "Study Shows That Country Radio Leads In Listeners," p. 86.

14. Merle Haggard, "Okie from Muskogee," Capitol, 2626, 1969.

15. Paul DiMaggio, Richard A Peterson, and Jack Esco, Jr. "Country Music: Ballad of the Silent Majority," in *The Sounds of Social Change*, eds. R. Serge Denisoff and Richard. A. Peterson (Chicago: Rand McNally and Company, 1972), p. 38–55.

16. Jimmie N. Rogers, *The Country Music Message: Revisited* (Fayetteville: University of Arkansas Press, 1989).

17. Terry Teachout, "Country Music for the Uninitiated," p. 1F. The historical background of populism and its relationship to contemporary country music lyrics is discussed in Jock Mackay, "Populist Ideology in Country Music," in *All That Glitters: Country Music in America*, ed. George H. Lewis (Bowling Green, Ohio: Bowling Green State University Popular Press, 1993), p. 285–304.

18. Florence King, "Red Necks, White Socks, and Blue Ribbon Fear," *Harper's*, July 1974, pp. 30–31, 34; John L Jellicorse, "Myths and Values in Southern White Racist Music," (paper presented at the Conference on Rhetoric of the Contemporary South, Boone, N.C., June 1974); Raymond S. Rodgers, "Images of Rednecks in Country Music: The Lyrical Persona of a Southern Superman," *Journal of Regional Culture*, 1 (1981): pp. 71–81.

19. David Browne, "No. 1 with a Bullet," *Entertainment Weekly*, November 8, 1996, p. 65.

11 / The Collapse of Popular Culture and the Case for Censorship

ROBERT H. BORK

The distance and direction popular culture has traveled in less than one lifetime is shown by the contrast between best-selling records. A performer of the 1930s hit "The Way You Look Tonight" sang these words to romantic music:

> Oh, but you're lovely, / With your smile so warm, / And your check so soft, / There is nothing for me but to love you, / Just the way you look tonight.

In our time, Snoop Doggy Dogg's song "Horny" proclaims to "music" without melody:

> I called you up for some sexual healing, / I'm callin' again so let me come get it. / Bring the lotion so I can rub you. / Assume the position so I can f... you.

Then there is Nine Inch Nails' song, "Big Man with a Gun." Even the expurgated version published by the *Washington Post* gives some idea of how rapidly popular culture is sinking into barbarism:

> I am a big man (yes I am). And I have a big gun. Got me a big old [expletive] and I, I like to have fun. Held against your forehead, I'll make you suck it. Maybe I'll put a hole in your head. . . .

The obscenity of thought and word is staggering, but also notable is the deliberate rejection of any attempt to achieve artistic distinction or even mediocrity. The music is generally little more than noise with a beat, the singing is an unmelodic chant, the lyrics often range from the perverse to the mercifully unintelligible. It is difficult to convey just how debased rap is. Not even printing the words adequately expresses that. There have, however, been some noteworthy attempts to get the point across. The music industry, Michael Bywater writes as part of an extended piece of masterful vituperation, "has somehow reduced humanity's greatest achievement—a near-universal language of pure transcendence—into a knuckle-dragging sub-pidgin of grunts and snarls, capable of fully expressing only the more pointless forms of violence and the more brutal forms of sex." He contrasts this with the remarkably subtle and emotionally precise popular music of only a few decades ago: "If Bach is the sound of God thinking, then perhaps Gershwin is, at least, the sound of St. Anthony of Padua whistling as he works."[1]

The difference between the music produced by Tin Pan Alley and rap is so stark that it is misleading to call them both music. Rock and rap are utterly impoverished by comparison with swing or jazz or any pre–World War II music, impoverished emotionally, aesthetically, and intellectually. Rap is simply unable to express tenderness, gentleness, or love. Neither rock nor rap can begin to approach the complicated melodies of George Gershwin, Irving Berlin, or Cole Porter. Nor do their lyrics display any of the wit of Ira Gershwin, Porter, Fats Waller, or Johnny Mercer. The bands that play this music lack even a trace of the musicianship of the bands led by Benny Goodman, Duke Ellington, and many others of that era.

Rap songs like "Horny" and "Big Man with a Gun" are not, as one might hope, culturally marginal; they produce best selling records. Nor is this "black music." Some of the worst rappers are white, and by far the *Eminem* largest number of records are sold to white suburban adolescents. What is one to make of these facts? One obvious answer has been mentioned: bored, affluent people in a society that no longer possesses the disciplinary tools of shame and stigma will indulge the most primitive human emotions. Sex, violence, and domination qualify.

Beyond that, it is possible to think these songs reflect a generalized rage, particularly rage against social authority. That seems to be the theme, expressed in obscene language and mixed with the celebration of violence in records like Ice-T's "Cop Killers." There is continuity with the '60s hatred of authority and in particular of the police, expressed in the phrase "Off the pigs." That may also explain the fury directed at women in this music. In that part of the black community where men are absent from the home, women are often figures of considerable power. White adolescents, with similar rebellious impulses, may resent the authority figures of mothers and female teachers, and the domineering whining feminists. The songs can be heard as paeans of revenge. No doubt the young have always chafed under authority; the difference now is that obscene assaults on authority have become culturally acceptable. . . .

What we hear in rap is paralleled elsewhere in popular culture in varying degrees. That the movies feature sex, violence, and vile language is not news. Car chases ending in flaming crashes, the machine gunning of masses of people, explosions of helicopters, the liberal production of corpses, language previously not heard even in semipolite society, these are now standard fare. It is no doubt true that Hollywood is appealing to profitable adolescent audiences, which appear to think that dismemberments and obscenities are an excellent evening's entertainment. But there is probably more to these developments than that. Many in Hollywood insist upon a liberal lacing of foul language in their films because they regard brutality and obscenity as signs of "authenticity." . . .

Television, not surprisingly, displays the same traits as the movies and music, though because it is viewed by families in the home, not to the same degree. Television viewing still resembles a bit the days when the family sat around the radio console, and that places a few restrictions on the medium. Still, things have changed here, too. Language is increasingly vulgar. A major study of changes in program content over the life of television finds, as might have been expected of a medium that has recently come under the influence of the '60s generation, that "[B]eginning from a relatively apolitical and traditional perspective on the social order, TV has meandered and lurched uncertainly along paths forged by the politics of the populist Left."[2] That has dictated changes in the way sex, social and cultural authority, and the personifications of good and evil are presented. Recreational sex, for example, is pervasive and is presented as acceptable about six times as often as it is rejected. Homosexuals and prostitutes are shown as social victims. Television takes a neutral attitude towards adultery, prostitution, and pornography. It "warns against the dangers of imposing the majority's restrictive sexual morality on these practices. The villains in TV's moralist plays are not deviants and libertines but Puritans and prudes."[3] The moral relativism of the '60s is now television's public morality.

Though it cannot begin to match rap, TV undermines authority in gentler ways. Families are relatively egalitarian; at work, subordinates ridicule their bosses and usually prevail over them. Businessmen are depicted negatively: they were three times more likely to commit crimes and five times as likely to be motivated by pure greed as people in most other occupations. Politicians fare no better. The military suffered a great fall in prestige beginning in the '60s. Law enforcement officials are now shown as corrupt and as likely to commit crimes as anyone else, but criminals are portrayed sympathetically. This has begun to change. Police and prosecutors are now more often seen as heroes, which, it has been suggested, may be due to the widespread and justified fear of crime in this society.

Perhaps popular culture is inevitably vulgar but today's is more vulgar than at any time in the past. Sex in sitcoms, previously pervasive, has recently exploded. A Super Bowl halftime show staged an elaborate sequence in which the central feature was Michael Jackson writhing and clutching his private parts for the edification of family audiences. . . .

Television becomes the equivalent of rap and movies on Music Television Videos and some of the pay channels. MTV is the more pernicious because it is usually part of the basic package that subscribers get automatically. They pay nothing extra and, unless the parents are vigilant, children will watch it. A rap song, for example, is accompanied by a video that may or may not illustrate the words of the songs. Images often follow one another at breakneck speed, images of guns, killings, police baiting, and sex. Like the movies, MTV is all the more dangerous because it is brilliantly produced.

One evening at a hotel in New York I flipped around the television channels. Suddenly there on the public access channel was a voluptuous young woman, naked, her body oiled, writhing on the floor while fondling herself intimately. Meanwhile, a man's voice and a print on the screen informed the viewer of the telephone number and limousine service that would acquaint him with young women of similar charms and proclivities. I watched for some time—riveted by the sociological significance of it all. Shortly after that, men only slightly less nude advertised homosexual prostitutes.

Art, by adopting many of the techniques and much of the content of popular entertainment, is becoming popular entertainment. And popular art, paintings of tomato cans, is taken as high art. James Gardner notes the incongruity that art has never been more admired, more adulated, than it is now, that it draws larger crowds and attracts more money than ever before, and yet the art itself is impoverished.[4] Here, as in popular music and television entertainment, it is not that there is no genuinely serious art at all; it is that there is so much that is meaningless, uninspired, untalented, or perverse. Perhaps the '60s brought in a fascination with the perverted, but lack of meaning was evident well before that decade. In a prestigious New York museum in the early 1950s, a piece of black burlap nailed to a board was presented as art. In a London museum, I thought I had come upon leftovers from a carpet laying: strips of brown felt in a heap in the middle of the room. Then I saw that the pile had a title. I asked a sculptor on the Yale faculty what his sculpture, which looked like a half-melted tree stump, represented. He said quite seriously: "Whatever you want it to be." Yale was willing to support a man whose idea of art was a three-dimensional Rorschach test. It is thus no cause for surprise that our great universities now offer courses on comic books.

These may be taken as manifestations of an individualism barren of substance, expressions of selves that are empty. But what are we to make of art that is both popular and perverted? For instance: a plastic puddle of vomit; piles of papier-maché excrement; jars of the artist's actual excrement; a painting entitled *Shit Faith* in which "crudely drawn excrement emerges from four abutting anuses."[5] We are informed that a "reinvigorated London art scene . . . began to be the envy of the contemporary art world in the late 1980s" with such offerings as a dead fourteen-foot shark floating in a tank of formaldehyde, a portrait bust of the artist in his own frozen blood, and "Everyone I've Ever Slept With: 1963–1993," which is a small tent "whose interior is lovingly appliqued with the names of [her] past loves and bed mates."[6] The object as always, one supposes, is to shock the bourgeoisie, but the bourgeoisie eagerly buy it. As we will see shortly, fascination with such materials as urine and excrement seems to be characteristic of today's bourgeoisie, if that is any longer the proper term for such people.

The hostility to traditional culture was manifest in the arts long before the '60s. "Anyone who thinks that fatuousness, nonsense, and obscenity in the arts are wholly recent, NEA-sponsored affairs," Roger Kimball, managing editor of the *New Criterion,* writes, "should look back for a moment at some of the numerous avant-garde movements that captured headlines in Europe from the turn of the century through the 1920s."[7] Reviewing a book that praised the Dadaist movement for subverting the values of bourgeois society, Kimball remarks: "Consistent with its attack on 'bourgeois values' (e.g., order, reason, honesty, propriety) is its fascination with violence, the scatological, and the obscene. This it shares with its close cousin, surrealism." While this is undoubtedly true—Gardner says that art began to direct its anger at the bourgeois state in the last quarter of the eighteenth century—

it does appear that the proportion of art that assaults bourgeois values is far higher today than in the days of Dadaism and surrealism. When the object is to attack bourgeois culture by delivering shocks to its standards, and when that culture keeps revising its standards by assimilating each new outrage, it is necessary to keep upping the ante by being ever more shocking. It seems clear, however, that large sections of the bourgeoisie, like drug-resistant bacteria, are approaching a state of being unshockable.

There is resistance in the public to the downward spiral we are riding. But it was not until the critic John Leo called Time Warner "our leading cultural polluter"[8] that the process of galvanizing public opinion really got under way. Senator Robert Dole found political capital in denouncing the more outrageous motion pictures and forms of rap music. But the most instructive episode was the behavior of the management of Time Warner when C. DeLores Tucker, a Democrat and head of the National Political Congress of Black Women, and William Bennett, former secretary of education and drug czar, met with the top Time Warner executives to protest the filth they were putting on the market. Tucker passed copies of the lyrics of Nine Inch Nails' "Big Man with a Gun" to the Time Warner executives and asked them to read the words aloud. None of them would. One of the Tucker-Bennett party did read out the words and asked if the executives found the lyrics offensive. The discussion included such modern liberal gems from Time Warner as "Art is difficult to interpret," "What is art?," and "Who decides what is pornography and what isn't?" The answers are simple: to the first question: "Big Man with a Gun" is as easy to interpret as an obscenity scrawled in a public lavatory; to the second: whatever art may be, this isn't it; and to the third: the public acting through its designated representatives can decide.

The executives talked about finding the "root causes" of crime and violence. That is the standard liberal diversion when anybody suggests doing something serious about an obvious problem. They said Tucker and Bennett were talking about symptoms. Of course, because it is the symptoms and not the root causes that kill, physicians treat the symptoms. My favorite Time Warner response was: "Elvis was more controversial in his day than some rap lyrics are today."[9] That is less a justification of today's music than a measure of how far our culture has fallen. The very fact that we have gone from Elvis to Snoop Doggy Dogg is the heart of the case for censorship.

Bennett asked the executives "whether there was anything so low, so bad, that you will not sell it." There was a long silence. But when Bennett said "baloney" a couple of times to the vapid responses he was getting, Time Warner's chairman, Gerald M. Levin, in a sudden onrush of sensitivity about words, objected to such language and walked out of the meeting.

The industry's responses to the criticism were even more instructive. Michael Fuchs, then chairman of Time Warner Music Group, shot back that offensive lyrics are "the price you pay for freedom of expression."[10] But obscenity in word and thought is a price that should not be paid simply so we can say there are no limits to what may be said. Fuchs might as well have said that crack addicts are the price you pay for a free market. Danny Goldberg, chairman of Warner Bros. Records, said: "Nine Inch Nails is a Grammy Award–winning, critically acclaimed artist [sic] who millions of people love. Why should a corporation listen to a bunch of middle-aged people who don't like the music and don't listen to it, and ignore the people who do love it and who do buy it?"[11] The reason the corporation should listen to those middle-aged people is that they are attempting to uphold some standard of decency for the protection, among others, of those who love and buy the filth. It says something frightening about this culture that lyrics like "Big Man with a Gun" win Grammy Awards, critical acclaim, and the love of millions. . . .

Though there certainly is a simmering dissatisfaction with popular culture, that apparently does not portend any effective action. The Tucker-Bennett episode was entertaining, but Time Warner, apparently embarrassed, sold the unit that produced gansta rap. The beat apparently goes on as before under new management. In any case, the confrontation tactic had such success as it did because it was new. Attempts to repeat it will have less and less impact, and the music executives will begin to refuse to meet with critics. Popular culture remains just that, popular. The American public watches, listens to, and makes profitable art forms it agrees are debased. That is an important point. The entertainment industry is not forcing depravity on an unwilling American public. The demand for decadence is there. That fact does not excuse those who sell such degraded material any more than the demand for crack cocaine excuses the crack dealer. But we must be reminded that the fault is in ourselves, in human nature not constrained by external forces. If that were not so, the problem would not be so dangerous and difficult to solve. . . .

A LIBERATED OCEAN WITH INFORMATION?

It is a question we all must soon ask, and not just about the racism and violence of hate rock, the violently obscene and brutal lyrics of rap music, and the obscenities and violence of motion pictures. Technology is now bringing worse material than we have ever seen or imagined, and as technology develops further, the material will become still worse. The Internet now provides users access to what Simon Winchester calls "an untrammeled, uncontrolled, wholly liberated ocean of information."[12] He thought it wonderful. Then one day he came upon a category called <alt.sex>, which has fifty-five groups including <alt.sex.anal>, <alt.sex.intergen> (intergenerational: the pedophile bulletin board), <alt.sex.snuff> (the killing of the victim) which includes subcategories for bestiality, torture, bloodletting, and sadistic injury.

The first category Winchester tried was <alt.sex.stories>, which contained a story about the kidnapping of two children. The castration of the six-year-old boy is "reported in loving detail" and occurs before he is shot. The seven-year-old girl is then repeatedly raped by nine men before having her nipples cut off and her throat slashed. There were two hundred such stories and the number was growing daily. "You want tales of fathers sodomizing their three-year-old daughters, or of mothers performing fellatio on their prepubescent sons, or of girls coupling with horses, or of the giving of enemas to child virgins? Then you need do no more than visit the news group that is named 'alt.sex.stories' and all will reliably be there, twenty-four hours a day, for everyone with a computer and a telephone, anywhere on (or above) the face of the earth."[13] The stories are written by pseudonymous authors and are filtered through two or three computers so that the authors and the points of origin are not known. The material is not only disgusting, it is a dangerous incitement. There is, for example: "A long and graphic account of exactly how and at what hour you wait outside a girls' school, how best to bundle a seven-year-old into your van, whether to tell her at the start of her ordeal that she is going to be killed at the end of it . . . how best to tie her down, which aperture to approach first, and with what—such things can only tempt those who verge on such acts to take a greater interest in them."[14]

Users can download pornographic pictures as well as prose from the Internet. And there is a lot of both available. The demand, moreover, is for material that can't be easily found elsewhere—pedophilia, sadomasochism, eroticized urination, defecation, and vaginal and rectal fisting. Among the most popular are sex acts with a wide variety of animals, nude children, and incest. The adult bulletin board service describes videos for sale and also provides over 25,000 pictures. The material is too obscene to be quoted here, but it involves girls defecating, girls eating feces (in both cases far more obscene language is used), oral sex with animals. One video is described as "Rape, torture, pussy nailed to table." It is impossible in short compass to give an adequate idea of the depravity that is being sold, apparently profitably.

The Internet, Stephen Bates informs us, offers plans for making bombs, instructions for painless suicide, the anti-Semitic forgery *Protocols of the Elders of Zion* (compressed for faster downloading), and racist diatribes, along with sexual perversion. There are certain to be offline harms from this material. "Pedophiles will abuse children they first met online, kids will blow off fingers with Net's bomb recipes, despondent teens will poison themselves using recipes from <alt.suicide.holiday>. Maybe all these tragedies would have occurred without the Net, but that's tough to prove."[15] It would be even tougher to prove that this material has any social value. Only the most radical individualism imaginable could countenance these uses of the Internet. . . .

But the situation is likely to get still worse than this. The pornographic video industry is now doing billions of dollars worth of business and volume is increasingly rapidly.[16] Companies are acquiring inventories of videos for cable television, and a nationwide chain of pornographic video retail stores is in the works. This may, however, be only a transitional phase. George

Gilder predicts that computers will soon replace television, allowing viewers to call up digital films and files of whatever they may desire from around the world. He discounts the idea that "liberated children [will] rush away from the network nurse, chasing Pied Piper pederasts, snuff-film sadists, and other trolls of cyberspace."[17] (The "network nurse," as a matter of fact, looks increasingly like a lady of the evening.) The computer will give everyone his own channel to do with as he wishes, and Gilder predicts a spectacular proliferation of programs on specialized cultural, scientific, and practical subjects.

That will certainly happen, but the presence of wholesome films and files does not rule out the presence of the corrupt and even diabolical. The Internet is proving that. The more private viewing becomes, the more likely it is that salacious and perverted tastes will be indulged. That proposition is demonstrated by the explosion of pornographic films and profits when videocassettes enabled customers to avoid the embarrassment of entering "adult" theaters. An even greater surge in the demand for perverted sex with violence will certainly occur when customers don't even have to check cassettes out of a store. Calling up films in their own homes, they will not have to face a clerk or let other customers see them browsing through X-rated films.

When digital films become available for viewing on home computers, we are likely to discover that Gilder's "trolls of cyberspace" are very real, very popular, and a very great menace. Imagine Internet's <alt.sex.stories> on digital film available on home computers anywhere in the world. The dramatization, in living color with lurid special effects of men castrating and then shooting a six-year-old boy, then gang-raping and killing a seven-year-old girl, is certain to trigger imitations by borderline perverts. Don't think such films won't be made; they will. Don't think that they will not be defended on First Amendment grounds; they will. And don't suppose it will not be said that the solution is simple: If you don't like it, don't watch it. That, too, will be argued.

A great many people are willing to deplore such material but unwilling to take or allow action to stop its distribution. When the Senate Commerce Committee approved a proposal to impose criminal penalties on anyone who transmits on the Internet material that is "obscene, lewd, lascivious, filthy, or indecent," ferocious opposition immediately developed from a coalition of business and civil liberties organizations. The wording of the bill leaves much to be desired, but that is not the primary objection these groups have. They do not want restrictions, period, no matter how carefully drawn. The coalition includes, of course, the ACLU and the ubiquitous Time Warner, which John Leo has said is "associated one way or another with most of the high-profile, high-profit acts, black and white, that are pumping nihilism into the culture. . . . We are living through a cultural collapse, and major corporations are presiding over that collapse and grabbing everything they can on the way down."[18]

We are still on the way down and they are still grabbing. I do not suppose for a moment that Time Warner would produce films of the material to be found on the Internet's alt.sex. Nor would any major entertainment corporation. Not today or tomorrow, but as we grow accustomed to brutal and perverted sex, inhibitions will be lowered still further. Some businesses will make such films and some civil libertarians will deplore them, adding, of course, that they should not be banned. In the absence of restraints of some sort, however, everything that can be imagined, and some things that can't, yet, will eventually be produced and shown.

Reflecting on where we have come, Maggie Gallagher wrote: "Sex was remade in the image of Hugh Hefner; Eros demoted from a god to a buffoon. Over the last thirty years, America transformed itself into a pornographic culture."[19] Gallagher accepted Angela Carter's definition, stated in somewhat more basic Anglo-Saxon, that pornography is basically propaganda for fornication, and offered a definition of her own: "[A] pornographic culture is not one in which pornographic materials are published and distributed. A pornographic culture is one which accepts the ideas about sex on which pornography is based."[20]

That is quite right, as far as it goes, but our popular culture has gone far beyond propagandizing for fornication. That seems almost innocent nowadays. What America increasingly produces and distributes is now propaganda for every perversion and obscenity imaginable. If many of us accept the assumptions on which that is based, and apparently many do, then we are well on our way to an obscene culture. The upshot is that American popular culture is in a free fall, with the bottom not yet in sight. This is what the liberal view of human nature has brought us to. The idea that men are naturally rational, moral creatures without the need for strong external restraints has been exploded by experience. There is an eager and growing market for depravity, and profitable industries devoted to supplying it. Much of such resistance as there is comes from people living on the moral capital accumulated by prior generations. That capital may be expected to dwindle further—cultures do not unravel everywhere all at once. Unless there is vigorous counterattack, which must, I think, resort to legal as well as moral sanctions, the prospects are for a chaotic and unhappy society, followed, perhaps, by an authoritarian and unhappy society.

THE CASE FOR CENSORSHIP

Is censorship really as unthinkable as we all seem to assume? That it is unthinkable is a very recent conceit. From the earliest colonies on this continent over 300 years ago, and for about 175 years of our existence as a nation, we endorsed and lived with censorship. We do not have to imagine what censorship might be like; we know from experience. Some of it was formal, written in statutes or city ordinances; some of it was informal, as in the movie producers' agreement to abide by the rulings of the Hayes office. Some of it was inevitably silly—the rule that the movies could not show even a husband and wife fully dressed on a bed unless each had one foot on the floor—and some of it was no doubt pernicious. The period of Hayes office censorship was also, perhaps not coincidentally, the golden age of the movies.

The questions to be considered are whether such material has harmful effects, whether it is constitutionally possible to censor it, and whether technology may put some of it beyond society's capacity to control it.

It is possible to argue for censorship, as Stanley Brubaker, a professor of political science, does,[21] on the ground that in a republican form of government where the people rule, it is crucial that the character of the citizenry not be debased. By now we should have gotten over the liberal notion that its citizens' characters are none of the business of government. The government ought not try to impose virtue, but it can deter incitements to vice. "Liberals have always taken the position," the late Christopher Lasch wrote, "that democracy can dispense with civic virtue. According to this way of thinking, it is liberal institutions, not the character of citizens, that make democracy work."[22] He cited India and Latin America as proof that formally democratic institutions are not enough for a workable social order, a proof that is disheartening as the conditions in parts of large American cities approach those of the Third World.

Lasch stressed "the degree to which liberal democracy has lived off the borrowed capital of moral and religious traditions antedating the rise of liberalism."[23] Certainly, the great religions of the West—Christianity and Judaism—taught moral truths about respect for others, honesty, sexual fidelity, truth-speaking, the value of work, respect for the property of others, and self-restraint. With the decline of religious influence, the moral lessons attenuate as well. Morality is an essential soil for free and democratic governments. A people addicted to instant gratification through the vicarious (and sometimes not so vicarious) enjoyment of mindless violence and brutal sex is unlikely to provide such a soil. A population whose mental faculties are coarsened and blunted, whose emotions are few and simple, is unlikely to be able to make the distinctions and engage in the discourse that democratic government requires.

I find Brubaker and Lasch persuasive. We tend to think of virtue as a personal matter, each of us to choose which virtues to practice or not practice— the privatization of morality, or, if you will, the "pursuit of happiness," as each of us defines happiness. But only a public morality, in which trust, truth-telling, and self-control are prominent features, can long sustain a decent social order and hence a stable and just democratic order. If the social order continues to unravel, we may respond with a more authoritarian government that is capable of providing at least personal safety.

There is, of course, more to the case for censorship than the need to preserve a viable democracy. We need also to avoid the social devastation wrought by pornography and endless incitements to murder and mayhem. Whatever the effects upon or capacity to govern ourselves, living in a culture that saturates us with pictures of sex and violence is aesthetically ugly, emotionally flattening, and physically dangerous.

There are, no doubt, complex causes for illegitimacy and violence in today's society, but it seems impossible to deny that one cause is the messages popular culture insistently presses on us. Asked about how to diminish illegitimacy, a women who worked with unmarried teenage mothers replied tersely: "Shoot Madonna." That may be carrying censorship a bit far, but one sees her point. Madonna's forte is sexual incitement. We live in a sexdrenched culture. The forms of sexual entertainment rampant in our time are overwhelming to the young, who would, even without such stimulations, have difficulty enough resisting the song their hormones sing. There was a time, coinciding with the era of censorship, when most did resist.

Young males, who are more prone to violence than females or older males, witness so many gory depictions of killing that they are bound to become desensitized to it. We now have teenagers and even subteenagers who shoot if they feel they have been "dissed" (shown disrespect). Indeed, the newspapers bring us stories of murders done for simple pleasure, the killing of a stranger simply because the youth felt like killing someone, anyone. That is why, for the first time in American history, you are more likely to be murdered by a complete stranger than by someone you know. That is why our prisons contain convicted killers who show absolutely no remorse and frequently cannot even remember the names of the persons they killed.

One response of the entertainment industry to criticisms has been that Hollywood and the music business did not create violence or sexual chaos in America. Of course not. But they contribute to it. They are one of the "root causes" they want us to seek elsewhere and leave them alone. The denial that what the young see and hear has any effect on their behavior is the last line of the modern liberal defense of decadence, and it is wilfully specious. Accusing Senator Dole of "pandering to the right" in his speech deploring obscene and violent entertainment, the New York Times argued: "There is much in the movies and in hard-core rap music that is disturbing and demeaning to many Americans. Rap music, which often reaches the top of the charts, is also the music in which women are degraded and men seem to murder each other for sport. But no one has ever dropped dead from viewing Natural Born Killers, or listening to gangsta rap records."[24] To which George Will replied: "No one ever dropped dead reading 'Der Sturmer,' the Nazi anti-Semitic newspaper, but the culture it served caused six million Jews to drop dead."[25]

Those who oppose any form of restraint, including self-restraint, on what is produced insist that there is no connection between what people watch and hear and their behavior. It is clear why people who sell gansta rap make that claim, but it is less clear why anyone should believe them. Studies show that the evidence of the causal connection between popular culture's violence and violent behavior is overwhelming. . . .[26]

[These] studies confirm what seems obvious. Common sense and experience are sufficient to reach the same conclusions. Music, for example, is used everywhere to create attitudes—armies use martial music, couples listen to romantic music, churches use organs, choirs, and hymns. How can anyone suppose that music (plus the images of television, movies, and advertisements) about sex and violence has no effect? . . .

The entertainment industry will battle ferociously against restraints, one segment of it because its economic interests would be directly threatened, the rest because, to avoid thinking, they have become absolutists about First Amendment freedoms. Then there are the First Amendment voluptuaries. The ACLU is to the First Amendment what the National Rifle Association is to the Second Amendment and the right to bear arms. The head of the ACLU announced in a panel discussion that the Supreme Court's failure to throw protection around nude dancing in night clubs was a terrible blow to our freedom of speech. Some years back, when I suggested to a law school audience that the courts had gone too far in preventing communities from prohibiting pornography, the then-president of the organization compared me to Salazar of Portugal and the Greek colonels. Afterward he said he had called me a fascist. It is fascinating that when one calls for greater democratic control and less governance by a judicial oligarchy, one is immediately called a fascist. The ACLU seems to think democracy is tyranny and government by judges is freedom. That is a proposition that in the last half of this century our judiciary has all too readily accepted. Any serious attempt to root out the worst in our popular culture may be doomed unless the judiciary comes to understand that the First Amendment was adopted for good reasons, and those reasons did not include the furtherance of radical personal autonomy.

It is not clear how effective censorship of the Internet or of digital films on home computers can be. Perhaps it is true, as has been said, that technology is on the side of anarchy. Violence and pornography can be supplied from all over the world, and it can be wireless, further complicating the problem of barring it. We may soon be at the mercy of a combination of technology and perversion. It's enough to make one a Luddite. But there are methods of presentation that can be censored. Lyrics, motion pictures, television, and printed material are candidates.

What we see in popular culture, from "Big Man with a Gun" to <alt.sex.stories>, is the product, though not, it is to be feared, the final product, of liberalism's constant thrust. Doing anything to curb the spreading rot would violate liberalism's central tenet, John Stuart Mill's "one very simple principle." Mill himself would be horrified at what we have become; he never intended this; but he bequeathed us the principle that modern liberals embrace and that makes it possible. We have learned that the founders of liberalism were wrong. Unconstrained human nature will seek degeneracy often enough to create a disorderly, hedonistic, and dangerous society. Modern liberalism and popular culture are creating that society.

REVIEW QUESTIONS

1. In the Introduction of this book a distinction was made between art imitating life and life imitating art. How would Robert Bork line up on this question?

2. One of the criticisms of this sort of critique of contemporary popular culture is that it is often generational; the "old folks just don't get it." Put a bit differently, some might argue the root of Bork's problem with today's popular culture is that he belongs to a different generation. On top of that, he is, after all, a well-to-do, white man. What is your view, is Bork simply out of step for the times or does he hit on something much bigger than "different tastes?"

3. As you know, Bork argues for censorship. Is this a viable solution? If so, where would you draw the line?

Notes

1. Michael Bywater, "Never Mind the Width, Feel the Lack of Quality," review of *The Faber Book of Pop, Spectator,* May 13, 1995, p. 44.

2. S. Robert Lichter, Linda S. Lichter, and Stanley Rothman, *Prime Time: How TV Portrays American Culture* (Washington D.C.: Regnery Publishing, 1994), p. 416.

3. Ibid., pp. 404–405.

4. James Gardner, *Culture or Trash?: A Provocative View of Contemporary Painting, Sculpture, and Other Costly Commodities* (New York: Carol Publishing Group, 1993).

5. Ibid., p. 183.

6. Roberta Smith, "A Show of Moderns Seeking to Shock," *New York Times,* November 23, 1995, p. C11.

7. Roger Kimball, "The Heritage of Dada," *Public Interest,* Fall 1994, p. 120.

8. John Leo, "The Leading Cultural Polluter," *U.S. News & World Report,* March 27, 1995, p. 16.

9. All quotes not citing a periodical source are from "notes" taken by Pete Wehner at the May 18, 1995 meeting between William Bennett, DeLores Tucker, et al., and Time Warner executives.

10. Howard Kurtz, "Time Warner on the Defensive for the Offensive," *Washington Post,* June 2, 1995, pp. A1, A18.

11. Ibid.

12. Simon Winchester, "An Electronic Sink of Depravity," *Spectator,* February 4, 1995, p. 9.

13. Ibid., p. 10.

14. Ibid., p. 11.

15. Stephen Bates, "Alt.Many.Of.These.Newsgroups.Are.Repellent.," *Weekly Standard,* October 30, 1995, p. 27.

16. John R. Wilke, "A Publicly Held Firm Turns X-Rated Videos into a Hot Business," *Wall Street Journal,* July 11, 1994, p. 1.

17. George Gilder, "Breaking the Box," *National Review,* August 15, 1994, p. 37.

18. Leo, "The Leading Cultural Polluter," p. 16.

19. Maggie Gallagher, *Enemies of Eros: How the Sexual Revolution Is Killing Family, Marriage, and Sex and What We Can Do About It* (Chicago: Bonus Books, 1989), p. 251.

20. Ibid., p. 252.

21. Stanley Brubaker, "In Praise of Censorship," *Public Interest,* Winter 1994, p. 48.

22. Christopher Lasch, *The Revolt of the Elites and the Betrayal of Democracy* (New York: W.W. Norton, 1995), p. 85.

23. Ibid., p. 86.

24. "Mr. Dole's Entertainment Guide," *New York Times,* June 2, 1995, p. A 28.

25. George Will, "This Week with David Brinkley," *ABC News,* June 4, 1995.

26. Michael Medved, *Hollywood vs. America: Popular Culture and the War on Traditional Values* (New York: HarperCollins, 1992), pp. 239–252; Vincent Ryan Ruggiero, *WARNING: Nonesense Is Destroying America* (Nashville, Tenn.: Thomas Nelson Publishers, 1994), pp. 91–125.

12 / A Filmmaker's Credo: Some Thoughts on Politics, History, and the Movies

OLIVER STONE

My first encounter with the distortions of history, with the power of mass illusion, was when I was eight years old and visiting my mother's relatives in France. Her grandparents and other family members would tell me stories about how they had fought the Nazis as members of the French resistance and about how many of their relatives and friends had literally been put up against the wall and executed. These were heroic tales, and I quite naturally believed them.

It wasn't until years later, when I returned to France in the 1960s and 1970s that I began to learn that none of the stories I'd heard were true— *none* of them. Most of the people I'd known as a kid were, in fact, collaborators who had worked for the Germans or else were people who had remained "neutral." I was shocked to discover that I'd been a victim of what we now call disinformation. In the 1970s, books and movies began to appear in France challenging the traditional view of French resistance. And when Francois Mitterrand resigned, we found out that he, too, had a hidden collaborationist past.

Such was my introduction to the possibility of mass denial by people in a society. Then as I grew older, I went through the shock of my parents' divorce. Life, it seems, as it goes on, is about this disillusioning process.

At eighteen, I went to Vietnam as a teacher, then at twenty-one I went back as an infantry soldier in the army. During my two tours there, I saw firsthand what the people at home were learning in a much more gradual fashion: that the war was a lie—a lie on a scale so massive that I never could have imagined it.

I had entered the war as a patriot. I supported the Gulf of Tonkin resolution (although twenty years later, we found out that the "incident" which led up to it was really a sham). As young men fighting in the jungle, we didn't really spend too much time thinking about the morality of the war— we had enough to do just trying to stay alive. And so sometimes we killed the wrong people. We hurt. We burned.

Sometimes you don't realize what you're doing or what you've done until years later. Self-consciousness is slow in coming.

And, in a sense, Vietnam veterans were doubly hurt, because not only had we taken part in a very confusing war but, after returning home, we became involved in a second war—a war for which we simply weren't prepared. I tried to show the effects of that in my film *Born on the Fourth of*

July, which was based on Ron Kovic's book. I can't tell you how cold a homecoming it was. Some people were against the war—and we definitely heard from them—but many people were for it. In my experience, however, the majority of the American people didn't really care either way because they were making an enormous amount of money at the time; under Lyndon Johnson, the Great Society had started and an economic boom was underway. But Vietnam veterans—many of them without skills—were denied entry into that economic paradise. So we fought two wars back-to-back, and the one at home was, in some respects, a struggle against our society's indifference to and denial of the one overseas: a denial of Vietnam, a denial of pain, a denial of people like Ron Kovic and myself.

I didn't know how to deal with my own pain at the time. Eventually I took it and wrote the screenplays for *Platoon* and *Born on the Fourth of July* relating these experiences. But neither of those films would be made in the 1970s, which was very depressing to me as a young filmmaker because I had hoped that such films would help bring the truth home to people. *Apocalypse Now* and *The Deer Hunter* were made, but they were both more like grand operas: beautiful but very unrealistic. They didn't deal with the stark, brutal, ground-level realities that I and others had known as soldiers. So the film industry became yet another means by which our society denied what was really going on in Vietnam and what was happening back home to the people who had fought there.

This was all very confusing to a young man. I began to think that maybe this was the way the world really was—that maybe I was the one who wasn't seeing the truth. I was young, full of self-doubts, and I began to think that maybe I had gotten things screwed up backward like my father said. There were a few times I almost gave up. It was hard to keep going—very hard.

But then my screenplay for *Midnight Express* won an Academy Award. That allowed me to continue as a writer in Hollywood. And I had an opportunity to go to Russia and write a screenplay about dissidents under the Brezhnev regime. In nearly a dozen Russian cities, under very difficult circumstances, I met with a number of Soviet dissidents. These people were being jailed for speaking their views. Many were thrown into psychiatric hospitals and drugged; some even incurred brain damage. Nevertheless, they continued to fight with tremendous courage against the Soviet regime. But once I finished the screenplay, nobody in American wanted to shoot it. So here was yet another impasse; once again, I couldn't seem to do the movies that meant something to me.

Eventually, however, I did get three or four screenplays filmed, including *Scarface* and *Year of the Dragon*. But that still wasn't getting me where I wanted to be as a filmmaker, so one day I just decided to chuck it all, to give up my attempts to work within the Hollywood system. I went down to El Salvador with a rascal friend of mine, a so-called journalist named Richard Boyle, and we started to do a movie called *Salvador*. We had no money and were going to do it independently—very cheaply, without a studio behind us—just to challenge the situation that we saw developing in Central America.

Though I had had considerable experience with disillusionment by this point, what I saw and heard in Central America really came as a shock to me, especially the sprawling American militarization of the region. Seeing young American soldiers—women now as well as men—in their green fatigues in the streets of San Salvador, I would approach them and ask, "By any chance, do you remember what happened in Vietnam to kids like you?"

Their responses were chilling. They were of two kinds. One was a blank: "I really don't know anything about that," they would say, and it was clear to me that they had never read anything about Vietnam. Sure, they knew vaguely that something bad had happened there, but they didn't want to know more about it. The other response was more negative and hostile: yes, they remembered Vietnam, but they didn't want to talk about it—especially with people like me who questioned the morality of the war. The idea of such a question raises the idea of independent thinking, and independent thinking is sometimes contrary to military purpose.

Well, you remember that we almost had a war in Nicaragua. *You* remember. But it's amazing to me the reaction I get when I travel the college circuit. Usually twice a year I talk to some of the kids, and I discover that they don't know much about U.S. involvement in Central America ten years ago, much less Vietnam in the 1960s. We were on the edge of war in 1986, with President Reagan making pronouncements on national television to the effect that, if the communists succeeded in Nicaragua, pretty soon their tanks would be rolling over the Rio Grande. The U.S. Army Reserves were actually being sent down, the tension level was extremely high throughout the region, and spies were everywhere. El Salvador was being ripped apart by a brutal war; Honduras was turned into a gigantic American military base and pretty much screwed up forever; and even Costa Rica—the one nation in the region without a military—was transformed, becoming very much a part of the web of espionage, bombings, terrorism, paramilitary activity, and CIA operations that had become a way of life for its neighbors.

And then came an extraordinary stroke of luck: the Iran-Contra scandal broke. Just by accident, we saw the surface of it: Richard Secord and Oliver North were called to testify before Congress and the momentum went out of the preparations for war. Elliot Abrams and the rest had to cool their heels for the next two years, and the Reagan administration barely hung on to the end of 1988. They couldn't provoke a war at that point, although warfare followed under George Bush.

Remember, too, that both Reagan and Bush had been quoted as saying that we had to "put Vietnam behind us." I think that's such an insult by those two men to the veterans of that war. The reason those fifty-thousand-plus names have been inscribed on that wall in Washington, D.C., is because we *must* remember what happened in Vietnam; if we don't, we soil the memory of the people who served there. We fail to acknowledge the sacrifices those veterans made, in good faith, for their country.

In any event, *Salvador* made the difference for me. After some eighteen years of getting nowhere, the dam broke. I got a bit of wind behind my back and was lucky enough to be able to make two films I really wanted to do: in 1985 I made *Salvador,* and then in 1986 I made *Platoon,* which I shot for very little money in the Philippines.

I didn't expect either film to be successful. Actually, *Salvador* flopped theatrically, and I didn't expect *Platoon* to do much better because of the nature of the subject. So I was completely unprepared for what happened next. *Platoon* was enormously successful. I've never seen anything like it, nor have I had anything similar happen to me since, either critically or financially. The film was a huge success not only in the United States but in New Zealand and Russia and places that had no particular interest in Vietnam. People lined up to see it everywhere in the world.

So you'd think that that would have been a good time to call it quits, to retire or die or start playing baseball or something. Instead, I went into the JFK business. The Kennedy assassination has obvious ties to Vietnam, but I also did *JFK* because I had a passion and a love for the man and the time, as well as an honest sense of outrage and shock at the dissident material about the assassination that I'd been reading over the years.

Had *JFK* been examined intelligently by its critics, they would have discovered that the body of thought presented in the movie wasn't original and certainly wasn't invented by me; it was a compendium of facts and findings that have been made by people who have been challenging the Warren Report and conducting their own citizen investigations into the murder since the 1960s. What was unique about my film was the style in which it was made; even so, it shocked the political establishment incurring their wrath in a way I had never imagined possible. After all, this was old material to me, but for some reason it seemed new and radical to others.

Perhaps we can see, in the reaction to this 1991 film, how much the country has changed in the last two decades. If I'd made *JFK* in the 1960s or 1970s, it would have been considered normal by the standards of the time. But by the standards of the 1980s and 1990s—years of real political reaction—the film is regarded as some kind of mad, liberal, insane attack on America. I have been criticized for everything from anti-Americanism to making up history. I have been called a revolutionary (apparently a bad thing) and charged with brainwashing the young—even though I have found, in my travels around the country, that the young don't know about history anyway because their teachers haven't taught them anything.

That's why so many people seem to be threatened by the movies I make. Yet a good movie is merely a good first draft: something you use to get into a subject, to begin to learn about it. Remember *Lawrence of Arabia?* There was a tremendous debate about it back when it was first released; some people objected to the movie's portrayal of T. E. Lawrence participating in the massacre with the Turks. But that doesn't make it a bad movie. As a result of seeing it, you need to go out and read. I read *The Seven Pillars of Wisdom* after seeing it. The film itself raises questions, and that's all to the good.

Then, too, everyone of the protagonists in my movies—from Jim Morrison to Richard Nixon (and I can't think of two more opposite personalities)—goes through a crisis of conscience and ultimately achieves some form of enlightenment through the travails of this life. And that, I think, is one of the noblest and enduring themes we have in art, be it movies or any other form. It is the very purpose of our existence.

At any rate, *JFK* ended my fifteen minutes of being a good guy and placed me forever in the ranks of the damned. It's an interesting experience to go both ways, to see the wheel turn, to be loved and then reviled. Not that it's been easy or fun, mind you—but it's been necessary. Because information in the country is, to a large degree, bought and controlled. It's very difficult, for example, to find reasonable argument on television. Conversation has been replaced by shouting matches or sound bites; quotes are misinterpreted or taken out of context. The Socratic form of dialogue isn't much evident in the media to me. That's part of the reason why I made *Natural Born Killers*.

I think our culture has really degenerated and I hold television and the rest of the corporate media largely responsible for it. It seems that the average attention span has shortened considerably in my lifetime, and with it we have lost the ability to argue and to accept dissent. So *Natural Born Killers* was my attack on television. It came from seeing the wall-to-wall trivia and sensationalism that passes for information these days. Advertising space was sold all over the airwaves because of coverage of the Menendez brothers, Lorena Bobbitt, Amy Fisher and Joey Buttafuoco, and, of course, the O. J. Simpson case. To this day, I would love to know the amount of money that was made by the networks off the Simpson trial and all these other stories. There was no overriding social issue of significance in any of them; compared to the more profound things that have been going on in recent years, they were all relatively shallow events. They were simply used as bait—jammed down the throats of the public—for the purpose of making money.

That's because the news, fundamentally, is about profits. So my much-reviled *Natural Born Killers* was a kind of vomiting up of what I felt was being force-fed to us at the time. And I did it in the style of the television programming I was watching. I wanted the film to be like holding up a mirror to something ugly and getting it back full in the face. Of course, Bob Dole called *Natural Born Killers* "a film of revulsion and decadence," and I don't think I'll ever be accepted into the Republican Party as a result of that.

Heaven and Earth, which I believe is a beautiful film, also came at the wrong time. It raised questions about immigration, among other issues, and what we did to Vietnam. It came at a time when the political parties were becoming very anti-immigration and the issue was in the forefront.

Nixon, of which I am very proud, is a film which, again, was mugged by the media. Its critics said I made up history—a hard charge to defend against, because the more specific you try to get (and they never give you adequate time to begin with), the more they come after you on general grounds. We worked very hard to research *Nixon* but, as with any dramatic composition, you have to condense a huge amount of material into two or three hours. As long as historical drama has existed, that has been the case. But the media won't accept that I had a right to use such dramatic license, to make up conversations between characters behind closed doors and so on. They'll accept it with *Schindler's List* or *Lawrence of Arabia* (let alone *Braveheart* or *Richard III*), but never with *Nixon*. Yet *Schindler's List* is particularly vulnerable to this sort of criticism, many people who knew Schindler continue to believe he was a Nazi and that the film was overly sympathetic to him. Being set in Germany, though, *Schindler's List* wasn't a challenge to the American political establishment.

In any event, we will continue to have these debates about history in films—and that's good. Because debating over cinematic representations of history is far better than having our minds numbed watching *The Terminator* or *Money Train* or all the other mindless movies which have come out of Hollywood. Not that film critics are any help in this area. I find that most movie critics are shallow and conservative and all too willing to attack as pretentious or presumptuous or self-absorbed those of us who are trying to inject some intelligence into mainstream Hollywood films. And what do we get as a result? Certainly not movies that will inspire our kids to ask these kinds of questions.

In many ways, we've become prisoners of conformity, the thing I feared most as a child. School was like that, the army was like that—everything I saw in my life in the 1950s and 1960s emphasized conformity. I was a conformist then and in many ways still am. I am scared of breaking taboos and going against the rules, but when the rules are wrong and you know it through your life experience and in your gut, then you have to be willing to break the rules and damn the consequences. And that's the only way you can live with yourself.

I fear a society that's becoming increasingly captive to money—especially in the communications industry, where we now see four or five major corporations buying up everything. And once they have bought up VHF, UHF, and all the available cable space, they will turn on each other, and then there'll be three, and then just two—and maybe one day there'll be only one. But that one will own everything, including the power of dissent. Even today, there's barely any real dissent—only the kind of "dissent" we see on television, where ABC, CBS, and NBC have pretty much the same consensus on the news: they ask the same questions and frame the same paradigm.

Meanwhile, the hard questions aren't being asked: Where is the money? How does it work? Who owns the world? Who owns America? What are these corporations up to? Which politicians do they have in their thrall?

We have fascism now. We don't call it that, but that's what you get when corporations own governments. The only democracy that American citizens are left with is the choice between Fab or Tide, ABC, CBS, and NBC: turn the channel to your favorite show, access more cable channels, but it basically only a consumer choice. It's merely a comfort zone—and if you're comfortable, there is no revolution, not even much evolution.

But I will continue to make films because there *are* people out there who respond favorably to them. I will continue to make my movies under the economic system that now exists, if they let me. And if they don't, I'll try to make films cheaper and in alternative ways, like I did with *Salvador* and *Platoon.* It can be done, though the distribution will be tough—maybe next to impossible—because theaters and TV are so monolithically controlled. But I will try because, everywhere I go, I see people—such as yourselves—who are responsible and who care and who are involved in the good fight somewhere in this world.

One of the great highlights of my life came in meeting the commandants of the Mexican guerilla Zapatista Liberation Army in late March of 1996. These people are tough: they live in jungles filled with insects and disease and are fighting against a much stronger Mexican army aided, once again, by American advisers and weapons. Perhaps it is another Vietnam in the making. And yet these kids and women and men, some of them even grandparents, are just indomitable. Though they miss their families, they have given their lives to this cause and so have taken on noms de guerre: Commander Tacho, Commander David, Commander Marcos. Because, in effect, they are dead to their old world; their old names no longer reflect the people they have become. And standing there in the jungle with them only renewed my faith in the power of the human spirit to overcome tremendous odds. When Commander Tacho said to the crowd of reporters, "We are little people," I responded, "No, you are not little people. You are giants."

REVIEW QUESTIONS

1. Would you agree that Oliver Stone challenges the establishment—the government, the military, and the film industry? Perhaps, as others have suggested, he simply has found a novel means for making money?

2. Why do you think cinematic representations of history enjoy a kind of debate that other types of films do not? Why is it that *Natural Born Killers* and *Nixon* provoked a response whereas *Schindler's List* did not? What does this say about our political culture?

3. Stone argues that our culture has degenerated. He holds the media, newscasters who sensationalize the news, and filmmakers who work within the system responsible. Do you agree? Is the media responsible for cultural decay, or is the media, like any other industry that needs to make a profit, simply responding to market forces?

13 / TV Vice? Sex and Violence Aren't the Problem

MICHAEL MEDVED

Most Americans who fret over television focus on its seedy content, often waxing nostalgic for the innocent fare of yesteryear. If only the Beaver hadn't transmogrified into Beavis, they sigh, then TV might still function as a source of harmless diversion and even reassuring uplift.

But this argument crashes head-on into a wall of contradictory history. The generation nourished on such wholesome family fare as *Ozzie and Harriet, Make Room for Daddy, The Mickey Mouse Club, The Real McCoys, Father Knows Best,* and of course, *Leave It to Beaver* did not grow up as well-adjusted, optimistic, family-affirming, solid citizens. Instead, children of the '60s went more or less directly from *The Donna Reed Show* to campus riots, psychedelic experimentation, love-ins, long hair, and all-purpose looniness. Could it be that TV itself, rather than the specific content of its programs, erodes American virtues?

The most significant fact about the '60s kids is not that they were the off-spring of specific shows like *Howdy Doody* or *Captain Kangaroo* but that they were the first TV generation. The boob tube arrived in most American homes in the '50s, just as baby boomers turned old enough to watch in earnest, which suggests that TV's destructive force lies in the medium, not the message. This insight should force us to reconsider our approach to the battles over television content, the new ratings system, the abandoned family hour, and the rest. If the family-friendly programs of the '50s and '60s led a generation directly to Woodstock, Abbie Hoffman, and the illegitimacy explosion, why try to reproduce those shows' conservative themes today?

Consider a simple thought experiment. Imagine that cultural conservatives manage to install Bill Bennett or Robert Bork as national TV "czar." Henceforth, every show must pass some rigorous virtue test before airing. Sure, TV would thereafter exert a less harmful influence on our children, but would it suddenly become a force for sanity and character-building? If children continued to watch the tube for dozens of hours each week, should their parents be entirely reassured by the programs' improved quality? Or does the sheer quantity of TV viewing represent a deeper, more intractable problem for this society?

These questions are uncomfortable precisely because the answers are so apparent. It is the inescapable essence of television, rather than a few dozen incidentally destructive shows, that undermines the principles most parents strive to pass on to their kids. When consumed in the American pattern of several hours each day, TV inevitably promotes impatience, self-pity, and superficiality.

IMPATIENCE

The most recent analyses reveal that the major cable and broadcast networks titillate viewers with a new image every nine seconds on the average. This quick editing contributes in an obvious and unmistakable manner to the alarming decline in the American attention span. Andy Warhol's "fifteen minutes of fame" seems to have shrunk to perhaps fifty seconds.

The effect of TV's rapidly flashing images is most obvious in preschool classrooms. America's three- and four-year-olds seem less able than ever before to sit still for a teacher—in part because no teacher can reproduce the manic energy or protean transformations of the tube. But those teachers can easily identify the children in class who watch the most TV. Please note that when it comes to this crucial issue of attention span, the admired *Sesame Street* exerts the same worrisome influence as the universally reviled *Power Rangers*. Even sympathetic studies of *Sesame Street* worry over the way that breathlessly fast-paced show encourages restlessness in its young viewers.

Television promotes impatience in other ways for older audience members. The very structure of televised entertainment—with most shows contained within action-packed half-hours—undercuts habits of deferred gratification and long-term perspective. In the world of TV, every problem can be solved within thirty minutes—or, if it's a particularly formidable and complex, then sixty will suffice. It's hardly surprising that many Americans feel frustrated when their personal projects—in romance, weight loss, or career advancement—fail to produce results as neat and immediate as those they witness on TV.

The commercials that consume so much of each broadcast day also foster the peevishness and unfulfilled desire suffered by many viewers. The purpose of these cunningly crafted messages is to stimulate impatience—to nurture an intense, immediate desire for a hamburger, an electronic toy, a beer, or a luxury car. If advertising does its job effectively, it will leave the mass audience with a perpetual attitude of unquenchable yearning for a never-ending succession of alluring new products.

SELF-PITY *feeling sorry for yourself*

The inevitable inability to acquire enough of these products helps to produce self-pity and insecurity, an attitude reinforced by even the most acclaimed and purportedly constructive "public affairs" programming. That programming, like all other "reality-based" television, offers a wildly distorted vision of the contemporary world: TV doesn't broadcast the news;

it broadcasts the bad news. A 1996 report in *USA Today* determined that 72 percent of that year's local news shows from around the country led off with stories of violence or disaster, living up to the rule of broadcast journalism, "If it bleeds, it leads."

Contrary to popular belief, this obsession can't be blamed on the blood lust and ratings hunger of unscrupulous news directors. It is a built-in, unavoidable aspect of the medium. If a father comes home after a long day at work and lovingly tucks in each of his five children, asking God's blessing on their slumber, that's not news. But if the same father comes home and goes from bedroom to bedroom shooting each child, it is news.

Television has an especially intense effect because of the medium's affinity for portraying horror and pain. Depicting love or heroism usually requires some sort of background or explanation, and visual media can't easily explain anything. Their strength is immediacy, especially in the impatient, rapid-fire world of contemporary TV. Even if a news broadcast were determined to balance its footage of mutilated bodies and burning buildings with equal time for noble parents and dedicated teachers, which images would make the more visceral impression, or remain longer in the public memory?

The same preference for the dangerous and the bizarre inevitably shows up in "entertainment" television as well, reflecting an age-old tradition. After all, Shakespeare focused on murders and witches and scheming villains and transsexual masquerades, not functional families and upstanding individuals. Nevertheless, the disturbing behavior in novels and plays and even radio shows of the past never enveloped an audience in the way that television does today, when an average American family owns multiple TV sets and keeps them on for hours a day. One pioneering Chicago station, WTTW, based its call letters on its chosen designation as a "Window to the World." For many viewers, that's the function the tube still performs.

The vast number of vivid images that pour through that window enter our consciousness with little distinction between the factual and the fictional. Whether it's the evening news, a sit-com, a daytime talk show, a docudrama, a cop show, or *60 Minutes,* TV blurs the dividing line between the real and the imaginary and shapes our notions of the wider reality and prevailing behaviors that exist beyond our homes. Producers of soap operas report that they regularly receive letters from devoted viewers who address comments to their favorite characters. And literally tens of millions of Americans will instantaneously (and often unconsciously) imitate catchy phrases or gestures from popular TV shows.

This tension between televised "reality" and the actual lives of ordinary Americans prompts self-pity. On the one hand, the impression people take away from regular viewing is that the world is unpredictable, menacing, full of violence, deviance, excitement, and compelling chaos. Decades of research at the University of Pennsylvania's Annenberg School of Communication suggest that the principal legacy of TV's emphasis on violence is a "mean world syndrome" in which people become more fearful about the present and future. This helps to answer the question posed in a celebrated *Forbes* cover story: "Why Do We Feel So Bad When We Have It So Good?" Real-life trends have recently been improving in numerous areas, including unemployment, the deficit, crime, air quality, and even teen pregnancy and AIDS affliction. Have you noticed a comparable brightening in the public?

If TV's dangerous world leaves people needlessly frightened and insecure, it also makes them resentful that their personal lives are vastly more "boring" than what they see on the tube. Our national epidemic of whining is aided not only by TV's natural emphasis on bad news, but by the way most citizens remain relatively untouched by these disasters—and so their quiet lives can't live up to the excitement, drama, and sexual adventure that television advances as a new American entitlement.

SUPERFICIALITY ✳ *Living in a dream world*

In television, there is only the thrill of the moment, with no sense of the past and scant concern for the future. Venal programmers hardly deserve blame for this tendency; it's a given in a medium that by its nature emphasizes immediacy and visceral visual impact. Flashbacks in a TV drama, no matter how artfully constructed, can never compete with the power of a live broadcast, no matter how insipid. How else can one explain the embarrassing fact that millions of Americans interrupted their lives to watch long-distance shots of a certain white Bronco lumbering down an L.A. freeway?

The O.J. idiocy illustrates another aspect of TV's superficiality: the all-consuming concern with physical appearance. Those who believe our fascination with Simpson's murder case stems from his sports-star status miss the point: Does anyone honestly suppose that the trials would have generated equal interest if O.J. and his murdered wife had resembled, say, Mike Tyson and Janet Reno? The preoccupation with glamour and good looks is nowhere more painfully apparent than in TV news, where the overwhelming majority of these supposedly brilliant and dedicated professional journalists just coincidentally happen to be exceptionally attractive physical specimens.

In real life, we rightly associate "air heads" with an abiding obsession with looks and grooming, but TV doth make air heads of us all. Currently, the most popular show in the world is that profound and probing melodrama, *Baywatch*. Its appeal can hardly be explained by the vividness of its characterizations; it has everything to do with gorgeous bodies abundantly displayed. TV trains us to feel satisfied with surfaces, to focus our adoration on characters who make the most appealing visual presentation, without examination of their ethics or accomplishments. Given the lifelong television training of most Americans, it's no surprise many voters readily forgive the misdeeds of political leaders who look cute and compassionate when they emote on the tube.

Beyond bad politics, beyond misleading glamour, television emphasizes another form of destructive superficiality: setting fun as the highest human priority. As my friend Dennis Prager points out, fun is fleeting and unearned—a thrill ride at a theme park, an engaging video game, a diverting half-hour sitcom on TV. Happiness, on the other hand, requires considerable effort and commitment, and in most cases proves durable and long-lasting. Fun can never be counted upon to produce happiness, but happiness almost always involves fun. Casual sex, for instance, may (occasionally) provide a few hours of fun, but it will never lead to the long-term happiness that a permanent marriage can provide. Similarly, watching professional sports on TV can be fun, but it hardly compares to the benefits of actually playing on a team yourself.

TV viewing represents the most empty-headed, superficial sort of fun in an increasingly fun-addicted society. It is meaningless precisely because it demands so little of its viewers—in fact, physiological examination of TV watchers suggests they are three-quarters asleep.

Sleepers, awake! It is high time we all woke up, especially those families who attempt to honor Jewish and Christian teachings. In each of the areas described above, TV contradicts the fundamentals of faith-based civilization: While TV promotes impatience, restlessness, and a short-term horizon, our religious traditions command a serene, steady spirit and a view toward eternal consequences. Where television encourages self-pity and fear, religious teachings emphasize gratitude and rejoicing in our position. And while electronic media inspire superficiality and shallowness, believers know to look below the surface at the cause lying beneath the confusing effects. Instead of transient, unearned fun, Judaism and Christianity stress the permanent good of achieving happiness through a full and virtuous life.

The increasingly unmistakable conflict between investing time in television and the religious priorities that most parents hope to pass on to our children brings us to a potentially historic crossroads. The current situation of TV addiction resembles the situation of nicotine addiction thirty-five years ago. Shortly after the surgeon general reported that cigarettes are a health hazard, the initial impulse from the tobacco industry and the public was to make the "cancer sticks" safer by improving filters or reducing tar and nicotine. Of course, such measures probably succeeded in saving a few lives, but these expedients were hardly a long-term solution.

Today, efforts to reduce televised levels of shock and stupidity resemble those old attempts to reduce tar and nicotine in tobacco. It may be worth doing, but it's hardly the ultimate solution. The most important response to the dangers of cigarettes was a long-term, overall decline in the number of smokers, even though millions of Americans continue to smoke to their own detriment. Similarly, the most significant reply to TV's malign influence will involve exhortations that lead to a long-term, overall decline in the rate of TV viewing—even though many millions will be free to continue in their television addictions.

This is not a pipe dream. A recent *Wall Street Journal*/NBC News poll found that an astonishing 65 percent of Americans say they are "watching less television altogether" than they were five years ago, despite the explosion of entertainment choices and cable and satellite technologies. Nielsen ratings and other studies confirm the encouraging news that Americans are spending a bit less time with the tube than they did ten years ago.

In fact, today's wide array of televised possibilities has done nothing to inspire public appreciation for TV. When asked whether "TV has changed for the better or for the worse over the past ten years," 59 percent thought it had worsened; only 30 percent said it had improved.

There just may be a receptive audience for a new campaign to reduce TV viewing—to give back a few years of life to the average American who will currently spend an uninterrupted thirteen years (twenty-four--hour days, seven-day weeks) of his life in front of the tube. After all, no one would consciously choose as an epitaph, "Here lies our beloved husband and father, who selflessly devoted thirteen years of life to his television set."

Fortunately, one of the most respected and moral philosophers of our time has courageously stepped forward to enlighten humanity about TV's danger to our children. "Television is pure poison," she declares. "To be plopped in front of a TV instead of being read to, talked to, or encouraged to interact with other human beings is a huge mistake, and that's what happens to a lot of children."

So says Madonna, in an interview with the British magazine *She*. When even the most publicized princess of popular culture appreciates the pitfalls of television, surely more conventional parents will consider pulling the plug and liberating their families from the tyranny of too much TV.

REVIEW QUESTIONS

1. How does Michael Medved's argument differ from other chapters in this book? Is it convincing or simply a new slant in a long line of television-bashing diatribes?
2. Would it be possible to extend Medved's argument to other forms of popular culture, such as music listening, playing video games, or attending sporting events? Put a bit differently, do other forms of popular culture promote impatience, self-pity, and superficiality–or is it just television?
3. If the author is correct about the harmful effects of television, how might it be connected to our political culture? Taking it one step further, are there connections between endless hours of television viewing and public policy?

14 / The Shelter of Each Other: One Big Town

MARY PIPHER

In the past forty years the United States has undergone enormous demographic changes. All over the prairie the lights have gone out as young adults have traveled to cities and never returned. Farmers have moved to the suburbs and little towns have dried up like tumbleweeds. Downtown cafés have closed and the locals now drink coffee at the Arby's on the highway. As we travel the interstates which Paul Gruchow called "tunnels without walls," we see the same stores, cafés, and hotels everywhere. It makes life convenient, but dull.

McKibben defined a working community as one in which it would be difficult for outsiders to fit in. That's because the information in the community would be specifically related to that time and place and grounded in the history of its inhabitants. Songwriter Greg Brown said "Your hometown is where you know what the deal is. You may not like it, but you understand it. You know the rules and who is breaking them."

When I think of a working community, I think of my father's Ozark town. Cousins lived near each other and everyone knew everyone. Outsiders had a tough time getting information about locals because, for most of this century, the only outsiders were salespeople or IRS agents and FBI employees looking for moonshine stills. On the other hand, sixty years after my father left the Ozarks, I can still go there, explain who my family was and extract special privileges—a campground on private property and advice on where to fish and pick berries.

Our country has moved from small, isolated communities to one big company town. Wal-Marts have replaced the small stores and Pizza Hut and Taco Bell have replaced the city cafés. We are united by our media and by what we consume. All over America, regional dialects and ethnic accents disappear as children learn generic language from television.

Civic organizations such as the Elks, Lions, and Moose—what we call the "animal clubs"—are being replaced by mailing list organizations. Shopping channels and televised auctions, even for cattle, keep local folks from gathering. Televised college classes allow students to get degrees without interacting with professors or other students. Our phone book offers numbers to call to discuss personal problems, hear weather reports and celebrity trivia, find new recipes, and hear consumer information and jokes. These calls mimic the kinds of things real people used to discuss when they met on street corners and in cafés. The need for connection is there, but it's filled via tape-recorded messages.

We've changed from a nation of primary relationships to one of secondary relationships. Primary relationships are ones in which people know each other in a multiplicity of roles—as neighbor, coworker, in-law, and schoolmate. Secondary relationships are ones in which people are strangers. We don't know their parents, their religion, where they live, or if they have a dog. We know only about their role at a particular moment.

By 1990, 72 percent of Americans didn't know their neighbors. The number of people who say they never spend time with their neighbors has doubled in the last twenty years. More people do what John Prine called "live in their heads." They fantasize affairs with people they will never meet. Our children move among strangers.

It's not yet clear what it means that so much of our experience is vicarious. Sociologist James House reviewed relevant literature and concluded that social isolation is just as dangerous as smoking, high blood pressure, or high cholesterol. A companion, any real-life companion, is a buffer against stress. I wonder if children learn different lessons from vicarious relationships than they do from real ones.

Real communities give people a sense that they are all in this place together. People who live together have something that is fragile and easily destroyed by a lack of civility. Everything you do matters. Protocol is important. Relationships are not disposable. People are careful what they say in real communities because they will live with their words until they die of old age. Accountability is different in the electronic community. Over the Internet people can be deleted the second they become annoying or tiresome. Names aren't necessarily even real names. One never needs to see or talk to anyone again.

Parenthetically, demographic shifts explain much of our obsession with looking good. As we've moved from primary to secondary relationships, appearance has become much more important to us. In an earlier time, we had various kinds of information about the people we encountered. We knew their families, their house, their work habits, religion, and amiability. Now often appearance is all we have to go on.

Electronic villages are not located in particular places. Cable channels from all over the world blare into our living rooms. Midwesterners hear the weather in Florida. New Yorkers hear the crime statistics from Austin. Domestic-relations court is filmed so viewers can watch other people's lives unravel. We work crossword puzzles to the unwinding of the Rwanda massacres. We hear of the rape of Bosnian women as we sweep our kitchens.

Nonstop data blurs many boundaries that hold our lives in place. As Stoll says, "Data isn't information any more than fifty thousand tons of cement is a skyscraper." Boundaries are blurred between places and times, between sexual and violent material, between funny and sad, trivial and important, news and entertainment, and fact and fiction. Public and private behaviors are blurred and the boundaries between childhood and adulthood disappear.

Time is a boundary that's been blurred. Shops used to be closed on Sundays and after six at night. Town whistles signaled when to rise, eat, and go home for lunch and dinner. News and weather were broadcast in the morning, at six, and again at ten. Everyone's life had more or less the same structure. Now television channels broadcast nonstop and every small town has an all-night convenience store. Banks have twenty-four-hours-a-day, seven-days-a-week automatic teller machines.

As Joshua Meyrowitz noted in *No Sense of Place*, backstage and frontstage have blurred into a twilight-zone middle stage where all of us operate all of the time. With video cameras everywhere, all of us are potentially on frontstage. Our private behaviors can be made public. We see ordinary citizens in their most private moments. The prayers of parents whose daughter was murdered are gobbled up for video. While being filmed on a camcorder, a man commits suicide.

From the point of view of this book by far the most important lost boundary is that between children and adults. George W. S. Trow wrote: "We are becoming more childish. We're falling out of the world of history into the world of demographics where we count everything and value nothing." Often in the media, parents are portrayed as adult survivors, as lost as children and as unsure of what is right or important. Age no longer implies wisdom.

When we erase lines kids have no protection and adults have no dignity or obligations. Thus, we see children defined as consumers and sold sugary alcoholic drinks and chocolate chewing tobacco. The cover of a Nirvana album showed a baby swimming toward a fishhook holding a dollar bill. When kids are defined as consumers they have no protected space in which to grow. Everyone becomes the same—a stressed victim of forces larger than themselves, i.e., a consumer or prey.

In the *Geography of Childhood*, Gary Nabhan writes that in 1900, 10 percent of our people lived in big cities. By 1992, 38 percent of Americans lived in cities. Most children gain their knowledge of the natural world vicariously. In the history of the world this distance from the natural world is a new phenomenon. The natural world teaches many lessons but fewer children have access to its lessons. Even a generation ago most Americans were related to country people. Families visited farms on a regular basis. Children saw cows being milked, pigs fed, chickens plucked, grain planted, corn harvested, and apples picked from family orchards.

Public space has disappeared as well. I thought of this recently at a Dairy Queen. I watched tired, stressed teens who barely knew each other waiting on lines of customers whom they didn't know. The customers didn't know each other and were clearly in a hurry to get their cones and be out of there. I contrasted these teens' experience with my own as a carhop at the A & W root beer stand in my hometown. The other employees were my classmates. We knew the customers; they were our friends, teachers, and parents. The customers knew each other and visited car to car while they waited for their pork tenderloin sandwiches and root beer floats. Work was connected to the rest of our lives. We worked hard because adults we knew were watching. But we had fun, too. We were at the center of our town's social scene.

Children are more frightened in electronic communities. They do not know the adults around them and have been taught that strangers may be dangerous. Most children think they are in danger. A study of children in Ohio found that 43 percent of them thought they were likely to be kidnapped. In the last few years, basic facts have escaped us. We've emphasized the perils of "bad touch" and forgotten the importance to children of "good touch." We've focused on the dangers of strange adults and ignored the danger to children of not having loving adults involved in their lives.

With our warnings, we probably have protected some kids, but at a considerable expense. The children have lost opportunities to interact with interesting adults and genuine characters. I think of the Yo-Yo King from Detroit as I write this. He was my cabdriver in from the Detroit airport. We talked about his long career. For three years in a row he was the winner of the Detroit yo-yo championship. A yo-yo company sponsored his tours in this country and abroad. He performed yo-yo tricks in stadiums. Mostly, though he went from school yard to school yard, teaching kids tricks and selling yo-yos. Now school policies don't allow him on school yards. He was bitter and said, "Perverts ruined everything for me and the kids." I felt sad as I listened. I knew that the policies were probably necessary, but much had been lost.

Children need to believe that the world is an interesting and safe place. Without it they cannot grow and explore. When we rear our children to fear other adults we truncate their growth. Lev S. Vygotsky, the great developmental psychologist, taught us that learning is fundamentally social. The relationship between children and their teachers isn't incidental, but rather is the central component of their learning. Human development occurs within the context of real relationships. We learn from whom we love.

NEW TOOLS

There is no direct connection between convenience and happiness.
—Dr. Suzuki

I remember a story from my undergraduate days in anthropology. Missionaries who settled near a tribal culture gave the native women metal knives. Prior to this the men had made knives from stone and this had been an important source of their power and wisdom. But these new knives in the hands of the women were far superior. This upset the gender balance of the villagers, and ultimately the society was disrupted. Men's rituals were rendered meaningless and the women's place, while elevated, changed in ways that unsettled relationships with their families. Unwittingly, the missionaries had overturned a culture. If that can happen with a few metal knives, what about a culture in which we all are bombarded with hundreds of new "tools" every decade?

The electronic revolution is as significant as the invention of the printing press. It has changed our world as dramatically and much more quickly. The important elements have changed; where they once were snow and rain, they are now car phones and fax machines. We are not yet ready psychologically. We are just beginning to consider how human communities are affected by the new tools. We have no protection from the elements.

New products often erode our sense of community in unpredictable ways. For example air-conditioning has changed neighborhoods. Adults no longer sit on their front porches to cool down in the evenings. Streets have become more dangerous without the supervision of neighbors. New tools have sped up the pace of our lives. Everyone seems stressed about time. When people communicate by E-mail and fax, the nature of human interaction changes. While some people use computers to communicate with those they know and love, many users communicate with people whose names and faces they do not know, in places they've never been, about people they've never met. I just read that soon we will be able to shop for food via computers. People will be able to pick out strawberries from their own home. When this happens we will be even less connected to those around us.

All the technology of our times has its good uses. The computer, for example, helped find the families of people killed in the Oklahoma City bombing and it helped coordinate medical and relief efforts. But the computer also has made it possible for militia groups to teach each other how to make bombs. Any one invention probably wouldn't do that much damage. The problem is the whole pile. It's the cumulative effect of all this equipment that has changed the very ways we live in families. Eventually quantity becomes quality and the integrity of our lives is altered.

As Clifford Stoll said in *Silicon Snake Oil,* "We program computers but they also program us." I don't think we should throw our machines into the sea, but we must analyze the effects of our technology and choose our tools carefully. We need to ask: Do we like the ways we are changing? How will this new technology affect humans? We need to be in charge of technology, not vice versa.

The speed of change is as dizzying as our lack of reflection on its consequences. To argue that change is inevitable is to say that planning is impossible. But there are precedents for making conscious choices about what tools to accept and reject. The Amish make conscious choices about technology. When the Japanese saw the havoc that guns wreaked on their samurai society, they threw their guns away and lived for hundreds of years without Western weapons.

Before the Seneca tribe made changes, the elders would ask, "How will this affect the next seven generations?" No new tools or customs were introduced without a thoughtful conversation about the future. We are not even asking how our explosion in technology and media is affecting the current generations.

Television

In a college class I asked "What would it be like to grow up in a world without media?" A student from the Tonga Islands answered, "I never saw television or heard rock 'n' roll until I came to the United States in high school." She paused and looked around the room. "I had a happy childhood. I felt safe all the time. I didn't know I was poor. Or that parents hurt their children or that children hated their parents. I thought I was pretty."

Television has probably been the most powerful medium in shaping the new community. The electronic community gives us our mutual friends, our significant events, and our daily chats. The "produced" relationships of television families become our models for intimacy. We know media stars better than we know our neighbors. Most of us can discuss their lives better than we can discuss those of our relatives. We confuse personas and persons. That is, we think a man who plays a doctor on TV actually knows something about medicine. We think a chatty talk show host is truly good-natured. This confusion is especially common with young children, who are developmentally incapable of distinguishing between reality and fantasy. But even adults get mixed up about this.

Most real life is rather quiet and routine. Most pleasures are small pleasures—a hot shower, a sunset, a bowl of good soup, or a good book. Television suggests that life is high drama, love, and sex. TV families are radically different from real families. Things happen much faster to them. On television things that are not visually interesting, such as thinking, reading, and talking, are ignored. Activities such as housework, fund-raising, and teaching children to read are vastly underreported. Instead of ennobling our ordinary experiences, television suggests that they are not of sufficient interest to document.

These generalizations even fit the way TV portrays the animal kingdom. Specials on animals feature sex, births, and killing. Dangerous or cuddly looking animals are favored. But in reality, most animals are neither dangerous nor cute. Sharks and panda bears are not the main species on the planet. Most animals, like most people, spend most of their time in rather simple ways. They forage and sleep.

TV isolates people in their leisure time. People spend more time watching music videos but less time making music with each other. People in small towns now watch international cable networks instead of driving to their neighbor's house for cards. Women watch soaps instead of attending church circles or book clubs. When company comes, the kids are sent to the TV room with videos. Television is on during meals and kids study to television or radio.

Parents are not the main influences in the lives of their children. Some of the first voices children hear are from the television, the first street they know is Sesame Street. A child playing Nintendo is learning different lessons than a child playing along a creek or playing dominoes with a grandfather. Many children have been conditioned via the media into having highly dysfunctional attention spans.

Adults too have diminished concentration. Neil Postman in *Amusing Ourselves to Death* writes of the 1858 Lincoln-Douglas debates. The average citizen sat for up to seven hours in the heat and listened to these two men discuss issues. People grasped the legal and constitutional issues, moral nuances, and political implications. In addition, they could listen to and appreciate intricate and complex sentences. Today the press and the public decry President Clinton's speeches if they last more than an hour. To an audience socialized to information via sound bite, an hour seems like a long time.

The time devoted to violence on TV in no way reflects its importance in real life. In real life, most of us exercise, work, visit our friends, read, cook and eat, and shop. Few of us spend any significant amount of our time solving murders or fleeing psychotic killers. On television there are many more detectives and murderers than exist in the real world. A rule of thumb about violence is "If it bleeds, it leads." Violence captures viewer attention. Our movies have become increasingly violent, and as James Wolcott wrote in the *New Yorker,* "Violence is the real sex now."

Some might argue that there is nothing new under the sun. Of course in a narrow sense, they are correct. There have always been murderers and rapists, and stories about violence have been themes of literature and song. But things are different now. Children, including toddlers, are exposed to hundreds of examples of violence every day. The frequency and intensity of these images is unprecedented in the history of humanity. We have ample documentation that this exposure desensitizes children, makes it more likely they will be violent, and increases their fear levels about potential violence.

Another difference is in the attitudes about violence. *Romeo and Juliet,* for example, was a tragedy. The deaths in the play were presented as a cause of enormous suffering to friends and families and as a terrible waste. When Juliet and Romeo died something momentous happened in the universe. The very gods were upset. Often today death is a minor event of no more consequence than say the kicking of a flat tire. It's even presented as a joke.

It is one thing to read Shakespeare, which at least requires that the person can read. It's another to, day after day, see blood splattered across a screen by "action heroes." It is one thing to show, as Shakespeare did that violence can be the tragic consequence of misunderstandings, and another to show violence as a thrill, as a solution to human problems or merely as something that happens when people are slightly frustrated or men need to prove they are men.

Of course, one could argue that parents can keep televisions out of their homes. This is extremely hard for the average parent to do. Even if they succeed, their children go from these "protected environments" to play with children who have watched lots of TV and who behave accordingly.

I don't often go to violent movies, but I do have a stake in them. I don't like living in a world where thousands of teenage boys, some of whom own guns, have been reared on them. Walking city streets, I may be accosted by a youth who has spent most of his life watching violent media. Unfortunately, needy children are the ones most affected. Children with the least available parents watch the most TV. Violent television is like secondhand smoke, it affects all of us.

Heavy viewers develop the "mean world syndrome." This leads to a vicious-circle phenomenon. Because children are afraid and the streets are not safe, they come home right after school and stay indoors. They watch more TV, which makes them more afraid and thus more likely to stay indoors. With everyone indoors the streets are less safe. Families watch more TV and are more fearful and so on.

Television and electronic media have created a new community with entirely different rules and structures than the kinds of communities that have existed for millions of years. Families gather around the glow of the TV as the Lakota once gathered around the glow of a fire on the Great Plains or as the Vikings huddled around fires in the caves of Scandinavia. They gather as New England families gathered in the 1800s around a fireplace that kept them warm and safe. But our TVs do not keep us warm, safe, and together. Rapidly our technology is creating a new kind of human being, one who is plugged into machines instead of relationships, one who lives in a virtual reality rather than a family.

Advertising

In therapy a young couple argue about what to buy their six-year-old daughter. Whenever they go out, Caitlan whines and begs for toys and gum. Dad says, "We can afford it, why not? It keeps her from fussing." Mom worries that she'll spoiled. As we talk, it's clear that no one in the family is enjoying outings anymore. Caitlan begs, the parents argue, the father gives in, and the mother gets mad. This reinforces Caitlan's whining and teaches her that products are the point of outings. A day will come when she begs for things the parents do not approve of and cannot afford.

I talk to my neighbor about her daughter, who has just started junior high. Mona says, "All of a sudden she's so money conscious. She wants to know how much we make. She keeps talking about who is rich and who isn't. And she wants expensive things that she doesn't need and we can't afford." Mona sighs. "We didn't teach her to think like this."

Since the 1950s, advertising has increased in amount and in sophistication. Much of what modern psychology knows about suggestion and influence has been usurped to sell products. We have t-groups and marketing polls. The general philosophy of ads—create a feeling of longing about a deeply human need, then suggest a product that will satisfy that yearning—works very well. Wishes are induced with the skill of a nightclub hypnosis, then elevated into needs. Your wish is your command. Ads elevate feelings over thinking and impulses over common sense. It's hard for parental calls for prudence to compete. The science of marketing is much more precise and focused than the science of parenting.

Ads manipulate us into being dissatisfied. A businessman B. E. Puckett said, "It's our job to make people unhappy with what they have." We are encouraged to feel anxious or sorry for ourselves. Advertising teaches us to live on the level of the pleasure principle. This leads to impulse-control problems and to feelings of entitlement. "I am the center of the universe and I want what I want now." This thinking creates citizens who are vulnerable to quick fixes. It leads to citizens filled with self-pity which is the flip side of entitlement.

Advertising teaches that people shouldn't have to suffer, that pain is unnatural and can be cured. They say that effort is bad and convenience is good and that products solve complex human problems. Over and over people hear that their needs for love, security, and variety can be met with products. They may reject the message of any particular ad, but over time many buy the big message—buying products is important.

Advertising trivializes the important and elevates the trivial. Crotch itch gets more attention than the famine in Ethiopia. Soft drink commercials receive more air time than global warming. We are taught to buy products to fill emotional voids. We hear weird messages about what we deserve.

The propaganda that life is made happier by purchases encourages adults and children to make bad decisions about their time and money. Parents may take second jobs to pay for things. Teenagers work at minimum-wage jobs for designer jeans. Children want things that parents know are not good for them. Children alternate between the belief that products will make them happy and a deep cynicism about the promises of the adult world. They develop a lack of trust and respect for adults. They know that adults lie to them to make money.

Philosopher Eileen Moody wrote that "the American dream has been rewritten in the language of advertisers." Advertising is our national religion, with parables that teach "Buy this product and you will be saved." Children recite jingles instead of poetry and they know brand names instead of the names of presidents. More students can identify Mr. Peanut and Joe Camel than can identify Abe Lincoln or Eleanor Roosevelt. They can identify twenty kinds of cold cereal but not the trees and birds in their neighborhoods.

VALUES

Over Christmas vacation I watched some talk shows. First I watched a show hosted by Gordon Elliot, a good-looking middle-aged man in a gray suit. He had an English accent and a smarmy manner. With his hand-held microphone he moved with ease between the panelists and the audience.

The topic was "Dealing with My Cheapskate Mate." Onstage were two working-class couples with large wives and scrawny, weather-beaten husbands. Tracy, with dyed hair and blue eye shadow, complained about her Gary. When he took her out to eat, he lied that it was her birthday to get a free dessert. Or he complained about the food or said he was an employee, just to get a free meal. Gary, a balding man with bad teeth and bad grammar, sat sullenly beside her. The audience booed when Tracy described Gary's tightness and cheered when Tracy put him down.

Loretta was a younger version of Tracy—also with dyed hair and heavy makeup. She spoke with a lisp and had a scar, probably from surgery to correct a harelip. As she spoke, she looked nervously at Earl who sat stiffly beside her. She claimed she was in therapy because of Earl's tightness. She was depressed because she couldn't go shopping with her friends. Earl defended himself by saying that they were maxed out on their Visa and that Loretta was a big spender. A friend of Loretta's stood up to testify that Earl was a cheapskate. The women in the audience booed.

Gordon urged the home audience to call his toll-free number, if they had a cheapskate mate. Then he broke for a commercial. "I don't know why I love you like I do" played behind a message about spaghetti sauce. There was an ad for an upcoming show with guests who had sexually transmitted diseases. An ad for appliances featured free financing with no payments for three months. A beautiful actress sold tampons with ultrasmooth applicators. The product motto was "trust." There was an ad for antacid and for Publishers Clearing House, "the House Where Dreams Come True."

We returned to Gordon and the couples sitting stiffly onstage. With their cheap clothes and clown smiles, they looked vulnerable and exposed. Underneath the couples the news flashed: "Thirty-one percent of women surveyed said they prefer money to sex."

Rita and Dennis walked onstage. Rita was heavy, with platinum-blond hair. Dennis limped and spoke English poorly. Rita showed the audience the $29.99 tag on her dress and said Dennis wouldn't let her cut that tag off because he wanted to return the dress after the show. The audience booed and Gordon gallantly offered to pay for Rita's dress. Rita's chin wobbled with emotion as she thanked him. Dennis looked scared and confused. He didn't seem to understand why he was being booed. He said that he gave Rita money whenever she asked—that is, if he had any money. More boos.

The audience crowded toward the mikes for their thirty-second spot on national television. The women in the audience looked like Rita, Tracy, and Loretta. They had stingy husbands too. One woman advised Rita to leave Dennis. Dennis tried to explain that he'd been fired from his job at the railroad, that he wasn't really a cheapskate, just broke. But since that point didn't fit with the day's topic, Gordon cut him off.

In a subtle but effective way Gordon encouraged tension, conflict, and drama. He said, "I'm really concerned about Rita. Should she leave Dennis?" Many in the audience shouted "Yes, yes." Soon Rita had a tear running down her cheek and the cameras zoomed in. Without waiting to hear if Rita would leave Dennis, I turned to another channel.

I watched an adult diaper commercial with the slogan "When you're comfortable, everything feels right." Then Sally Jesse Raphael explored the topic of daughters who had never met their fathers. Angela was onstage with her mother Maxine. They held hands as Angela explained that Maxine wouldn't talk about her ex-husband, Angela's father. Maxine, her voice quivering with emotion, said that it was because she was ashamed. However, with the coaxing of Sally, Maxine told Angela about her father in front of the television audience. She said she'd been physically and emotionally abused by him. As she spoke, her voice cracked with emotion and both mother and daughter wept.

Angela's father came onstage. He was a large, red-faced man who cried as he hugged his newfound daughter. Angela cried too and looked rather sheepishly at her mother, who stood nearby. Millions watched this family's most dramatic moment.

Sally held up the microphone. In a soft, coaxing voice she encouraged a fight. The father denied any abuse in the marriage and said he wouldn't have left if he'd known he had such a beautiful daughter. Maxine said that the reason he didn't know his daughter was that he'd skipped town and she couldn't find him.

I switched to another channel, where Maury Povitch interviewed people who had killed or had a family member killed by a drunk driver. Onstage sat six traumatized parents who had lost their children and a girl who sobbed as she told of maiming her boyfriend. She wailed, "He was an athlete in high school and now, because of me, he's in a wheelchair for life."

Povitch walked into the audience, put his arms around guests and glibly encouraged them to tell their stories. One woman's husband was in jail after killing their six-year-old daughter. She'd forgiven him. Another woman, whose son had been killed, hated drunk drivers. With Povitch's encouragement, she attacked the more forgiving woman. Meanwhile, the parents onstage looked shell-shocked, unsure where they were.

I was struck by how wrong these shows felt. Poor and needy people were manipulated into revealing personal information. People were selling their souls and their most private pain for a few minutes' celebrity. Their grief and tragedy were our momentary entertainment. People talked about their deepest traumas, their worst habits, their arguments, and sex lives. For a refrigerator or a trip to Los Angeles, they were encouraged to betray their parents or lifetime companions.

I wondered what happens to these people after they leave. Do they show the videos? Do the men beat up their wives? Do they divorce or pretend the betrayals never happened? What is left for people after they have shared their most private secrets with a television audience?

The shows reminded me of the Russian show trials of the Stalin era. In those trials, people betrayed their families and friends in front of cameras. Their motives were different. The Russians did it to save their own lives while Americans do it for their fifteen seconds of celebrity. But I'm struck with the similarities. Both talk-show culture and Soviet society foster the betrayal of family. By these public exposures of family secrets both cultures teach that families are neither private nor sacred.

In an article entitled "The Loss of Moral Turf" in *Rebuilding the Nest,* Coter and Jacobsen wrote of the daytime talk shows. "If for some reason a new federal law required television networks to do everything possible to cheapen the social value of the medium, to violate society's traditional understanding of childhood, and to inflict gratuitous harm on the family as an institution, the networks could do no better than simply to beam these programs each day into millions of American homes."

A capitalistic country, just like a communist country, has reason to view families as the enemy. In a communist system where people are defined as units of production, families often interfere with production. Parents want their children to go to school and play, to rest and to attend family events. Most parents care much more about the happiness of their children than the production quotas of the government. The Soviet system worked best when there was no intermediary between the individual and the state.

In a capitalistic system where people are units of consumption, families often interfere with sales quotas. Parents intervene between their children and the marketplace. Parents don't want their children to drink alcohol, use tobacco, or have sugar diets, even if the consumption of those products is good for the economy. Parents don't necessarily want to buy designer jeans or expensive toys. They have different values and different goals for their children than corporate society does.

Families are about love, relationships, and time. Of course parents make mistakes. But even at their worst most parents are not trying to make money off their children. They are not interested in exploiting their children for personal gain.

In their concern for children, parents are both deeply conservative and deeply subversive. Families are a buffer between individuals and the state and all totalitarian states attack families. In many such states young children are taken from their families for education. Often the values taught are contrary to what the parents believe and contrary to the interests of the children themselves.

In the former Soviet Union children were trained to work as informers and to betray their own parents. They were to listen to their parents talk and report it to authorities if it was seditious or even disgruntled. Children who "informed" on their parents were publicly revered. By this process children learned the supremacy of the collective over the family.

In America today people betray their families. As a member of Megadeth put it, "Parents are dickheads." All adult problems of whatever ilk are attributed to poor parenting. The message is that if people are having trouble or in pain, their parents must have failed. Both nations produce houses with no walls. Children turn to the broader culture for guidelines on how to live. In the former Soviet Union, children were encouraged to produce, while in America children are encouraged to consume. Both the Soviets and the talk shows demonize intellectuals, who are, by definition, people who might actually think about what is happening in the culture and argue articulately against certain activities.

In both cultures children grow into deeply cynical adults. Hedrick Smith wrote that Russians believe in their friends and little else. Alcohol then becomes a way to kill the pain of helplessness. This description fits young adults in the United States as well. And like the Russians, this generation uses chemicals to deal with their lack of influence. Many have been drinking heavily since junior high. They use alcohol to deal with all their emotions—bitterness, anger, insecurity, and despair.

Neither the communist state nor the money-driven corporate culture supports communities. Communities are for families. They teach proper behavior and good values. They give families a sense of history, of place, and they offer them a complex weave of people from whom to learn how to be more fully human. Communities provide children with good stories, with cautionary tales and moral fables.

Families need communities the way my corn plant needs soil. Since the beginning of time, humans have shared their lives with those around them. Families shared their fish from the sea, gathered reeds for thatched roofs, and looked at the stars. We have watched out for each other. Now for the first time in human history many of us feel alone and unconnected to groups. The world has changed but we have not. We all want love, respect, good work, and interesting pastimes. We want a safe, stimulating world for our children and friends and a planet that will survive. We humans are all more alike than we are different.

REVIEW QUESTIONS

1. Some feminists argue that the traditional family structure is oppressive and is conducive to relations in which women's work is devalued and in which women are abused. The media, in this view, might be applauded for bringing to the public's attention such issues as domestic violence and incest. Pipher notes, though, that the media has contributed to the demise of community and of family. With whom do you agree? Is it possible for the media to report these issues without destroying the family unit?

2. Pipher notes that television does not portray reality but rather sensationalizes and dramatizes. Should the media be condemned for adopting this approach, or is the media simply reporting that which is entertaining? Should we accept dramatic representations of reality for their entertainment value? Is there a way in which we can enjoy these representations while keeping them in perspective?

3. Pipher offers a commentary on talk shows, arguing that they exploit the guests. Yet others have praised shows like *Oprah* for their candid discussions of such issues as sexual abuse. Can these two positions be reconciled?

4. Do you find Pipher's argument that capitalism, the dissolution of the family and community, and the media are interrelated persuasive?